THE MARTIAL RACES OF INDIA

Owing to the antiquity and rarity of this book, certain pages are regrettably absent, and readability is compromised due to the blurring of the original text. If you possess any insights regarding the availability of these missing sections, kindly inform us. Your assistance is crucial in ensuring the completion of this significant work for the benefit of future generations.

COLONEL NAWAB MALIK SIR UMAR HAYAT KHAN, K.C.I.E., C.B.E., M.V.O. Chief of the Tiwanas (Rajput Mussalman clan of the Punjab). In uniform of his regiment. (Then the 18th K.G.O. Lancers.)

[*Frontispiece*

THE MARTIAL RACES OF INDIA

SIR GEORGE MACMUNN

GYAN

Published by

GYAN

Gyan Publishing House
5, Ansari Road
Daryaganj, New Delhi-110002
Phone: 011-47034999, 9811692060
E-mail: books@gyanbooks.com

Distribution Network
gyanbooks.com
India, USA, Canada, UK, Australia

ISBN: 978-93-7014-626-6 (HB)

First Published, 1933

2nd Impression 2025

Printed at: Gyan Press, Delhi.

THE MARTIAL RACES OF INDIA
Author: SIR GEORGE MACMUNN

THE MARTIAL RACES OF INDIA

THE MARTIAL RACES OF INDIA

BY

LIEUT.-GENERAL

SIR GEORGE MACMUNN

K.C.B., K.C.S.I., D.S.O.

Colonel Commandant The Royal Artillery

LONDON

SAMPSON LOW, MARSTON & CO., LTD.

INTRODUCTION

THE constant interest that people of Great Britain and the rest of the Empire take in matters Indian, their appreciation of the share that Indian soldiers took by our side in all theatres of the World War and our admiration of the way that they and the police have resisted inoculation with the Ghandi poison, have induced me to try to present to the English-speaking world some account of the Martial Races of India.

India unlike almost any other country has a vast mass of unwarlike people whose hand has never kept the head. In this class must be mustered many who have the brains and aptitude to assimilate Western education far more rapidly than the more virile races. But it is these virile races that have dominated India in the past, and as the Simon Report has stated, would do so again if British control were removed. It is moreover in these forceful classes that the real future of India for good must lie whether it be peaceful or whether it be otherwise. I have therefore endeavoured to draw the picture and tell the story of Rajput and Turk, of Afghan and Sikh, of Mahratta and Mogul, not as the scientist and ethnologist would want it, but rather as the ordinary reading and understanding public would wish to see it. I have therefore but drawn the outline, and tried to concentrate on the drama, the romance of the old time before and the times that have just gone, with all the fidelity to the British Crown and trust in British leaders that have been so phenomenal, and I have tried to gaze a little way into the future. I have endeavoured to draw the picture so that it may be useful to the younger officers of the Indian Army, and to those of the British Service who have, as most must, to soldier in India, while making it a book that parents whose sons will soldier in the East may like to see in their hands. I do not attempt to emulate the detailed knowledge that an officer in a Sikh regiment should have of his Sikhs or in a Mahratta corps of his Mahrattas, but I have served in close touch with most of the races, and try to show a reel, a hasty reel perhaps, that all who care for India may wish to glance at.

To me the whole story is so glorious, so stimulating and so rich in all that makes an active life worth while, that I should like to think that anything that I might write will encourage our sons still to seek their careers in this great Indian continent. It is their forebears, the British and the British alone who have rebuilt it, and are endeavouring to restore it in some part to those who are fit to inherit the estate.

Lest anyone should say that I am but a beater on a drum that has lost its sound, I would urge all and sundry to read what an American authoress, Patricia Kendall, has written on this subject of the British in India and their following there. For the first time America has got it 'straight off the ice' at American hands. It is called *India and the British. A quest for truth* (Scribner.)

The coloured illustrations herein are from the brush of Major (later Brigadier-General) A. C. Lovat of the Gloucester Regiment who illustrated for me *The Armies of India* (A. & C. Black, 1912) and are reproduced by special courtesy of Messrs. Black. General Lovat was the most succesful painter of Indian military types, but died some years ago from the results of the winter of 1914–15 in France.

CONTENTS

CHAPTER XV

ILLUSTRATIONS

MAPS

THE MARTIAL RACES OF INDIA

THE MARTIAL RACES OF INDIA

CHAPTER I

THE MARTIAL CASTES AND RACES

THE MEANING OF THE MARTIAL RACES—THE DIVERGENT RACES—OUTLINE OF INDIAN ETHNOLOGY—THE CONFLICTING RELIGIONS—THE ARYAN CASTES—THE RAJPUTS AND JĀTS—THE AFGHANS AND PATHANS—THE TURKS.

WHO and what are the martial races of India, how do they come, and in what crucible, on what anvils hot with pain spring the soldiers of India, whom surely Baba Ghandi never fathered? Who is the great bearded Sikh with his uncut Nazarite hair, his curling beard, and the enormous head-dress with encircling quoit? What brings the jaunty swaggering hill-man from the frontier, 'who treads the ling like a buck in spring', to the wars of the East and West? Where does the square-shouldered athletic Mussulman of the Punjab fit in the system of India, of the lithe Mahratta, with the uncouth *Prakrit*, whom Lord Lake's army in the beginning of the nineteenth century provoked to a fine Mahratta fury, by dubbing them the 'Untoo Goorgas' because of their out-land speech? Does the squat, pug-faced little Mongolian Gurkha with a Kilmarnock cap on the side of his little head fit at all with the tall Rajput longhead, and where comes in the Pariah of Madras who builds the Empire's frontier roads, dammed by some coal-black mammy of the South? Do they the '*gloriamur*' swell or the '*quare fremuerunt*'?

Who is the Afridi soldier who salaamed to the life-size crucifix in Belgium, for some reason he could not fathom, or the men of the lost patrol in Sinai?

Indeed, to understand what is meant by the martial races of India is to understand from the inside the real story of India. We do not speak of the martial races of Britain as distinct from the non-martial, nor of Germany, nor of France. But in India we speak of the martial races as a thing apart and because the mass of the people have neither martial aptitude nor physical courage . . . the courage that we should talk of colloquially as 'guts'.

India has a population of 350 millions. During the World War when the Empire asked India for some more men, the Army Recruiting Board at Delhi and Simla spread their net very wide, and searched into every possible pocket where men of martial proclivities and a modicum of galvanizable physical courage might be found. They estimated that not more than ten per cent., perhaps thirty-five million souls, men and women, old men and children existed, from among whose males of suitable ages soldiers could be found. That is a remarkable fact, and one that opens up on to a strange medley of causes, as scientific as the question of red corpuscles, as historical as the story of Aryan, Dravidian and Aboriginal. It also brings into the discussion the effect of prolonged years of varying religions on their adherents, of early marriage, of premature brides, and juvenile eroticism, of a thousand years of malaria and hook-worm, and other ills of neglected sanitation in a hot climate, and the deteriorating effect of aeons of tropical sun on races that were once white and lived in uplands and on cool steppes.

Three hundred and fifty million people, and perhaps of them thirty-five millions whose young men are manly young men, there may be three million males between the military ages of 20 and 35! Astounding! and at 35 in the East a man is even then ageing for work in the ranks!

This fact, astounding as it is now, begins to clear up the story of the conquerors from the North, the coming of the waves of Tartar, Turk, Mongol, Persian, and Afghan who have ridden through India to dominate, almost from all time and to a very definite extent, since days parallel with the Norman Conquest of Britain.

To follow the story and the romance of the martial races, to see the Rajput soldiery, the 'sons of Princes', struggling against Alexander of Macedon and his Greek phalanx, to read of the Rajput chivalry immolating their wives in the pyre of a burning castle rather than let them fall to the rude hands of Moslem invaders and Tartar pagans, to see them led by British officers to cross bayonets with the French in Java, in Egypt, and in The Mauritius, to watch them carry the Union Jack from the Great Wall of China to the flats of Flanders—a story, a brief story, of the India races is necessary. Things being such, it is possible to understand why Sir John Simon and his Commission reported that without the British officer and the British soldier, the Indian Army the races of the North, would once more eat up the people of the South.

The gentle yet merciless race of hereditary moneylenders, from which Lala Ghandi springs, only kept within bounds by an occasional flaying and roasting, have never been able or even tried to protect their own hoards. Not for them, nor for the classes whence come the political lawyer, was the troopship that led the martial men of India westwards, to fight in the war of freedom.

The clever trading classes of India have never borne the sword by their side, the tradesmen, the artificers, the goldsmiths, all that come under the ancient grouping of the Vaisya, twice-born though they be, have none of the instincts that answer blow with blow. It is one thing to suffer a blow and turn the other cheek, in humility and self restraint. It is quite another thing to do so from fear.

The martial races shall stride across the stage . . . as they swung through Marseilles with half the girls of France on their arms . . . that Marseilles that went beside itself to see the smoke stacks and masts of the mighty Armada that brought the Army of India. The Jăt Sikhs mighty and curled of beard, kin perhaps to the men of Kent, the Jutes from Jutland, with them Moslem and Hindu Rajput, the fierce hillmen from the frontiers, the Tartar from Nepal that we know as Gurkha, recking little else than that the Badshah or Padishah, the great White King, had summoned them and that his white officers would lead them and his white troops fight by their side. We will try to see them in their daily peasant life and working occasions as well as in their romantic warring past and in the disciplined lives that they lead within the ranks and cantons of the Army in India. In so seeing them let us remember that the great Arthur Wellesley himself led them, and brought the slighting term of 'Sepoy General' to everlasting fame, that Alexander of Macedon himself knew them well as ally and as foe, and that many marched with Xerxes to the slaughter at the pass of Thermopylae.

The Divergent Races

The races of India as we know, are many, divergent in origin, and extremely divergent in customs and languages, as indeed are the races of Europe. Unlike the races of Europe there is no universal religion, there is no religious rule of life. Europe is guided in general ethics and its laws are founded on the Decalogue, a rule of Righteousness received of God. The usual conduct of this divergent continent of India is not. Even were it all a Muhammadan or all a Hindu country, it would still, like Europe, have its different races, its intensely divergent climates, its high mountains, and its sweltering watered valleys and its hot and healthy upland, some rainy, some dry. Its agriculture and its fruits vary with its climates, and grow the kindly fruits of the earth, both those of the tropics and those of the far north. But across the ethnic and climatic differences in a bend sinister, lie those of religions. The white races that forced their way through the mountains of Solomon from Central Asian steppes, evolved a faith which we call Hinduism but which they do not. They impinged on a far older faith, and met a far older colonization mixed with earlier folk still. To the working or quarrelling melange of white and darker races, came in due course that portent of the Eastern world, the warring, proselytising faith of Islam, the Submission to the One God, conceived of an earlier tradition, and explained in desert metaphor, and to meet this conquering faith that set the East a-roar, there existed south of the Indus a civilization and a religious system entirely different. The new-comer came in his millions and with him came power and might and dominion, and many colonizing men of hardy race. To this day the followers of Islam and those of the early complicated faith that never dies, glare at each other, across the table, in the council chamber, and in the streets of the crowded cities. There is only one set of people among whom live and let live is a principle, and only one place where cameraderie is a practice. The martial races of India live side by side in friendliness so long as there is a strong hand of Government to prevent their stouter hearts joining more seriously in the quarrel, and this place where cameraderie exists is curiously enough in those homes of content and enthusiasm, the regiments of the Army of India.

To understand then the martial races a bowing acquaintance is necessary, and will be set forth in brief sequence, with the history of the races and the rise of the religions. In this light the puzzling fact of the martial and non-martial races and the almost impassable line between them will, to some extent, be intelligible.

An Outline of Indian Ethnology

It is almost a commonplace of knowledge to speak, as has just been done, of the move of the Aryan races from their cradle somewhere on the steppes of Asia, but it is the keystone of the Indian population problem. Nowhere else on the world's surface does the story of thousands of years ago still have every day repercussions and echoes in the every day social life of the people.

Until quite recently it was held that the Aryan races, simple, pastoral, but of an intellectual brain structure, entered an India populated by an earlier emigrant race of no great culture, and by negroid and Mongoloid aboriginals, and that the white race of their own power had evolved a mighty culture, a complicated religion and an intricate philosophy. Now, after many centuries, the spade and the pick, on the lower Indus and in the Punjab, are showing us the remains of a civilization as old as and sib to that of the Babylon of Hammurabi and of Ur of the Chaldees. It may well be found therefore that the Aryan impinged on something far more developed, and as Goth and Vandal took on the polish of Rome, so they found some of their culture ready made. (*v.* p. 19).

That, however, is not very germane to the subject of this book, and the point here is that some four thousand years ago a white race akin to our British selves, which became the mother of the Hindu race of to-day, trekked up the Oxus with their ox and their ass and swirled up and round the mountains that we now call Afghanistan. Thence they welled through the passes to the Indus and the rivers of the Punjab, and thence over the district known as Sirhind the 'Head of India', down to the valleys of the Jumna and mighty Ganges.

Now as these people developed and settled, and conquered the earlier inhabitants, the hammer and spear head, the fighting man, became at some time or other, known as Rajputs, the 'sons of princes' or the 'clansmen of princes', and in the development that followed crystallized off into a separate race or people. It is as if the Scottish Highlanders and their chiefs, their clansmen and their dune-vassals remained cognate, aloof and separate from the rest, colonizing far and wide but remaining apart with great pride of place, from the rest of the world. Incidentally perhaps it may be said, if you had seen a Highland gathering in the Rocky Mountains or the Scottish regiments of Canada in their kilts and feather bonnets, you might feel that the Scottish clansmen have to some extent, remained wherever they spread as have the Rajput clans in India, but minus the inexorable religious spacing. The point of it is that, as we come to analyse the various races of India to-day, in various guises which merit the term and distinction of 'martial', we shall see that in some way or other they are the descendants of the warriors who carried forward the Aryan exodus and influx, and that mingled with them are another race somewhat cognate who came last whom we know as Jăt or Jāt. Such others as there be are of an entirely different biological origin and psychology, variant of the Tartars, who should be called Tātars, and pronounced like a postman's knock . . . the people of the Mongol fold, which we call the almond-eye, flat-nosed, high-cheeked folk, so different from the Aryan beauty and physiognomy of the Greek, to which the high-grade Aryan profile of India bears considerable resemblance.

THE CONFLICTING RELIGIONS

The conflicting religions are primarily those of Brahminism and Islam, because between these two, which the bulk of the people profess, so long as religious differences stir men minds, no real concordat is possible. A short description is needed if we are to see the repercussions that influence the martial races. Brahminism is the teaching evolved through the ages by the priestly classes of the Aryan incoming. It is a most subtle intellectual conception of the world, the universe, and the powers that control it, thrice distilled and complicated by the probing to the *n*th of the problems that puzzle mankind. Some 80 millions of the followers of Islam, the Moslems or Muhammadans, face 270 millions of people of whom the greater portion may perhaps be classed as Hindus, those people of Hind or Ind who follow the teachings in some sense of the Brahmin priests and leaders.

But this large body includes a thousand Hindu cults and castes, many of which are anathema to each other.

Islam has more than one sect, notably the division between the orthodox and those who follow Ali and the Prophet's family as the successors in the guidance. But besides these two main cults and the infinite variants of Hinduism, there are the Jains who follow the teaching of a contemporary of the Buddha, one Mahavira, the *Jinna* or 'Conqueror', several missions of Christians of varying denominations, the Parsees, a few indigenous Jews, and in addition many millions of aboriginal animists. But the greater variants in many ways are those that occur within the Hindu umbrella. The 60 million untouchables come nominally within Hinduism, despised and debased though they are, while even orthodox Hinduism recognizes such ranges as those from the salvation cult down to the realistic worshipper of female force. How each and all came to arise is outside the scope of this book, but it may be said, that the high-caste Hindu, with his theory of re-incarnation, and *karma* the effect of his doings on his next incarnation, is in his own opinion the only one who has the keys of the next world in his hands. His spiritual regard for others does not exist, thus his tolerant contempt for other religions is supreme. His worship, especially in its lesser variants, contains many deities, in themselves perhaps but aspects of the one, and to the Moslem, the fierce uncompromising unitarian, this is sheer idolatry worthy only of his unutterable contempt. Strange bed and board fellow then must they be, whose tolerance one with another rests on feeble props and stays.

The Aryan Castes

The martial races, as explained, are largely the product of the original white races. The white invaders in the days of their early supremacy started the caste system, as a protection, it is believed, against the devastating effect on morals and ethics of miscegenation with Dravidian and aboriginal peoples. The men of war were given to women it would seem, and the priest and leaders saw that that tendency must be kept within legitimate lines. The white people therefore, became stereotyped in three great pure divisions, first the race or clan that succeeded in arrogating to itself the priestly functions, but was far more numerous than priestly functions demanded. These were the Brahmins, and to this day many hundreds of thousands are non-priests. Those who are cultivators and have led a manly life are no mean soldiers. Then the tribes and clans that followed the chiefs and did most of the warring, became recognized as forming the great Kshattriya or warrior caste, a people of many clans who established themselves in many parts of India desirable and otherwise. Below them by reason of their peaceful callings, were the Vaisyas, traders, merchants, clerkly, servitors, artificers in clean material and the like. These three represent the ancient divisions of the 'Twice-born' a term which means little more than baptized, in the same sense as the Christian is 're-born' of water and the Spirit. Below them came the great army of the Sudras, those beyond the pale, descended of Aryan sires and out-caste dams, innumerable as the years rolled on, and within it innumerable sub-castes of its own, of no import to the white world, of immense import to themselves. As among the Sudras so among the 'twice-born' Vaisyas whose innumerable occupations tended to mix trade-union principles with religious conceptions of man's value on earth, many castes arose, and all the while war, rule, power, might, and dominion was with the Kshattriyas, now the Rajputs, who had many clans but one main caste, that of the warrior, the man who dealt with realities, and as warrior held the land in military and feudal tenure. Behind them, the power behind the throne, the hand that rocked the cradle, were the Brahmin's brains, priestly and lay, scheming, subtle, patriot.

From this faint impression of the story we begin to get some glimmer of the crucible whence the martial classes arose and how they came to be supreme. A complication and a change whose ramifications will never be known, came with the strange downfall of Brahminism, which commenced when that complicated and intense religious and social system was at its zenith, and was then driven to the wilderness for a thousand years. In the sixth century B.C., was born Gautama Siddatha of the Kshattriya family of a ruling prince in what is now Nepal. From him emanated the wonderful philosophy that men called Buddhism. Gautama eventually became known as 'Buddha' 'the enlightened', and the noble humane philosophy 'Enlightenment' that he taught eventually drove Brahminism into pockets and pot-holes. How Buddhism took five hundred years to rise and five hundred years to wane, and became a 'religion' will be outlined hereafter.[1]

It was not till about the sixth century A.D. that Brahminism was paramount once again, and India was ruled by Hindu princes obedient to the priestly control.

The religion-gripped divisions of the people when free from Brahminism during the prevalence of Buddhism, must have retained some portion of their social status, so that they took on the old form fairly easily. But it would appear that the Brahmins had the power of classification and could enact higher or lower status within certain limits as they thought fit. It is to be presumed that those who early re-embraced the old faith were assured of status thereby, and that many were classed as Rajput for political rather than hereditary reasons. The caste grouping of India to-day

[1] See p. 41.

therefore, dates from about the times of the comings of the Saxons to England.

The Rajputs and Jăts

The Rajputs, the 'sons of princes', the modern remnants of the Kshattriyas, were and are grouped in three great divisions, those of the Sun, the Moon, and the Fire, and there is no doubt that they dwelt far up in the mountains of Afghanistan, as well as in India. The people as far north as Kabul were Hindu up till the eleventh century and Rajput or Jăt at that. This brings us to the Jăt race who to this day are so mixed up with the Rajputs in the martial story of India.

The story of this people is not a very clear one, but it is certain that they, a somewhat cognate white race, followed the Aryans into India perhaps a thousand years behind them, and coming by the southern roads ousted or pushed further south the Aryans on the lower Indus and in the southern Punjab, reaching eventually below Delhi. At some time in their history they entered the Hindu hierarchy as high-caste men, but were never acknowledged to be of Rajput origin. They must also have settled in some of the valleys of what is now Afghanistan, and there is little doubt that the majority of the Pathan tribes of the frontier hills are of Jăt or Rajput origin.

When Alexander of Macedon entered India he came to enforce his control over the Persian province of Northern India which Darius had captured five hundred years before Christ, but which after Eastern custom, had more or less broken away from his freak successors. From the vicinity of what is now Kabul he summoned the chiefs of Northern

India to come and pay him fealty as the ruler of the Empire of Persia. Some did and some did not.[1] Among those who did was Rajah Taxiles of Taxila, that ancient city of Hindu Greek and Buddhist culture, which has of late been unearthed not far from the great modern military station known as Rawalpindi, the *pind* a village on the Rawal stream.

It would even appear from the Greek historians that the very same tribes who occupy the hills to-day were there in Alexander's time, the inhabitants of the Khaiber region, being referred to as Aparoetae, which is the way the folk we call Afridi pronounced their own name.

When Islam came to India a large number of the Rajput and Jăt tribes adopted that faith, the Muhammadan Rajputs to-day form the bulk of the fighting men of the Punjab, and it is probable that the tribes of the frontier hills are as stated above for the most part the same, viz., Jăt and Rajput Muhammadan tribes who had done likewise.

The Jăt race are known as Jāts south of the Punjab, most of the Sikh fraternity are Jăts to whom the teaching of that religion especially appealed, but the race is to be found in the Punjab as Hindu Sikh and Moslem. The Maharajah Runjhit Singh, the Sikh baron, who turned the Afghan province of the Punjab into a kingdom for the space of his life only, left miserable sons behind him. They all met their deaths at the hands of his unruly soldiery and nobles, with the exception of the boy Dhulip Singh, the putative, but not accredited son of his old age. Runjhit Singh was a Jăt. When, after his death, his army insisted a year or so later on rushing onto the bayonets of Lord Gough and the Indo-British Army, and were destroyed for their pains, the British Government endeavoured to restore and maintain

[1] See p. 22.

the Sikh kingdom. It will be remembered how the Sikh chiefs and the old Sikh Army that survived insisted on trying their fate once more, only to be destroyed in 'the crowning mercy' of Goojerat. Then was the Punjab annexed and the boy, Dhulip Singh, eventually sent to be brought up in England with ample revenues. To him his friend, Colonel Sleeman, the famous Indian political officer, wrote, "I see you are going to live in Kent. You will be among your own people there, for you are a Jăt and the men of Kent are Jăts from Jutland," and no doubt he was speaking ethnological truth.

How the Jăts have kept up their war-like proclivities through the ages, how the Jăt who is a Sikh has been so prominent and faithful a soldier of the Crown, or how the Hindu Jāt came to such great fame in the World War, for one of their battalions to receive the title of 'Royal', will be told in the course of this book.

Afghan and Pathan

Reference has been made to the Muhammadan conquests and invasions of India, from the hills in the North-west, which began when Sultan Mahmud Ghuznavi was king of Ghuzni the hill-girt city which lies in the uplands between Kabul and Kandahar.

Mahmud of Ghuzni, to give him his usual historical name, was a Turk, but when he rode to India there rode with him every lad who could raise a horse from Turkestan and from what we now call Afghanistan. Afghanistan means the 'country of the Afghans', and is in itself a modern word, the actual country so designated being long part of the Empire of Delhi or the kingdoms of the Punjab. It takes its name from a race who gave the country an emperor. Ahmed Shah the Afghan, of the Abdali tribe, a leader of horse in the pay of Nadir Shah the Persian Turk, it will be remembered, seized after his master's murder in 1747 his treasure and the provinces of Kabul, Kandahar, Herat and also those bordering on the left bank of the Indus, carving therefrom the Durani Empire. This was a name of his own invention, for he dubbed himself *Dur-i-Duran*, the Pearl of Pearls and his people *Duranis* 'the people of the Pearl'. His own people, the Afghans proper, are an Arab or Semitic folk who came into the Mountains of Ghor and the vicinity of Kandahar somewhere about the time of the Prophet and his teaching (seventh century). They call themselves, to this day, the Children of Israel, the '*Ben-i-Israel*', and claim descent from one Afghana, a grandson of Saul of Israel and a commander-in-chief of Hebrew Armies. They evidently took the new faith fiercely, as did all its converts, and must have taken a considerable part in conquering and converting the people whom we call Pathans, the remainder of the non-Turkish people of the hills and valleys on the right bank of the Indus. So much so, that all the people who have already been referred to as being in all probability the original Rajput and Jăt colonists of those hills, now claim relationship with the Afghans; Afghan genealogists have framed a largely fictitious, yet ample table, showing that all the tribes who speak Pashto or Pakhto, which is what the word 'Pathan' means are descended from one Kish or Kais who was eighteenth in descent from Saul.

Together they claim to be the Afghan race, although the *Durani* is usually of Semitic type while the non-Durani Pathan is often of Aryan and even Greek profile.

However, these people, who all became Moslem, followed Mahmud of Ghuzni and his successors to India and settled all over the land, carving estates for themselves and helping to establish the Muhammadan dominion that reached as far as the Bay of Bengal on the one side and down to the Dekhan in the South, and even to Mysore.

Lest the term Moslem be not clear, let it be explained that the Prophet Muhammad preached the doctrine of Islam which means 'The Submission', the submission to Allah, the ancient God of the patriarchs whose recognition had been obscured by the worship of countless idols and sub-gods by the Arab of the desert. Moslem by the derivative system of the Arabic language means 'he who practises Islam'. By another derivative the Moslem is also often referred to as a Mussalman, which contains the same root as Islam. Moslems and Mussalmans are but Muhammadans, the followers of the faith taught by the Prophet Muhammad, which is also spelt by older writers as Mahomet.

Now the Afghan and Pathan settlers of India were long the material from whom many of the princes found their soldiery, princes of their own race and faith. Indeed in a vast sense the Muhammadan conquest followed the ways of the Norman conquest save that it was religious as well as racial. The Moslems of India are divided into four main classes, *Sheikh*, *Sayad*, *Mogul*, *Pathan*. *Sheikh* meaning lord is a euphemistical name for the Hindus who became Moslems, not always from fear of the sword but from admiration of the teaching. *Sayad* is the descendant of the original Arab evangelists of the sword. *Pathans* are the speakers of Pashto, Afghan or otherwise. *Mogul* is the name for the many and various Turks, Tartars or Mongols, who flocked into India from the days of Mahmud of Ghuzni onwards, and were indeed drawn from many of the differing Turki peoples from Central Asia and Mongolia, who show the almond eye that is called the Mongol Fold.

So Sheikh, Sayad, Mogul, Pathan are the Moslems of India and under Sheikh come those Rajput clans who accept Islam and who form the backbone of the Indian Army to-day.

THE TURKS IN INDIA

The Turks in India have been many, but they have ceased to be as distinct from the ordinary Moslem population as perhaps the Afghans. Since Genghis Khan the great Tartar conqueror was of Mongol stock, and many of his followers of that branch of the Turkish race known as Mongols, therefore Baber and his successors of the great Mogul Empire took that name, because it was a name of fear. Baber himself, was a Chagatai Turk descendant of Timur, although on his mother's side he traced descent from Ghengis Khan. In India this dynasty is known as Chagatai. For this reason all Turks in India whether Turk, Tartar, Usbeg, Mongol or Uirghur (the word of dread from which we derive ogre) came to be called or called themselves Mogul.

The almond eye has largely died out in India itself, though we find it in the hills on the confines of Tibet where Aryan and Dravidian blood has met Mongolian blood of old strains.

The word Turk is, of course, used in many non-descript and differing senses as is that Tartar. Turk or Tartar is really the term for all the many clans, tribes and races that have the almond fold, except so far as miscegenation has carried that fold into many aboriginal and other peoples. Thus Mongols, Uirghars, Usbegs, Kirghiz, are all Turks. The country that they belong to is Turkestan whether Russian Afghan or Chinese, and their story one of strange romance. Time and again have they swept Europe; far into

Russia, up the Danube and along the coast of the arctic seas have they penetrated as Turks and Huns, and even the Prussian has the cruel Hun blood in his veins.

In India many of the nobles and barons are of Turkish origin. The Nizam of Hyderabad is a Turk, for instance, the descendant of the only one of the revolted Mogul Viceroys who made his peace with the British and remains. In Mogul days the quarrels and factions of the Turkish Lords, the 'Lords of Turan' and the Aryan chiefs the 'Lords of Iran' were a constant theme and anxiety. The Turki language stretches from the Pacific to the Bosphorus and four Turkish dynasties quartered Asia, the Manchus at Pekin, the Moguls at Delhi, the Khajjars at Teheran, and the Ottoman at Constantinople, of all of whom it may now be said 'none so poor as do them reverence'.

But the Turkish military strain has almost died from those who claim martial status in India, the Moguls of the Salt Range in the Punjab being the principal modern presentatives. Yet round Delhi there are settlements of Mogul graziers who drove the conquerors' flocks and who still call to their sheep in the Indian plains with the peculiar cry of the Steppes and not the cry of India.

The Turkish stock in the Indian Army is represented by these Mogul, and by foreigners from the highlands beyond Ghuzni, the Tartar folk known as the Hazaras. The only other exponents of the Tartar blood are the Gurkhas, the Mongoloid tribes of Gurkha or Nepal, from the Rajput state which is outside India, of whom more anon.

With such a glance from the air on the racial past, we may now more easily turn to the story, the romance and the drama of the martial races through the later centuries and to-day.

CHAPTER II

THE EARLY WARRIORS OF INDIA

THE KSHATTRIYAS—ALEXANDER ENTERS INDIA—THE ROCK OF AORNOS —THE DEFEAT OF KING POROS—THE STORY OF THE BRAHMIN RECRUIT—THE RISE OF CHANDRA GUPTA—THE EMPIRE OF ASOKA— BETWEEN ASOKA AND HARSHA.

THE KSHATTRIYAS

THE doings of the war-like Aryan clans in their earlier days of colonization are wrapped in legend and mystery in which the persons of deities, spirits and incarnations change piquets continually. The great epics of the Ramayana and the Mahabharata mix legend and what must be history inextricably, but only the patience of German students working for generations could possibly sift any of the grains of truth from the accretions of the fantastic. But we know from such glimpses that come through that they found castles to storm and we know too that as the centuries rolled on, farther did they penetrate into the mountains and jungles of Central India through the ranges of the Arravallis and Vindhyas, to the country of the demons and the black people.

The discoveries of the last few years, in the ancient city sites at Mohenjo-Daro in Sind and Harappa in the Punjab, show us cities revealing a culture akin to that of Ur of the Chaldees three thousand years before Christ, or that of Babylon in the days of Hammurabi and Sargon I. These discoveries have entirely upset the comfortable conception that Indian thought and Aryan civilization sprang from the acute and highly developable brains of the incoming whit migrants. We now know, though the spade of the archæologist and the studies of those who interpreted his unearthings have hardly yet spoken to us clearly in the matter, that these discoveries are going to demonstrate how a very advanced civilization of a kind did exist in the East two thousand years and more before it was hitherto suspected. Whether that civilization had disappeared, whether it had developed steadily, or whether it had deteriorated so that the white Aryan races swept into a rotten 'troll garden' to use Kingsley's expression, as Goth and Vandals swept into the Roman Empire, is yet to be determined. We cannot yet know, if ever, whether our white Aryan nomads fought merely against half civilized folk, or whether great dynasties broke before their bows and spears. We know that they found an earlier emigrant dominion which we call Dravidian in the land. What it consisted of is as yet a sealed book.

But let us turn over the pages of a thousand years or so, and we find the Aryan civilization in full swing, such a civilization as has been unveiled for us at Taxila close to Rawalpindi at the entrance to the Hazara valley. Here we begin to meet the precise history of the Greek writers which modern discoveries in India as in Mesopotamia, have been able to countercheck in a remarkable manner.

Alexander Enters India

When the civilization of Kshattriya and Brahmin were highly developed, there came a remarkable contact with the West, in the coming of Alexander of Macedon.

The historians of the Alexandrine Legend obviously

ALEXANDER IN INDIA (*By courtesy of the Indian Archaeological Dept.*)

Remains in Taxila, the capital of his Indian ally

compiled their narratives from contemporary accounts, and just as modern excavations and researches have proved the truth of many of the accounts of the Hebrew writers, and of the inscribed claims of Babylonian Kings, so have the Greek writers gained by cross and counter reference. It is to be remembered with interest, since logical pretexts for adventurous conquests are as modern as they are old, that Alexander came to India in his capacity as the holder of the Persian throne. In the battle of Arbela by the Greater Zab, now known of men as Erbil, the defeat of the Issus had been turned to crushing disaster. The magnificent road and staging system of Persia, already honeycombed with Greek clerks and traders, was at the disposal of the conqueror and up the great route to Khorassan and what are now Kandahar and Kabul, Alexander led his Macedonians supplemented with levies of Aryan Persians.

Five hundred years B.C., what is now known as Afghanistan and the Indus valley was conquered by the Persian general Skylax and became a Persian province. In the generations that followed no doubt the Aryan chieftains faltered in their allegiance whenever the Persian power waxed feeble. It was close on two hundred years later that mighty Alexander of the Two Crowns, in the year 327 before Christ to be precise, marched up the road from Kandahar and what was later Ghuzni to the vicinity of the present Kabul, to re-assert the Persian dominion over Northern India. This march was not so wonderful as is often supposed. The roads for the most of the way were superb, the routes well known, and Greeks had probably often traversed them, while the pack systems of the period and of the countries traversed were equal to the occasion.

From his camp near Kabul the Macedonian summoned those chiefs whom Skylax had conquered in the old time afore, to come and renew their homage to their ancient Persian overlord in the person of himself. Several obeyed his summons, others did not, and it has been surmised that those who did were later arrivals, of Jăt or Scythian origin, outside the normal Aryan fold as later comers to India, their hands often against their older neighbours, among whose landed possessions they had probably played cuckoo.

However that may be, Alexander then marched for the Indus, avoided the Khaiber route, whose inhabitants, the Aparoetae were as kittle cattle to deal with then as the Apriti or Afridi are to-day. Crossing the Kabul river near Jalalabad, and moving up the Kunar river, he entered the Peshawur valley by the Swat and probably over what is now the Malakand pass.

The Indian people of Swat contested his advance with ill success, Alexander then made to cross the Indus, and join at Taxila his ally Prince Taxiles, apparently one of those who had accepted his summons and recognized him as his ruler. But beiore he did so, he realized that the tribes with whom he had been fighting had withdrawn to a mountain fastness, where they with all their families and flocks could live and sally forth on the communications of the invaders. The Great King was too good a soldier to accept this situation and while the bulk of his army were making preparation to cross the Indus at Amb above the modern Attock, he himself with his lightly equipped and other selected storm troops set about to attack this fastness in the mountains.

The Rock of Aornos

Chief among the Alexandrine historians, perhaps is Flavius Arrianus who we speak of as Arrian. But Arrian was born in A.D. 96 and Alexander invaded India in 327 B.C. The astounding story of the storming of the Rock of Aornos, was compiled apparently from accounts by that Ptolemy who founded the Greek dynasty of Egypt, and that by Aristoboulos, both of whom took part in the deed.

Ever since the British came to this part of India in 1849, historians and archæologists have searched for the Rock of Aornos. Many have been the mountain sites along the Indus suggested but none of them filled the bill of the historians' detailed account. Then for some years the forbidden mountain top of Mahabun in the inaccessible independent hills was looked on as the spot, that hill, which can be seen from the Attock railway bridge, snow-topped in winter and always blue and provocative. But some years ago Sir Aurel Stein of the Indian Archæological Department visited the mountain under tribal escort, arranged by the Chief Commissioner on the Frontier. Alas! he came back to report that by no stretch of imagination could he fit the place to the account. Such few ruins as there were must be of far later date.

However, the years rolled by, and peaceful influences increased, so that a few years later Sir Aurel was able to go much further into these tumbled mountains known as the Trans-Indus Kohistan, or 'Hill Country', searching more especially for Buddhists sites referred to by the famous 'Chinese Pilgrims', into the water-parting between the Indus and the Swat, to Ghorband and Chakesa.

When his venture to Mahabun proved a failure, Sir Aurel Stein was at last inclined to think that Aornos and its storming must really be a travellers' tale, but Colonel Wahab of the Royal Engineers, a well known frontier road-maker and geographer, had always thought that the site might be still further up the Indus gorges, and though hanging with grim cliffs over that mighty river might be accessible from behind.

This conjecture proved to be right and Sir Aurel from the reverses slopes, after much climbing found the great plateau of refuge with a peak called Una[1] and even the little col connecting it with the outer world. He found too the actual bluff on which Alexander's engineers had built up the erection from which their marksmen kept down the fire of the defenders while the gorge between was sufficiently filled up with tree trunks cut and carried from the forests below. In every way it filled Arrian's description, and is still the place to which the graziers move their flocks in summer. Here is Arrian's account which it fulfils: "The rock is said to have a circuit of about 200 stadia (23 miles), and its lowest elevation a height of 11 stadia (6,700 ft.). It was ascended by a single path cut by the hand of man, and yet difficult. On the summit of the rock there was, it is also said, plenty of pure water, which gushed out from a copious spring. There was timber besides, and as much good arable land as required for its cultivation a thousand men."

How the desperate storming was done by the Greek veterans and their Bactrian levies, and how desperate was the struggle for the col, Arrian tells us, and we who have seen Highlanders and Sikhs vie with one another to scale the goat-foot path that led to Dargai know that the tale can be true, and that as it is described so it occurred, twice a thousand thrice a hundred years and more ago.

The Defeat of King Poros

Having safely crossed the Indus, with no enemy left in being behind him, Alexander halted awhile at Taxila, and

[1] Which may be "Aornos."

held an assault-at-arms. In other words his army wanted rest, and some re-equipping after the arduous passage through the hills. The tribesmen with whom he contended were, we may be sure, very much the same folk as the British Indian Army of to-day knows so well, and their methods would be, at any rate, not dissimilar to the mountain tactics of the frontier tribes, say fifty years ago, before a plethora of breech-loading weapons made them shun the impact of steel. We may be confident that the Aparoetae referred to were but the Apriti of to-day, that being the Afridi's own pronunciation of his modern name[1], while the Păctiae were no doubt, the folk who spoke as to-day that language of the frontier of the same stock as the Indian tongue which we know as Păctu or Păshtu.[2]

Coming through the passes the slingers on the hill-tops no doubt took tally of the convoys whenever the heights were not piquetted by the light troops, the *hypaspae*, and bunches of swordsmen hung about the ravines waiting lest a convoy escort snoozed and gave an opening. The ways of mountain warriors all the world over remained the same for countless years, until villainous saltpetre taught them even better ways of battle, murder and sudden death.

So at Taxila the Macedonians and their Aryan levies led by eager young Aryans of the West exactly as the Aryan Rajput soldiery are led to this day by their enthusiastic Western Aryans of Britain, halted a while and recovered from the strain of the mountain passage and the storming of Aornos. No doubt, as we ourselves know so well, cattle needed rest and more had to be hired.

The next task before the invaders was to tackle the Kshattriya overlord of the country, to whom the chieftains had transferred their allegiance when Persian rule waxed

[1] *v.* p. 22.

[2] Which comes from the *Zend*.

feeble, but who was probably always outside the original Persian acquisition.

In these matters of Eastern conquest it is to be remembered that from ancient to quite modern times, conquest and over-lordship meant merely the paying of revenue and the supplying of military contingents on demand to the overlord, who if not interfered with did not himself interfere with local governments and people. We may here compare the system of Napoleon when Europe lay at his feet. It was not indeed, until the fanaticism of the earlier Islamic conquerors brought religion as well as dominion into the scales, and slaughtered the people they conquered rather than made them revenue payers, that this situation altered. The lesser barons in the days of Alexander sided with the strong man armed, especially if, as seems to have been the policy of Alexander, reasonable political treatment was meted out to those who submitted.

The good King Porus who ruled the Northern Punjab was not, however, to submit without a trial of strength, and so Alexander accompanied by Taxiles with 5,000 of his own men started off to the most nor-westerly of the five rivers, the River Hydaspes which is now the Jhelum, on the eastern side of which, dominating the crossing, King Poros had massed his forces, estimated as the Alexandrine historians record at 4,000 horse, 30,000 foot, 300 chariots and 200 elephants. The latter two may indeed be considered as the whippet and heavy tanks of the period.

The passage across the Punjab will have followed to a great extent the line of the Grand Trunk Road which our troops know so well, filing through the gorges of Jani Ka Sang, and thence down to the plains of Rawalpindi, where, no doubt, the *pinus longifolia* which is still seen in patches covered a wider area. The River Jhelum after emerging from the mighty Pir Panjal range and cutting across some open country then finds itself tearing its way through the gorges of the Salt Range, those hills that have bred and nurtured men among men, warriors and yeomen from earliest days. Here were the Aryan Kshattriya tribes and their henchmen established, and from far and near were in the Rajput, to use the more recent word, ranks of the Punjab King. Under the gorges of the Salt Range, hidden perhaps by the alley ways that they afford, the Macedonians reached what is now Jallalpur, amid raw red rocks, broken ravines, patches of arable silt and certain habitable flats and islands. As it was now summer and the Hydaspes was heavy with molten snow-water, Alexander, to lull the Indians to security, gave out that he did not intend to attempt the passage until later in the year when the floods would have subsided.

The Indian host in the meantime faced him on the hither-bank opposite Jallalpur, while Alexander constantly moved forces up and down the right bank so as to keep the Indians in doubt as to his intentions. Seventeen miles to the north of Jallalpur, where the main army of Porus faced the Macedonian camps, the Jhelum takes a sweep, and on the right bank stood a great mass of rock, and opposite in mid-stream a wooded island.

Here Alexander decided to make a crossing, leaving Craterus in charge of his main camp at the Jallalpur fords. He started for the rock aforesaid, reaching it apparently unseen by the Indian host. Under cover of night he regained the island to find at dawn that a rushing branch of the river still lay between him and the left bank. A deep ford however, was shown him, which his horsemen managed to negotiate, his infantry crossing as best they could by boat, and some neck-high in the river.

With Craterus Alexander had left orders to cross to his

front, if the Indians had sent away all their elephants to meet his own turning movements, saying that if any elephants remained Craterus would not be able to get his horses to ford the river.

Across the river, Alexander formed a line facing down the stream with his right thereon, which as his infantry struggled over, gave him some 4,000 horse and 6,000 foot. By now Porus knew of the crossing of at least a Macedonian detachment and sent his son with 2,000 horse and 120 chariots to oppose it. This inadequate force, as might have been expected, received very rough handling from the invaders' cavalry, losing its leader, 400 men and all the chariots which had stuck in the river sand.

Porus now hastily moved the bulk of his army some five miles up river, and formed into line of battle about the present mud village of Moong.

Moong, it is interesting to note, is practically the scene of the desperate soldiers' battle of Chillianwallah, fought in January, 1849, between a Punjabi army, many of them the Rajput descendants of the very men who fought against or for Alexander at this battle of the Hydaspes, and Lord Gough with his mixed force of British and Hindustani soldiers. The historical parallel was well known to the British Army for, by the camp fires, the following was lustily roared:

> Sabres drawn and bayonets fixed
> Fight where fought Alexander
> O'Paddy Gough's a cross betwixt
> Bull-dog and Salamander.

The Rajput army of King Porus thus hastily threw itself in array and faced up the Hydaspes as the Macedonians moved down. It must have been much such an army as is to this day to be seen in some of the Indian states, and certainly resembled, let us say, that of the Mahrattas at the last battle of Panipat in 1761. It must also have resembled that portion of the Punjabi armies eighty years ago as had not had a European military training. Masses of spearmen and archers, gaudy colours, plenty of banners as each chieftain led forward his henchmen—the great elephant tanks in the intervals, the whippets of the chariots waiting to gallop forward en masse—plenty of colour, steel helmets, bright scarves and baldricks, axe and lance and mace. How far there was discipline and power of manœuvre is not known, but other details we do know from the pages of Arrian.

Alexander, writes the historian, pressing forward with cavalry, his infantry following steadily behind, halted in view of the Indian army till they came up and deployed. Then engaging the enemy's left he sent a force of cavalry under Coenus to envelop the Indian outer flank and rear. Holding back his frontal attack till his cavalry, as highly trained and equipped as those of modern armies, had plunged into the rear of the Indian masses, he joined battle on the whole front. It was the old story, the disciplined West, those solid, imperturbable phalanxes were too much for all the wild valour of the East. The elephants were disconcerting to the Macedonian and broke up the lighter formations, but the masses of the phalanx could withstand them, and galled beast and howdah tower with their arrows. In vain the Indian cavalry returned to the charge. The disciplined ranks of horse and foot were too much for them, the elephants penned up among the infantry lost their tempers and damaged friend as much as foe, trampling hundreds under foot, their own mahouts slain by the arrows of the Macedonians. The Indian horse bunched helplessly, lost their pace, and were surrounded by the Greek cavalry, into the midst of whom now advanced a mass of infantry covered by their shields.

Craterus had now crossed the river and come up to take part. Long was the afternoon of slaughter in the heat haze of an Indian summer's day. Twenty thousand Indians were said to have been killed, and all their chariots and elephants captured. It was another Sobraon. The more accurately stated casualties of the victors were said to be less than a thousand, and however that may be, the fate of the Punjab was for the time settled. Porus accepted a state of vassalage and was thus restored to his throne while Alexander passed on. We need not follow him across the Punjab to the Chenab, the Ravi and the Sutlej and the day when after further victories, his army 'fed up' with its years of marching, refused to march for Hindustan.

The story has been told thus far because it tells of the same martial races of India as we know them battling in much the way we also know, and shows the Western Aryans leading their Indian or Eastern Aryan soldiers just as do the British to-day, for there is no new thing under the sun. Then the conqueror was persuaded to return West leaving garrisons, only to die of malaria in Babylon. The 'C. 3' men, to use the modern army jargon, whom Alexander left in India were soon slain or absorbed and India returned to its own Kshattriya allegiance. But the Greeks left kingdoms north of the Indus which endured for generations and mingled the civilizations, of which traces still remain. Among the villages of the tribes in Swat are the ruins of the Graeco-Buddhist settlements and the carved temple friezes like to those of the Parthenon, and to this day also do aged peasants untie the tail of their shirts and offer to sell you the coins concealed therein which they have turned up at the tail of their plough-shares.

There were 216 mints in which Greek coins are known to have been struck. The writer in the early 'nineties was visiting the mint at Jammu in the State of Jammu and Kashmir, with the Accountant General. New Kashmiri rupees were beings truck then, known as *Chilki* rupees, and bags of old hoarded treasure were being melted down. The last bag of an old hoard was being poured forth, and we asked to look. They were all Graeco-Bactrians, and were rescued and formed a joyous find to the Punjab numismatists. The bags that we were too late to save were ever a matter for chagrin.

THE STORY OF THE BRAHMIN RECRUIT

Here is a story which is wafted about in quiet circles in the Punjab by officers who know, which some day I hope to tell at length. The legend runs that once upon a time during his Indian campaigns Alexander was collecting elephants, and there came a Brahmin maid to petition that her father's elephant might be excused. Dazzled by the girl's beauty the King consented on condition that she remained with him. Now Brahmin families do not easily preserve the legends of such happenings, but the philanderings of so powerful a king solace family pride and to this day a certain Brahmin family cherishes a bend sinister as redounding to its glory. The Great King was a man of moods and violent tempers and was in fact, an epileptic, as historical records hint at. The modern story runs somewhat as follows. One Duni Chand, a Punjab Brahmin, had enlisted into a Punjab regiment, a stout, well grown, hearty lad, but the bane of the drill sergeant and his adjutant. Drill as they could, set him as they would, he had the trick of suddenly going askew with one shoulder hunched. The question of his discharge as physically unfit as one having an epileptic taint, was held over for love of his uncle, an old Indian officer of the corps. While he was away as orderly to an officer attached to a frontier column, he fell a victim to a Waziri sniper's rifle, and that was the end of Sepoy Duni Chand.

A year or two later two officers of the regiment visiting a picture gallery in Florence, stopped before the picture of a man, a head and shoulders with a slight upward hunch of one shoulder.

"Why," exclaimed one, "I'm hanged if that is not our Duni Chand, the lad shot when with me up the Tochi."

But the gallery catalogue said, "Alexander the Great (Painter unknown.)"

The Rise of Chandra Gupta

It is necessary to follow in brief outline the centuries that supervened on the Alexandrine invasion, as they have all contributed to that Rajput revival in the first millennium of the Christian Era, which laid the foundation of the martial races and their divisions as we know them to-day. Far down the Ganges valley, while Alexander was harnessing King Porus to the Persian Empire, there flourished the great Hindu Kshattriya kingdom of Magadha, its capital being Pataliputra near by the modern Patna. Magadha, then ruled by the Nanda dynasty, had been extending its influence and had absorbed many of its lesser neighbours. It stretched over the greater part of Bengal and up the Ganges to the confines of the Punjab, and the river Sutlej.

At Taxila Alexander had heard of this great state still to conquer, and the victory over Porus seemed to put even its kingdom within his reach. It is said that a refugee Kshattriya there, one Chandra Gupta whom the Greeks refer to as Sandracottus, urged the enterprise in him, with a view no doubt to holding the satrapy under Alexander, a view as old as the world yet as modern as modern can be, in Eastern politics.

The mutiny of his over-marched soldiery however, put any further conquests outside the realm of immediate possibility, but when the Macedonian authority east of the Indus, faded as quickly as it had arisen, some turn of the wheel, without Greek assistance, brought Chandra Gupta to the throne of Magadha where he established the famous Mauryan dynasty.

In the break up of Alexander's Empire that followed his death at Babylon in 325 B.C., one of his commanders, Seleucus, assumed control of Bactria, the province which is now Afghan Turkestan. Thence he endeavoured to repeat his master's feat and re-entered India. Here he was met by a confederacy with Chandra Gupta at its head, and was so severely handled that he was glad to come to terms with Chandra Gupta and even to give the latter his daughter in marriage, resigning his call to all lands south of Kabul. That was a happy enough proceeding and incidentally it gave the opportunity for more recorded history, which would never have been extant had not Seleucus sent an envoy Megasthenes to reside at the Mauryan court.

Megasthenes remained five years at the headquarters of King Chandra Gupta, and portions of his account remain. He gives many details of what came under his own observation, of the system of law and taxation and administration, and of the vast standing army which presumably alone as in Mogul days secured the adhesion of the component parts of the Empire. According to Megasthenes the army was over 600,000 strong with an immense number of chariots and several hundred elephants, and those conversant with any of the larger 'Princes' States' to-day, will note how little such matters have changed with the ages.

The Empire of Asoka

Chandra Gupta was succeeded by his son who reigned twenty-eight years, and in 267 his famous grandson Asoka came to the throne which Chandra Gupta's heir had still further extended. Under Asoka the empire of Magadha became the greatest Hindu Empire which India has ever seen, before or since. Not only was his reign notable for further conquests, which took it down to the Bay of Bengal and the Krishna river and up to the confines of Bactria itself, but in light and law giving and wisdom it also transcended.

Like so many Indian princes, in succeeding to the throne of Chandra Gupta he had to do so over the body of his elder brother, with whom he had a fierce quarrel. The Buddhist writers of the day say that he murdered his brother to clear his own way to the throne, but other legends represent the elder, who was Governor of Taxila, as being killed in battle with the forces of his brother. These fierce struggles between brothers are a pitiful feature in all the stories of the succession of dynasties, whether Hindu Buddhist or Moslem, and are without doubt due to polygamy. The quarrelling brothers are almost always half brothers, while own brothers are usually friends and allies. The ambitions of the various mothers, added to the custom governing succession whereby the legal heir was often the son nominated by the ruler, are responsible for the struggles which were as disastrous to the state concerned as they were to the unsuccessful claimant. In fact it was for hundreds of years, nay still is, an axiom in the East that no wise king allows his brothers to live, or if he does so deprives them of their eyesight by one of the accepted methods, the red hot iron or the needle. In Turkey it will be remembered under the eyes of civilization, the brothers of the rulers lived in 'the cage', from whence at times they were withdrawn to fill a vacancy on the throne after years of enforced withdrawal from the affairs of the world. In Kabul, the blinding-iron and the knife provided a simpler method.

During his reign Asoka first became a Buddhist layman and then later a Buddhist monk, so that under him Buddhism became practically the state religion and began to spread over the whole of India. His edicts, carved on conspicuous sheets of rock throughout Aryan India, remain to this day, proclaiming the rules of Buddhist life and well-doing. Under him Buddhist missionaries were welcomed all over the civilized world. He died in 232 B.C. after a monumental reign of 41 years, and after him there ruled six more Mauryan kings in 48 years, under whose inferior rule the great empire decayed sadly, so much so indeed that an invasion by a Greek prince Menander of one of the small states west of the Indus into which Bactria had subsided, penetrated to the very gate of Pataliputra itself. With the death of Asoka military power had passed away for a while from Aryan India. Sungas succeeded to Mauryas, and Kanvas to Sungas, and went down in their turn to a great and rising power in Central India and the Dekhan known as the Andras.

Between Asoka and Harsha

Very little is really known of the Andras except that under that dynasty sea trade from the coast both East and

West developed greatly. Along the Indus there were many happenings of which we have but confused information in the centuries immediately before and after the Birth of Christ. The Greek kinglets in Bactria had been engaged with the Parthians who now controlled the Persian Empire, and also with a new set of invaders, the nomadic Sakas whom European writers refer to as Scythians. A Parthian ruler of Persia, one Gondophares, had gained control down to the Indus and made the local chiefs satraps, while the Greek kinglets and their westerners were driven down to the Indus also. To the Indus also came the 'Sakas' about this time. There is some confusion concerning the latter, who are often spoken of as if they are a Tartar people. With them are always bracketed the Jăts or Jāts. This is probably correct, but that the mass of the Sakas Scythians or Jăts were Tartars, is probably wrong. They were apparently of stock much akin to the earlier Aryan invaders and Ibbetson says that the Jăts are indistinguishable from Aryans, a statement with which all who know them will agree. There is no possible trace of the Tartar in the tall Jăt Sikh or Jāt of Delhi.

It is quite possible, however, that this term Scythian was used for all nomads, and that some Tartar nomads were tacked on in their wake. Indeed this Jăt infiltration *via* what is now Kandahar and the passes to the southern Punjab seems to have been steadily in progress since before the days of Alexander.

We shall probably never attain to any more precise knowledge on the subject, but we do know that the Sakas towards the end of the first century did form a rule in Guzerat that waxed to some importance, spreading south to combat with the Andras, and that at the commencement of the first century A.D. they were living under the overlordship of the

Gondophares referred to, who had made them into a Kshattrapa or Satrapy.

The real Tartar invasion comes a little later, when a race known as the Yuechi drove fiercely both Graeco-Bactrians and Sakas before them, and when a portion of them known as the Kushans took possession of what is now Afghanistan and Bokhara under one Kadphises. His son Kadphises II having failed to penetrate into China from Turkestan turned his attention to India, overthrew the Parthian authority and established a capital at Peshawur, whence by the end of the first century he had extended his conquest as far as Benares. This meant the end of any real Indian dynasty or central control, and the Andras in the south and centre were able to increase their territories. About this year Kanishka succeeded to what was large enough to be known as the Kushan Empire. He and his Tartars became Buddhists and Buddhism flourished mightily in Northern India. The kaleidoscope in these centuries was never to come to rest, for by 150 A.D. the Kushans were falling and the Saka kingdom in Guzerat, now Hindu, was coming to power as already mentioned, and the Aryan power was recovering once more on the Ganges. Quite how is not known, but by 250 A.D. another Chandra Gupta starts the Gupta dynasty and again his authority is over a tract big enough to merit the description 'Empire', . . . an empire which lasted to the famous days of Chandra Gupta Vikramaditya, the 'Sun of Victory'. We have a detailed account of the state of affairs at that period when the first of the famous Chinese pilgrims to record his journeys wrote his itinerary. Buddhism he describes as flourishing, but Hindu temples and centres were reviving, and the various dynasties indeed, so far as the mass of the people and the countryside were concerned, were of no great account. The folk merely paid their cess to a new master, the local barons sent their levies to serve a new lord, and marrying and giving in marriage, the reaping of the crops and the comfortable life in the monasteries continued. Indeed a study of England in the Wars of the Roses and even in the Civil War, shows that life went on in the countryside similarly unaffected. As long as you conformed to the demands and orders of the local major-general all was serene. So in Hindustan, in the plains of the Jumna and Ganges, it is a pleasant life that Fa Hien is able to show us, far away from the fiercer stramash on the Indus Valley where Sakas, Bactrians and Tartars struggled for mastery.

We now come to the fierce Tartar in-roads of the Huns and Toraman. The first coming of Turkish races in the shape of the Yuechi and their driving down to India the Greeks, Bactrians and Jăts, has been already related, and now in the middle of the fifth century to add to the medley, come into India the White Huns. These are but some of those hordes whom Attila led to Europe, and who, driven back from the West, in the middle of the fifth century, overflow the plateaux and come through the passes to the patient valley of the Indus, and its long suffering inhabitants. Fierce and cruel as were the conquests of these Huns under Toraman and his son Mihiragula, earning a name of horror still remembered in India, a couple of generations saw their power for evil destroyed, after a crushing defeat of Mihiragula, by the allied forces of several Kshattriya chiefs. Of these Yasodharma of Ujjain seems to have been the leader, a king who is believed to be identical with that Vikramaditya referred to, who figures in many Indian legends. After Chandra Gupta Vikramaditya, the north fell asunder into many small kingdoms, a period which lasted from about 528 A.D. till the first decade of the next century. The Huns who had remained had absorbed Buddhism, and were to some extent already merged with the older peoples and thus prepared for the greater merging that was coming, and which set the framework of the races that has lasted till modern times.

Chapter III

THE NEO-RAJPUT KINGDOM

THE RISE AND FALL OF BUDDHISM—THE EMPIRE OF HARSHA—THE HINDU AND RAJPUTS OF THE REVIVAL—THE JATS—THE GROUPING OF THE RAJPUTS—THE OUTER CONQUESTS.

The Rise and Fall of Buddhism

In the foregoing outline of the early centuries immediately before and after the commencement of the Christian Era, reference has been made to the existence and the spread of Buddhism. Martial history in India is as much connected with movements of religion and the struggles they engender as in the rest of the world, perhaps even more so. In India these movements have covered the face of so many centuries that they must either be swept over with a general glance by the student or else be entered on in considerable detail.

To follow the evolution of the martial races and the blending that produced the modern Rajput peoples, an outline of the rise and fall of Buddhism in India, is essential, but more than a mere outline is beyond the scope and purpose of this book.

The faith of 'Enlightenment' had its birth when Brahminism under the old dispensations was at its zenith, thrice complicated in subtlety and refinement. Throughout the land many teachers and many preachers were searching for

THE TRUE (ĀSĂL) HINDU RAJPUT
The Bikani Camel Corps, famous in Syria (1914–17)

THE SPORTING PUNJABI MUHAMMADAN RAJPUT

[*Face page* 40

light, girding at privilege and ritual, and the chains thus forged for mankind. They and the *Buddha*, thought not of new religion but only preached reform and simplicity within the existing order.

In the sixth century B.C. two teachers rose to prominence, Mahavira the *Jinna* or 'Conqueror', and the noble, eternally famous 'Buddha'. *Buddha* which means 'The Enlightened' was a Kshattriya princelet, a son of a ruler of Kapilavasthu in what is now Nepal, named Suddhodana, and is often referred by his names Gautama and Siddatha. He was of the Munia clan and is also often spoken of as Sakyamuni the 'sage of the Muni'. Having taken part in his youth in the field-sports and wars that his race so often enjoyed, a surge of horror entered his soul that such things should be. Turning to the gentle holy thoughts of the world, he spent many years searching for the 'way of life' at the feet of others and found it not. Then it was that he founded his own school and taught the 'Noble Eightfold Path'. Buddhism was a levelling philosophy and how and what it taught is again beyond the scope of this book of warriors. It was but one of the many teachings in this Hinduism and not intended to be the separate faith into which it grew. Suffice it to say, that it spread but slowly, yet with sure gathering force, till at last the great Asoka[1] who, as related, had brought under his one rule far more of India than had ever been unified before, became first a lay brother and eventually a monk. This was in the latter half of the third century B.C. Asoka having ascended the throne in 267.

When Asoka, whose famous edicts of morals have been referred to, actually adopted Buddhism, that 'Way', for it was not yet a religion in the strict sense of the word, was

[1] Now spelt Açoka by the scientific.

assured of dominance and started on its inevitable path of ecclesiastical agrandisement.

It spread and spread, till the ancient dominion of Brahminism was practically eradicated and driven under ground, remaining dormant among the never dying sacred race but confined to the pot-holes and rock temples or the gathering of the 'forest-dwellers', by then disappearing.

Buddhism in India reached its zenith about the time of the birth of Christ. Missionaries too, were carrying it far into Asia, and it is not too much to believe that India was, for a while, infinitely happier and better under the benificent teaching. But it was growing very complicated, because subtle minds still demanded the why and the wherefore, and human minds would not do without a 'religion', a belief in a worship of God, and some method of teaching regarding a mystical communion and 'way' and a word of power. The thinkers gradually produced such within the confines of Buddhism. Incarnations and saviours appeared in the esoteric story, and with a religion there arose the formalism that is inevitable when such things are handled by man. Great prelates came to authority, monasteries galore, powerful and wealthy, arose throughout the land. Then the new faith, now many centuries old was growing remarkably like the old one, without all the village fun that Hinduism had sanctioned. By a process that we do not know, the long wait in the wilderness of Brahminism had passed. Centuries of conservation of teaching and the strength of the old sacredness was to meet with its reward. Presumably there came a period of Buddhist apathy, and this enabled the old faith to come anew.

Because Buddhism was a philosophy, it seems quite possible that the old social barriers were never more than partially broken down, the princes and rulers became supporters of one faith or the other, while the priesthood arose again on political, social and private quarrels. For as the Prophet Jeremiah says—

> "The Prophets prophesy falsely, and the priests bear rule thereby, and my people love to have it so."

The story now passes to the stage where Hindu and Buddhist supporters quarrel one with another, the country slowly falls away from the peaceful, kindly, contented ways that Buddhism succeeded in engendering and the Indian world re-entered the period of strife.

It is under these conditions that the Rajput system as we know it to-day, which has given us in one form or another most of our martial races, and which was able to survive the long Moslem domination without more than partial absorption, began to assume concrete shape.

The Empire of Harsha

The Empire of Harsha, whose final capital was the then magnificent city of Kanauj, flourished when Buddhism was breaking up fast but was still a power in the land. Harsha himself, though a Rajput, was still a Buddhist but the wise men both Brahmin and Buddhist were encouraged to conduct discussions before him. We are singularly fortunate in knowing something of the greatness and also the colour of this period, not from Indian sources but from the itineraries of the second of the famous Chinese Buddhist pilgrim travellers who came to see the land of Boddhi. In A.D. 606 Harsha had ascended the throne of the Maurya dynasty, and it was in 630 that Houen Chang entered the country journeying by Kandahar and Kabul. Wherever he went he found Buddhism falling into decay, and existing side by side with a reviving Hinduism.

Houen Chang gives many details of what he saw, and is especially interesting in saying that Buddhism had fallen from its high estate in Afghanistan, and deteriorated into idol worship, where magical powers were attributed to images of Buddha. Beyond Bamian to this day, giant images of Buddha remain, carved in the solid rock of the hillside, hundreds of feet high, alongside which men appear as pigmies.

Houen Chang speaks of great dislike and distrust between Buddhist and Hindu. Nevertheless Harsha's kingdom, in which incidentally it appears that law and order were not so well maintained as in the days of Fa Hien's travels, was a great one, and he was in effect the last who could claim to be a 'ruler of India' till the days of the Moguls.

The Brahmins had learnt much in their many hundreds of waiting years, and had mastered two essential facts, the first that the world needs a religion, and not a philosophy, the second that a religion must be part of the life of the ordinary people. Under Buddhism far too many of the people had become monks, many of whom to the outer world were what in olden days in England were known as 'abbey-lubbers', and were living on the community. The drive of the Noble Eight-Fold Path was gone, and the Brahmins now encouraged a development of the old religion that was deeply wrapt up in the everyday life and joys of the people. They were ready to assimilate almost any cult and teaching, even Buddhism as a mode of thought, and in this guise it did and does remain. The Hinduism of the devout has much of the teaching of Buddha in its make-up.

The Hindus and Rajputs of the Revival

When Harsha and his dynasty passed away, in the seventh century, there came a period on which the curtain of oblivion has descended and we know remarkably little of what happened. But we can fairly well imagine these years in outline. The Tartars, Turks, Mongols, whichever name is applied to them, who had come into the country had accepted Buddhism. As Buddhists, whether conquered by Indian Buddhists as they eventually were, or when colonizing among Indians during the sway of the Tartar dynasties of the north, they had not the difficulties to overcome that would have presented themselves had the regime in India been Brahmin. When, therefore, the Indian peoples began to turn towards Brahminism, no doubt the Tartars were ready to come back to its fold with the Aryans and there had probably been much miscegenation.

The Rajputs were undoubtedly the Aryans of the old Kshattriya class, but recruited and blended with many another stout folk, who were admitted by their fellows and acknowledged by the Brahmins to be Rajputs 'the sons and followers of Princes'. Blended as Buddhists they remained as Hindus, and as Hindus of the highest class bar the Brahmins themselves. The new Rajputs appear to have been the dominating folk from the Indus to the Himalaya, but south also to the Aravalli hills and beyond, and even in the valleys of what we now call the frontier hills across the mighty Indus itself.

In Central India it would appear that the Rajputs were perhaps more generally pure Kshattriya, and in the north and west more mingled with the various Tartar races and with those Jăts who had arrived as many had, *before* the reclassification. Those Jăts who came later remained outside.

Many of the Kshattriya legends and ancestry were accepted, no doubt in many cases accurately enough, by the re-grouped clans. Descent from Krishna and Rama was accredited to certain clans, and these latter became grouped as Rajputs of the Sun *Surajbansi*, of the Moon *Yadubansi* and as a later grouping and not quite so exalted or of such high repute, the Agnicular Rajputs those 'descended of the Fire,' whatever that might mean. The legends of descent and origins were legion and the making of fictitious family trees was, no doubt, done to order in many a clandestine herald's office, recognition by the Brahmins being the price for supporting the warp and weft of the new regime. During this period it has been thought that it was from Kanauj, the capital of the Rahtores, as will be described later, that the whole modern Hindu system was forged and the 'En-Rajputment' planned, based on the old teaching, fortified by the experience that Brahminism had been through. All the chivalry was gradually brought under one umbrella, by the bribe of being accepted as *Fidei Defensor* and thus of a caste exalted beyond dispute. To be the 'sons of princes' appealed to all men of ambitious warrior instinct. As already explained, with the disappearance of Buddhism there was but one religion in India, however varied in its daily methods. Hinduism as distinct from another faith, only appears when Islam split the continent, after it was tight in the bonds of an occupational caste system hallowed by priestly and religious sanction, derived declared the Brahmins from an ancient code, that of Manu the law giver, which at this time was made of great account.

Thus the Brahmins spreading their grip wherever Rajput held dominion, took all the gods and totems of non-Aryan,

Dravidian India, into their system, as manifestations, or at least as part of the saintly calendar. Thus their influence became universal. The untouchable is one, who, not of Aryan descent, has accepted place in the web thus woven, a place granted contemptuously on his humble seeking. Outside are the aboriginal, the animist and the Christian, who are not even 'untouchable' since they come not within the organized heaven-born framework. They 'cut no ice' in this cruel complex and artificial frame-work that we call the caste system of India, a system, however, for which it is claimed that it has kept and did keep this great continent from falling irretrievably to pieces in the eight hundred years of strife that lay between the coming of the Moslem and British rebuilding. That is a claim which cannot be disregarded.

To follow it, however, except so far as it is incidental to the story of the martial races is outside the purpose of this book, and we may with this point in our minds now pass to the fabric of India in the tenth century.

The Jăts

Some reference has been made to the coming to India of the Jăt, and the probability expressed that his inclusion in the term Scythian is only permissible if we use that word for wandering cuckoo tribes from the Central Asian table land, pushed forward by pressure behind, and that while the Tartar tribes may be called Scythian, all Scythian tribes were not of Turk or Tartar ethnological origin.

These Jăts at the time of this re-building were long in position spread fanwise from Sind and what is so graphically known in the Punjab as the *Triniab* and the *Panjnad*. That means those great broad waters, first where three have joined and then where five, and in that form join the mighty Indus, before that river comes to the layer of rock and conglomerate about Sukkur Bhukkar which has made the astounding Lloyd barrage an engineering possibility. From the Panjnad and Sind the Jăts splay out to the confines of and eventually into Rajputana into the southern and Eastern Punjab down to Delhi and Bhurtpur, and on the west far down perhaps among races that are now of other name. The Jăts it would appear were more tenaciously Buddhist, and even when nominally Hindu, like the Gurkha of to-day in an unsophisticated state, bore their Hinduism lightly, and made no great account of Brahmins and their claims. They perhaps pooh-poohed the proposal that they should be classed among the Rajputs, considering their own racial and temporal position good enough for any man. So they lay apart although resembling the Aryan Rajput, gradually absorbing a Hindu outlook, universally admitted as the years passed to be men of birth and purity, but never evincing, at any rate, till too late, any desire to be within the magic circle. As the centuries rolled on, the position was that they were denied Rajput status in the opinion of the world, and the social privileges attaching, that only mattered if you cared about them. Stout farmers and stouter soldiers they knew themselves to be, always taking a forward hand in the affairs of their own piece of country side.

In modern times we hear of the old Brahmin weapon of the re-construction being used. "If you will become *Fidei Defensor* and general kicker up of dust, against the British, then perhaps it will be possible to admit that the Jăts were wrongfully and negligently regarded as having no Rajput status, and the matter can be put right." Hitherto it may be said that the voice of the charmer has been heard in vain. In common with most of the martial races, enthusiastic support of the British Government, and devoted and distinguished service in the World War has been the reply of the modern Jăt or Jāt, whether Sikh, Hindu or Moslem in religion, to such suggestions.

How this race failed in these various forms of religion Muhammadan and Sikh as the years went on will be referred to later. How closely, however, the race mingles with the Rajputs some of the stories to be told will show. The term to-day is used in ordinary parlance of that portion of the race who are under the Hindu umbrella, and fairly near the handle.

The Grouping of the Rajputs

In the phrase at the head of this section is to be understood for all practical purposes the making of the martial races of India north of the Aravallis and in the Ganges plains. In these five Rajput states referred to, Kanauj, Delhi, Lahore in the north and east, Mewar in the centre and Annul-warra in the west, were practically the whole of the men then fit by courage to bear arms, to handle sword and bow and pike and ride a war horse, either those who had received the Rajput ticket or those like the Jāts who remained outside but resembled them exceedingly. From the matrix thus established come the martial classes of India, other than those who came in with later invaders, whether they be Hindu, Moslem or Sikh. What probably happened in the Mahratta country, the Maharasthra of history, will be related later, but it may here be said that some of Aryan-Scythian Rajput folk penetrated farther south on the west side of India, to weld with an earlier indigenous people to form an unusually sturdy race, and that the Mahratta is only but an allo-tropic modification of the general Rajput principle. This brings us by a sideway to even another definition of a tenth century Rajput as one "who is prepared to fight under the priestly banner of the Brahmins", and now and again we get a glimpse of an idea analogous to that of the Holy Roman Empire. Indeed the saying of Voltaire regarding the latter days of that Empire might with equal sarcasm be applied to Brahminism.

Each of the five Rajput states had important cities round which the great clans grouped themselves to which the lesser tribes became affiliated. The three races have been referred to, the *Surajbansi*, the Rajputs of the Sun, the *Yadu* or *Chăndďbansi*, the Rajputs of the Moon, and the third the Rajputs of the Fire, the Agnicular races. Of the three the first two are definitely admitted to be Kshattriya and the latter derived from unions and absorptions of the Scythic races other than those Jăts who held all aloof. The names themselves are little more than fanciful, and do not seem to indicate any special origin, any more than the quite unintelligible but hostile divisions of some of the frontier tribes into the factions of Gar and Samil.

Indraprasthra, the first of seven Delhis, was the capital of the Chauhans and the centre of the Moon Races, while Kanauj and Adjudia on the Ganges and in Oudh were the capitals of the Sun Races, Kanauj being the capital of the great Rahtore clan. The central and eastern Punjab was in the hands of a famous Lunar Race, the Katoch. The state of Mewar was perhaps the greatest stronghold of the Sun Races, who all trace their origin from Rama the conqueror of Ceylon, that famous, almost mythical hero of Indian legend. At Mathura was also a centre of another branch of the Lunar Race whose origin was encouraged by priestly craft to date to the mighty man-god Krishna, around whom even more and happier legends and stories were and are current than of Rama. The wildest and most intricate legends of rapes, elopements, demons, snakes and tigers, were interwoven with genuine memories of early migrations.

The Lunar Race had at one period or another many other centres and capitals besides Indraprasthra and Mathura, one so far west as Dwarka in Kathiawar, and as far east as Hardwar where the gorge breaks from the main hills. Prag which Islam re-named Allahabad was another, thrice sacred to this day by the mystical and emblematical union of Jumma and Ganges, where the twain become one, and pilgrims still flock by the hundred thousand.

There it was that from north to south and from east to west, from Kashmir to the Narbudda, from the mouth of the Indus to the mouths of the Ganges there was the great fabric of an India, largely Aryan partly Tartar, but with Tartardom swamped by a stronger Aryanism. All the land and all the power were in the hands of Rajput Princes with barons great and small, with Rajput and Jăt farmers, tenant and yeoman all following the newly re-affirmed and improved Brahminical religion. Below this Rajput coverlet were of course, the countless hosts of the conquered menial useful depressed classes, of darker skin, whom we may for the moment call by the generic name Dom, but whose only claim to life and liberty was their usefulness. Working among both were too the hereditary Aryan and usually non-martial traders, bankers, money-lenders and so forth. It was not till the Islamic conquests that the destruction of the Hindu states, of which more anon, resulted in a mass migration of some of the leading tribes from their homes on the Ganges and Jumna, to the wild hills and rocky deserts of what is now Rajputana. Their original ground, in which the race and religion had developed since they came from the north, viz. the fertile plains watered by the Jumna, the Ganges and their tributaries, were abandoned to escape from a conqueror and a regime they abhorred. The abandonment took them to a land of rock and jungle where hard life was to be their portion and independence their guerdon. Between the 11th and 12th centuries then the Rajputana or Rajastan as we know it to-day was founded and formed, a land bordering on the already Rajput Mewar. In the Punjab the Rajput population, far less pure Aryan than the population of Hindustan, remained *in situ*, to bow to the storm of invasions, to accept the new faith, and generally to blend with new arrivals.

In the Hindustan that the clans as such deserted, many individual Rajputs however remained, the yeoman peasantry on the land to which they were wedded. But the clan as a whole with its chiefs and its organization, its feudal system and its pride went. Therefore the Rajputs of Oudh to-day, the Eastern Rajputs of to-day are what we know as 'broken'. They know their clan but are under no clan control, and have no clan psychology. Without that, much of the old time feudal system and ideas that it engendered have gone. Stout and sturdy though they be, they have not the instincts of the better men of Rajputana.

THE OUTER CONQUESTS

Before leaving the subject of the Rajput network spread over Northern India, a glance is desirable at the outer conquests or penetrations, which Kshattriya or Rajput has made, as they go to still further illustrate the general thesis of this book, viz., that almost all the martial races are drawn at long last from this Rajputization of all the fighting men who would support the founders of the Neo-Brahminism.

From the plains of Oudh the penetrating Aryans had spread up into most of the accessible valleys of the outer Himalaya, they had conquered the tribes of Nepal and introduced an Aryan system in ancient time, for as we know Gautama himself was the son of a Kshattriya prince in Nepal. They spread into the hills of Tehri Garhwal, and at the revival they and tribes of less certain origin were admitted into Rajputcy. All along the hills, as far up as the River Jhelum, we shall find the genuine Aryan Rajput, some of ancient habitation and some of the Sun and Moon Races who may have gone there and perhaps joined earlier and kindred settlers, when Islam destroyed the Rajput states already referred to. The clump of small states in what are known as the Simla Hills are full of Rajputs of sorts, and, as will be explained later, give in most cases a few Rajputs to the Army.

As you get into that bit of the Himalaya between Nepal and the Simla Hills Rajputdom is a more important matter, for you are in the Garhwal Hills where Kshattriya and the ancient race call Khas, of whom so little is known, have combined to produce a race to which the reformed stamp, 'Rajput' was well and truly given. How and what they have been in recent British times shall, in due course, be shown, with the crash of the German shell as chorus and the swish of the Flanders rain as accompaniment.

Farther north across the Beas are an equally fine Rajput folk who live in the *Dugar Desh*, the Country of the Two Lakes, and who probably migrated there from Rajasthan after leaving their homes on the Ganges, before the flaming sword of the Sons of the Prophet—willy-nilly we may be sure. There they found probably some older Kshattriya blood, for the Dogra hills are too desirable to have been passed by in the great trek back in the mists of time. How the Rajputs of the Dogra country have served His Majesty and his forbears this many a year, and how they came to dominate Kashmir and the Pamir states shall also be told in the warp and the woof of Northern India.

CHAPTER IV

THE WARRIORS AND PEOPLE OF ISLAM

THE FIRST COMING OF ISLAM TO INDIA—THE FERMENT IN THE AFGHAN HILLS—THE RAJPUTS INVADE GHUZNI—THE SLAVE DYNASTY OF GHUZNI—SULTAN MAHMUD GHUZNAVI—THE COMING OF MUHAMMAD OF GHOR—THE SLAVE DYNASTY OF DELHI AND AFTER—THE MOGUL PERIOD—THE MOSLEM PEOPLES OF THE MINGLING.

THE COMING OF ISLAM TO INDIA

THE next chapter that opens out for India is the saddest of all, and shows how completely ineffective the martial spirit of the land had become. Whether this was due to want of leading, to that streak of inefficiency perhaps of the Indian character, which the Westerner with Indian experience is so often perplexed by, can only be imagined. Perhaps too we may attribute the failure to some great defect in Brahminism as a stimulant and world force. Into this India just described, the India of the quarrelling kingdoms of Delhi and Lahore, of Kanauj and Mewar, came at the end of the tenth century the first of that series of raids that grew to invasions, and invasions that matured into conquests, which have so entirely altered the trend of Indian history.

We have seen that the reconversion of the peoples of India from Buddhism to Hinduism did not change their ways and natures, though it crystallised off all fighting men of any status of Aryan or part Aryan descent, as Rajputs, the 'Sons of Princes'. The sharp segregation of the martial classes, no doubt contributed to pride of race and behaviour, but it only recrystallised the old Kshattriya clans with such accretions as appeared worth while. The coming of Islam however was a very different matter. This severe monotheistic intolerant faith claimed to, and to a great extent actually did, wipe out all barriers. It admitted all men as equals in the sight of God and man, and admitted into the warrior class all whose heart could muster up sufficient pluck to wield a sword.

Islam burst on the world in the seventh century. Unlike the gentle and slow spread of Christianity, or the patient rise of Buddhism, it roared across the desert and the middle East, and westwards along the coasts of Northern Africa and into Spain and even France. About 711 it surged across the Indian Ocean from Bussorah and the Persian Gulf and ascended the Indus. What is now Sind, the 'Land of the Indus', was invaded by the Arabs from Bussorah, which we now write Basra, under Muhammad Ibn Qassim. A fortified temple which is thought to have been at the present Dwarka, was captured after a fierce struggle, and the Hindus pursued up the Indus to Multan which was also captured, that Multan which has been the scene of so many struggles, and which is still the inner strategic key, from its situation on the rivers that converge to the Indus.

For forty years Arab rule prevailed, leaving a strong trace on the Indus boatmen who so resemble those of the Tigris and Euphrates, and generally contributing to the make-up of the races in that corner of India. When they left they left behind them Islamic pockets, and some of those Sayads who are still to be found all over India, being putative descendants of the Prophet, but probably often basing their claim on the mere fact that they were among the earlier and most privileged of the Islamic missionaries.

Islam then left India as a driving proselyting force, and did not emerge from the mountains between the Oxus and the Indus and the uplands of Khorassan. There it swirled and lapped and conquered for two and a half centuries.

The Ferment in Afghanistan

Before turning to see the commencement of the period which saw the second coming of Islam to India, it will be well to glance at the ferment of races in Afghanistan, to use a more modern but intelligible term, that is to say the mountains and tablelands aforesaid between the Oxus, the Indus and Khorassan. We have seen the land in the hands of the Graeco-Bactrians, established in Bactria by Alexander, the land that is now called Afghan Turkestan, and how the struggles between Graeco-Bactrians and Sakas let in the Yuechi, one of the Tartar races. Parthians and Tartars gained some power along the Indus, eventually passing away before the growing Aryan strength, and while Tartars remained east of the Hindu Kush, the Aryans and possibly Jat tribes still occupied the valleys between the Indus, and at any rate the Kandahar-Kabul-Ghuzni road. Somewhere about the time of the rise of Islam we have seen the race that calls itself Afghan and Ben-i-Israel come into the mountains and uplands, north of Kandahar. They and the other races in the land were steadily absorbed into Islam, and the tide swept up to the valleys where Hinduism and Buddhism still dwelt, the latter perhaps in isolated pockets. At the time of Mahmud of Ghuzni, the Rajput kings of the Punjab held sway over a Hindu and perhaps Buddhist folk as far as

Kabul. But except on the road to Kabul, Islam had gripped Afghan, Israelite and Turk. Fermenting quarrelling, and perhaps pressed, or at any rate joined by any stray party or clan of freebooting horse, the upland peoples proceeded to share in the forays and after despoiling for several generations the idolators and their idols west of the Indus, at length came down to conquer, to colonize, and to hold fierce relentless sway over Aryan, and in time, Dravidian India.

That India was largely Hindu in the warp and woof we know, but what actually had been in progress between the days of Harsha and the coming of Sabaktigin we do not know, beyond the general consolidation of the Brahmin network, Whatever it was it had not produced as in the days of Asoka or even Harsha, a supreme Hindu ruler, who could compel a common front to a common foe.

The tribes in the hills between the Indus and Ghuzni, whether subject to Sabaktigin or not, had long been active in leading raids into Hindu India. Indian opinion was greatly enraged, and the first series of actual invasions of India, was possibly induced by the Rajput attempt to put a stop to the raids. Immediately here are we faced with the reflection that the raiding custom of a thousand years ago is the custom of to-day, and that our British frontier wars but spring from the same habits of the same folk.

The Slave Dynasty of Ghuzni

The Moslem conquest of India began with this said Sabaktigin, and here for a moment let us turn back to see the origin of the Slave Dynasty of Ghuzni. Among the welter of khans and their dynasties in Central Asia of which history and legend tell us, there arose in 903 that of the

Samanids, which incidentally lasted one hundred and twenty years. The fifth prince of this dynasty, one Abdul Malik, possessed a Turki slave, Alptigin. It may here be mentioned that the termination *tigin* or *tagin* indicates slave origin. Here also it may be explained what 'slave' actually means in this matter of courts, households, and dynasties, as we meet it in Egypt, in Delhi and elsewhere. It was the policy of many Eastern conquerors to surround themselves with bodyguards and huscarles of lads of good race and lineage, carried off in infancy in some raid or conquest, and so have about them a body of favoured troops who owned no country and no allegiance save to their master, protector and rewarder. From among them, commanders, governors and even sons-in-law might be drawn, and often enough at times some 'slave' planned and plotted to tip his master from his throne. Such were the 'Slaves' of the Ghuzni dynasty, the Slave Kings of Delhi, the Mamelukes of Cairo, and the Janissaries of Istamboul.

Abdul Malik, the Samanid, had made Alptigin governor of Khorassan. But on his patron's death, fearing the unfavourable attitude of the new ruler, Alptigin fled to Ghuzni, no doubt with some of his own troops and, maybe, his bodyguard of slaves of his own providing. He thus was able to establish himself as a chieftain in the Suleimans. About 976 he was numbered with his fathers, and his son Sabuktigin succeeded to his realm. Alptigin, rumour said, was the captive child of some royal house, and Sabaktigin did not belie his father's origin. Increasing his dominions in all directions we hear of him conducting something greater than a raid into India. He returned to India without new territory, but with slaves and booty. This much stimulated the desire for more in all the soldiers of fortune who would march in his or any other service to that promised guerdon. They had within them all the zeal of the early converts to Islam, backed no doubt by intense ignorance of any of its tenets. Like the immortal Captain Wattle 'who was all for love and a little for the bottle', they were 'all for Islam and a little for the booty'.

But before their raiding propensities developed from a habit to be almost a gift, the prestige of the defenders of India took a severe blow which greatly encouraged the initiative of the raiders.

The Rajputs Invade Ghuzni

The first incursion of Sabuktigin, undertaken in more serious manner than the constant hill raids, provoked great anger in Northern India, and Jaipal, the Rajput ruler of Lahore, proceeded to lead an expedition over the Indus, with a view to exacting reparations at the gates of Ghuzni. With thousands of foot and horse, with his elephants and guns he set forth, having almost as much impedimenta as hampered Sir John Keane in 1839, 860 years later. Sir John went round by Kandahar in the summer season, but Jaipal elected to cross the Indus valley and avoid its heats in the winter. Crossing somewhere by Dera Ismael Khan, or the ferry at Mari-Attak, he made through the Derajat, and used the Gomal or perhaps the Tochi route. Here he fell, as have British armies after him, on severe winter weather, and only saved his army by giving up all his elephants, promising large sums, and engaging to accept the envoys of Ghuzni at his Rajput Court at Lahore.

Safe from the perils of the snows, however, the Hindu went back on his promises and the Moslem forces entered India to enforce them again. Now the Northern Rajputs saw the need of some union, and Lahore, Delhi, Ajmere, Kalinga and Kanauj, all sent their chivalry, only to go down before the fierce *élan* of the sons of the Prophet and their pagan Tartar allies. The Ghuznivide was content however to take from the Rajputs the now Afghan valley Lugman, and the Peshawur valley, that age-old subject for dispute between India proper and India trans-Indus.

It was this victory which marked for the first time a division at the Indus of what had both east and west been originally India. Sabuktigin would no doubt have pursued his successes further had he not also, according to a custom that was to become a habit in the years to come, been called away from India to attend to trouble on his Turkestan frontiers.

In 997 he passed away at Termez on the river Oxus, and the throne was seized by his eldest though illegitimate son, Mahmud, while a feebler brother who had not the bend sinister to ban him from easy succession was driven forth.

Sultan Mahmud Ghuznavi

The coming of Mahmud of Ghuzni to his throne, the 'Sultan Mahmud Ghuznavi' of many a Moslem song and fable, sealed the fate of India. He burned with a holy zeal for the faith, he hated with a bitter hatred the idols of Indian temples and the many shrines, figures and carvings of Buddhas and Buddhisatvas that had to his mind so disfigured Afghanistan. Ghuzni he would make a glorious centre of the learning and the civilization of Islam. India the lascivious, the idolatrous, the *musherik*, the 'sharer of gods', should pay, and he, Mahmud, would make it so. Nor was he apparently among his own people savage and tyrannical, but cultured and reasonably humane. He collected at his mountain capital the learned. Alberuni, the scholar, lived at his court and Faruqi wrote his Shah-Namah in his honour.

Mahmud had heard from his father of the ill-organized valour of the Rajputs, and the agreeable stories of the wealth of the Hindu princes, and in the year 1001 made his first inroad. Jaipal, his father's old enemy, met him with the forces of many of the lesser chiefs. The Rajputs were defeated near Peshawur, and Jaipal was pursued to the Sutlej, where he was captured, but released on ransom and promise of tribute. Mahmud with his plunder returned in triumph, while Jaipal, who had now endured nothing but defeat, resigned his throne to his son Anangapal, putting an end to his own life, the story goes, by mounting his own funeral pyre and perishing in the flames. During the next few years Mahmud made several lesser expeditions to India in collection of tribute and to put down rebellion in the Multan province, which was subject to Ghuzni. As Anangapal had supported this rising, Mahmud in 1009 made his fifth entry into India to punish him, marching via Peshawur.

Northern India was now more than stirred. From every Rajput centre the chivalry marched, from Delhi and Kanauj, the Rajputs of the Sun and Moon, the Chauhans, and the Rhatores, from far Ujjain and from Gwalior. The women of India threw their gold and their silver ornaments into the military chest, and a host of lesser princes and barons rallied to the standards of the great Rajput chieftains. It was Islam and all that Islam stood for against Hinduism, the one and only God against the great Hindu deities and their countless emanations and affiliations. All the resources of equipment and clothing that could be collected were hurried up to the marching columns concentrating at the point of

BALUCH AND PATHAN
In the pre-war dress of the Scinde and Baluch Horse

[*Face page 62*

danger at Bhatinda, where the roads from the Gomal and Multan that led to Delhi drew together.

The battle that was to ensue is strangely like that between the Afghans and the Mahrattas at the last battle of Panipat, seven and a half centuries later. The opposing forces sat in their entrenched camps, watching one another for a wrestler's grip, for over a month. Then the Hindus, probably as before Panipat, were forced by starvation and the enemy's raiding horse, to attack. With them, as in all Eastern armies of the time, were many elephants, which were indeed as already explained the 'tanks' of that period. Where an elephant would push, no trench and parapet would stand up, and no mass of men resist, while from the castellated howdah the crew would work their engines of war. But . . . the but of the living tank, was whether or no he got frightened. If frightened and unmanageable the elephant is dangerous to his own side. The elephants at the battle of Bhatinda, it is said, tore back through their own ranks and the Moslem horse rode through the gaps. Long was the night of slaughter, great the Indian defeat, and loud the wail of mourning that swept south through the Rajput homes.

Mahmud however, stayed his penetration into India, merely destroying the famous temple of Nagarkot in Kangra, and returned to Ghuzni with more plunder to enrich his capital, and more captives to serve his people.

For five years the tormentor remained quiet, and then set forth on a well planned raid on Harsha's wealthy city of Thaneswar, which he carried after a brief defence, only to return to Ghuzni with his gains once more. In fact this sucking of India dry seemed only too easy a feat to these reiving mountaineers, whose next nest to plunder was to be Kanauj itself. In 1009 the Ghuznivide led forth an even larger number of his pirates, crossed the Punjab with ease, and appeared before the sacred cities of Bindraban and Mathura. These he razed to the ground, destroying the innumerable shrines and temples of these places of pilgrimages, shrines whose ruins and carving lie about even to-day just where the '*But-shikan*', the 'Idol-breaker', to use the proud intolerant title that Islam conferred on him, left them strewn in the dust.

After destroying also Baran, which is now Bulandshahr, Mahmud appeared before the Rhatore capital. But the Rajput chivalry had fallen on many a stricken field already. There were none to defend the city adequately, and its ruler, another Jaipal, surrendered to save it from the fate of Mathura which had been sacked without pity. Mahmud satisfied with the vast booty that even a cursory sack revealed, returned whence he came. Three years later however the son of Anangapal led the Lahore forces in rebellion against the Ghuzni suzerainty. Determined to have no such recurrence, he, for the first time declared Lahore and all its territories annexed, and installed a Moslem governor and garrison in Lahore itself.

This act was the foundation of Moslem power and dominion in India. The Muhammadan historians dwell with glee and pride on the vast slaughter of idolators that accompanied these victories, and especially in the famous sack of the temple of Somnath, which occurred in the '*But-shikan's*' sixteenth and greatest invasion. This time his enterprise took him over to the western coast, by a route in which the Rajput warriors had not all fallen in vain resistance. Somnath in the south of the country of Guzerat was a temple of Siva. It was also one of the holiest and most revered in India, and was also reputed to be the most wealthy. Mahmud's route lay through Rajputana and the town of Somnath was well garrisoned by the Western Rajputs, so that the defence was a stout one. Nothing, however, could stop the ruthless invaders. Suffering heavily themselves, they inflicted a loss, it is said, of 5,000 on the defenders, before the town fell and was given over to sack and slaughter. Temples were destroyed, images broken down, and the story runs that before the biggest of them all, the priests in charge besought the conqueror's mercy.

'Take their all, take their lives, but spare the great image of Holy Mahadeo'.

Grimly the Idol-Breaker ordered it to be broken, when from its head poured out priceless jewels.

The gates of the temple of Shiva made of sandal-wood, were carried off to Ghuzni to grace the entrance to a mosque. It will be remembered that the avenging army of Kandahar was ordered by Lord Ellenborough, the Governor-General in 1841, to bring back to India the Gates of Somnath from Ghuzni, where they were still supposed to lie. It pleased those who jest on inadequate premises, to deride Lord Ellenborough for his bombastic and quite banal gesture as one that stirred no feeling in Hindu India. They were unaware that five years before, Runjhit Singh, the Maharajah of Lahore, in promising help to Shah Shujah to recover his Afghan throne, had stipulated himself for the return of the Gates of Somnath as one of his conditions. When, therefore, the Governor-General and his Foreign Office searching for some dramatic feature in the ultimate Anglo-Indian victory after the disasters of the year before, bethought themselves of this, it was but because the Sikh himself had considered it a point of value. Incidentally it may be said that the gates duly carried down on elephants proved not to be the original ones at all. The defenders of India had this slight compensation that on his way home, Mahmud was severely handled by the Jăts of the Southern Punjab.

Thus ended in humiliation and disaster the first attempts of unorganized chivalry to defend India from the 'breakers from the north'.

With the spoils of Somnath, Mahmud was still further to adorn the great mosque in Ghuzni, which he called his 'Celestial Bride', but his course was nearly run. After a campaign to punish the Jăts for molesting his forces returning from Somnath, he passed away in the year 1030 after a career of 33 years, leaving two sons to quarrel for the succession. As has been said, Moslem historians are loud in his praise as a patron of civilization and learning, and despite his hatred of religions, of images, and his ruthless havoc wrought in India, it does not appear that he practised slaughter for slaughter's sake, as did so many of the Tartar and Hun world-stormers, who swept through Asia and parts of Europe.

The setting up of a Governor in Lahore as related did not really found the great series of Turkish rulers of Delhi, and that was not even to come from his own descendants, but from the dynasty that absorbed them, that of Muhammad of Ghor.

The Coming of Muhammad of Ghor

The sixteen invasions of India left, as we have seen, the Rajput fabric broken and exhausted, and had laid the better part of the warriors low in their vain attempt to repel and embank the said breakers from the north. The immediate event after the death of Mahmud was the impinging of the Seljuk Turks, a new wave and horde of the almond-eyed, which burst against the northern frontiers of the realm of Ghuzni. The Rajputs of Lahore took this opportunity to rise against their Turkish government, but the Lahore stronghold was retained. Before long Lahore became the actual capital of the Ghuznivide kingdom which included Balkh, Kabul, Ghuzni, Kandahar and Sind and the Punjab. This corresponded pretty nearly with the old Aryan Kingdom of the North at the time when Darius appeared on the scene. Early in the twelfth century nevertheless, the realm had passed into the hand of Ala-ud-din Sultan of Ghor, who, Moslem though he was, burnt the magnificent buildings in Ghuzni, and earned the soubriquet of *Jahan-suz* 'The World Burner'. The Punjab alone remained to the Ghuznivide. By 1180, Muhammad Ghori, nephew of the 'World Burner' came to the throne, and succeeded also in absorbing the Punjab, so that the dynasty of Alptigin, after 234 years of warring dominion, passed altogether.

Although the Rajputs had long lost the dominion of the Punjab the dying away of the conquering habits of Ghuzni and the lapse of years had allowed of a general Hindu recovery. The Rajputs continued their conquests and extensions farther south and west, and the work of completing the Hindu fabric went on south of the river Sutlej. Nagarkot, the shrine that Mahmud had sacked in Kangra, was recovered from the Muhammadan governor of the Punjab. Kanauj was reviving and continuing to be the great centre still from which the Puranic Hinduism was engineered, while all over the country Buddhism was being expelled from those out-of-the-way pockets in which it still lingered, and it seemed that there was still India enough left in the South for an Asoka to control an Indian India.

In the Punjab it was otherwise. By degrees most of the Rajput clans inhabiting the plains of the five rivers had become Moslem, but still retaining their proud, if often degraded, claim to be the 'sons of princes', and to this day call themselves Rajput before Moslem, the race before the religion. Wedged here and there are foreign tribes and clans who settled among them, but the mass of the Moslem gentry and yeomanry of the Punjab belong to that racial frame-work, which has been described.

Muhammad of Ghor was not content with his Punjab province and the conversion of its Rajputs to the 'Submission.' A Turk himself as had been the Ghuznivides, there were thousands of hardy Tartar, Turkish and Mongol soldiers released from Central Asia who were prepared to ride with him to Delhi. The Pathans and Afghans of the mountains, Semites, Jăts, or whatever their origin, were equally eager. The lure of the successive cities of Delhi and their wealth has appealed to all the soldiers of fortune and masterless men of Central Asia, since gold and jewels counted in the world's prizes. This lure brought more Turks to ride with Baber in the days of our Elizabeth, it brought the wild frontier tribesmen to join the British levies in 1857, and indeed the return of Her Majesty's Corps of Guides from Delhi after the storming of the Kashmir Gate is talked of with awe and admiration to this day. Rose-curtained carts with women who had been eager to join the conquerors, pony carts of *kincob* [1] and looted junk marched in the train of that famous Corps, while the lesser levies were not backward in their share. Even more so was it in the days when the Kings of the Mountain States rode south to Indraprastra and her successors. In the train of Muhammad Sultan also must have marched many of the converts with the burning zeal that ever distinguished their class.

It is not hard to imagine the enthusiasm that would arise when it was known in the camel's-hair tents on the Oxus, or in the mud and stone villages of the Afridi Tirah, that Mahmud Ghuznavi, Muhammad of Ghor, Kutb-ud-din Toork,

[1] A gold embroidered cloth, lit. *Kam-quab*—seldom seen.

A MUHAMMADAN RAJPUT OF THE PUNJAB
One of Colonel Sir Umar Hayat Khan's retainers

[*Face page* 68

or any other of the kidney were raising men for India, to sack Somnath, to capture Delhi or what not. If you have seen in our own times the enthusiam in Cape Town when it was heard that Methuen, or Schermbrucker, or Piet Retief were raising a commando to fight Basutos, Matabele, Zulus, or the like, and that too without the guerdon of sacked temples, you would understand it. "Sultan Mahmud wants men does he. Oh Ho! how many lads will ride with me". And Tartar lance and bow and sword would be furbished up and the spiked helmets with mail collarettes would be got out and all would be bustle. "Hey for horse and hound, lad, and round the world away." Delhi for its guerdon!

Then too the jackal tribes would be waiting, the *Chappar-bands* who made the armies' huts, and took their maids a-chambering, whose pack donkeys and bullocks were lean with waiting, the *Sikligars* who also marched on the flank among the followers, who sharpened the swords and spear and mended the mail, and now grind knives and scissors and tinker pots and pans in merry England, sure! the call to India found them all agog.

So since Hindu India *more suo* had fallen a-quarrelling in the north, Rajah Prithvi of Delhi and Ajmere, and Jai Chand of Kanauj were in jealous rivalry. The lesser chiefs clustered round them in two separate groups and seemed to have forgotten the forceful enemy at their gates. The Hindu forces however had learnt something from their troubles at Mahmud's hands and were better organized than in those frenzied days when nothing could stop the Moslem. The Rajput armies, disunited though they were, were not quite as sheep to the slaughter, and as dross before the organized valour of the north.

Marching to the old battlefield at Bhatinda in 1191, Muhammad of Ghor carried the town that was Rajah

Prithvi's. Then Prithvi himself led out a large force of mounted Rajputs and met him at Tarain on the banks of the holy Saraswati, a hundred miles north of Delhi, that long dry river which runs Indus-wards between Jumna and Sutlej, to lose even its flood waters in the sandy desert.

The Rajputs there utterly defeated the invaders, and Muhammad himself badly wounded, barely escaped to Lahore. For two years he licked his wounds, remustered his forces and prepared. One defeat would certainly not turn him from his purpose, and two years later he recrossed the Sutlej.

Not even after his victory was Prithvi able to command the support of his factious fellow countrymen in what, perhaps, was their last chance as a nation. Once again, but partially supported, he led forth his chivalry to stem the Ghoride on the banks of the Saraswati, and met him over against Thaneswar.

For some weeks the armies watched each other waiting for grip in the Eastern way. And then one morning, unexpected by their opponents, the Moslems attacked. Prithvi himself was captured, fighting at the head of his forces, and at his fall the Hindus made way, leaving many dead behind them, including Chawand Rai chief of Delhi itself, while Prithvi Rajah captive, found no mercy at the hands of his conquerors. With him perished once more the flower of the gallant but ineffective Rajput quality.

The Moslem victory was stained as was that at the Afghan victory of Panipat by massacres of prisoners. Muhammad himself after his victory returned across the Indus and left Qutb-ud-din Aibak, the 'moon-faced,' as ruler in India.

But the memory of Prithvi Rajah slaughtered to make a Turki holiday, was long cherished in Hindustan, and when the regiments in the cantonment on the Ridge at Delhi mutinied in 1857 they marched off to the slogan of '*Prithvi Raj ki Jai*', 'Victory to the rule of Prithvi', despite the fact they were marching to the Mogul palace.

The victory at Thaneswar did not at once involve the fall of Delhi, but only of Prithvi's own capital of Ajmere, but within a year of being left in charge of India, Qutb-ud-din had made himself master of that stronghold of Chauhan Rajputs as well.

Three years after the battle of Thaneswar, viz., in 1194, Muhammad was back in India, and then it was that Jai Chand of Kanauj had good cause to regret that he had not sunk his own differences to unite with Prithvi in the defence of their country. Gathering together all who would rally to the Hindu cause, Jai Chand faced the Turks at Etawah, but with no better fortune than Chawand Rai, for he too died on the field, and Rajput domination in Hindustan perished with him. Then it was that the Rajput chiefs and their clansmen, too weary to continue a struggle in which the dice were so heavily loaded against them, rode off to seek new kingdoms in the centre of India, in the hills and inaccessible deserts of the Aravallis and their neighbourhood. Thus was founded the Rajputana or Rajasthan as we know it to-day, their defeat in the plains of Ganges and Jumna being compensated for by the enduring nationality that they thus secured. Rajputs, it is true, remained behind them on the land as already related, but without organization and only those to whom their lands were more precious than their independence.

The death of Muhammad Ghori while suppressing a rising of Gukkhar clans on the Jhelum brought to an end the Ghori dynasty, and the kingdom broke up into its component parts. From this day dates the domination of Northern India by the Turkish dynasties of Delhi.

The Slave Dynasty of Delhi and After

When Qutb-ud-din 'The Star of the Faith', nick-named the Moon Face, found his master dead and none to take the reins, he became the actual ruler of Delhi and the founder of what is known as the 'Slave' Kings, because he and his successors were slaves, and Turkish slaves at that, as had been the dynasty of Alptigin, with this difference that the succession for the most part went afresh to a new slave. Under him the Muhammadan conquest of India continued apace, and ere long Bengal, Jaunpur, Sindh, Multan, Malwa, Guzerat, Khandesh Berar and parts of the Dekhan became what are generally called 'Afghan' kingdoms, using that word in the sense of those foreigners whether Afghan, Pathan, Turk or Tartar, who came to India as Moslems through the mountains of Afghanistan.

The Empire of Delhi, the provinces within hail and easy control of the capital, varied in extent with the range of the ruler's power, and more often the different outlying kingdoms were entirely independent. It was during the rule of the Slaves that the Mongols or Moguls in the mediæval sense of the word, still for the most part pagan, first appeared on the frontiers, Ghengis Khan himself did not actually enter India, though his generals reached the Indus, and kept the Delhi ruler hard at work to repel them. Herat fell to this particular world-stormer, to endure at the hands of his pagan hosts the most ruthless slaughter that history records, the deserted townships of those who suffered still standing as a memory and an object lesson in Seistan. Qutb-ud-din was succeeded by Altamish, who by 1236 had conquered India down to the line of the Vindhya mountains, capturing the famous fortress Gwalior, storming the Rajput fortress of

THE GRIP OF THE TURKS ON DELHI
The grim architecture of The Tuglaq Dynasty, Khirki Mosque
(A.D. 1387)

[Face page 72

Ratambhor, and even penetrating to Ujjain, the ancient Hindu capital of Malwa. The story of India now is the story of the dynasties of Delhi, the Khilji Dynasty still Turk, succeeding that of the Slaves in 1290, and lasting to 1320, when another Turki slave gained the throne to found the Tughlaq dynasty, which lasted for close on a century. Under the Khiljis, the Hindu kingdoms of Southern India were attacked, and it was not long before no Hindu ruler of any size remained outside the inaccessible Rajput principalities in Rajasthan.

The reconstruction of India by the Brahmins therefore cannot be said to have long contributed to the power temporal of their fellow countrymen.

It is not within the scope of this book to follow the fortunes of these dynasties of Delhi, almost all be it reiterated Turkish in one form or another. Sayads, Lodis and Afghans succeeding the Tughlaks, till the days of our Queen Elizabeth, when there came out of Ferghana and Kabul the greatest Turks of them all, the soldiers who formed the dynasty which is always incorrectly described as the Mogul Empire (as already explained) (p. 17).

The conversions to Islam which took place in the Punjab, were followed by that of many of the Rajputs remaining round Delhi, and were extended to a large number of the depressed classes of India, for whom Islam came with as great a social uplift to all who are poor and oppressed as Christianity had come to the slaves within the Roman Empire.

The Mogul Period

The new dynasty that was to weld India together into a gorgeous Empire, was commenced by Baber, Governor of

Kabul, and prince of Ferghana, who seeing that India was in a turmoil, and beseeched by many who sought a ruler, proceeded to demand that the ancient appanage of Timur should be his by right of ancestry. Marching to India in 1527, he defeated the last of the Khiljis and his effete troops; and ere long had received the allegiance of the greater part of India, conquering and treating with considerable duress the Rajputs and Hindus who resisted. On his death in 1530 an Afghan rising drove out his son Humayun, who thus became a wanderer, but by a turn of fortune's wheel, Humayun found himself in 1556 once more master of Delhi, only to die from a fall from his horse soon after. He was succeeded by his son Akbar, then a minor in the hands of ministers. It was not long however before Prince Akbar who had an old head on his very young shoulders, insisted on taking the reins.

When the turmoil of conquering the Afghan dynasty was over, then the young Akbar settled down to make the Mogul Empire the greatest India had seen. After his sack of Chitoor to be described hereafter, he had brought Rajput India actually to acquiescence and even alliance, by his wisdom, his broadmindness, and his numerous marriages with Rajput princesses.

As related, it was in 1527 that Baber's final victories brought him the throne of Delhi, and it was 1556 when his grandson Akbar succeeded in regaining all that his father having once lost had begun to recover before his death. The rule of the Chagatai, for the term Mogul, is not one used by India, Baber being a Chagatai Turk, ere long spread practically to the Oxus river, and Rajput princes were among the high commanders who led the troops of India, Hindu and Moslem, far afield. The succession now goes on steadily, the Mogul emperors being known by titles, which seem to sing themselves as they go, Jehāngīr, Shah Jehān, Alămgīr, the first two reigning from 1605–1627, and 1627–1658 respectively. From 1658 to 1707 well into the days of our Anne, ruled Aurungzebe Alămgir, usually known, unlike his father and grandfather, by his name rather than his title. He it was, as related hereafter under the story of the Mahrathas, destroyed the Moslem kingdoms of the Dekhan and thus brought about a state of affairs that was to result in the fall of his own dynasty. Alămgir was the last of the great Moguls to be great, and for a while he ruled nearly as much of India as do the British. When he died, an elderly son, Muazzim, succeeded, with the title Bahadur Shah, Shah Alăm, to rule by his father's prestige. With his death commenced the totter that was ere long to end in a crash, during which kingmakers and puppets toyed with the Imperial throne, and brought it in shame to the ground, the first to fall of the Turkish thrones that quartered Asia. During the days of the first of the emperors the change amongst Moslems of India was not remarkable. More settlers from Turkish and Afghan lands served the Mogul and settled on the land, and indeed the term Turk began to stand for a mercenary race of Moslem soldiery who received land in return for liability to serve. Most of them owned slaves who cared for their land when they went a-soldiering.

The Moslem Peoples of the Mingling

The outline of the coming of Islam to India and the influx of Islamic peoples from the north, that has been related, shows how the Moslem frame-work of India, and the martial races professing this faith came to be woven. The constituents of Moslem India at the time of the rise of the Mogul power must have been blended on the lines now to be explained.

We must remember that under the dynasties and empires referred to, what we now call the 'Frontier Hills', and indeed the best part of Afghanistan, was a part of the realm of India, and may be considered as much a part of India as it was in the ancient days before Darius made it a Persian satrapy. Afghanistan itself was an intricate network of races, then to some extent united so far as Eastern Afghanistan went by its Moslem unity, only broken by the Shiah and Sunni discord. Western Afghanistan on the Oxus side of of the Hindu Kush was a part of Turkestan, and that name applies now as then. There the races were of Tartar or Turki origin.

The hills towards Kabul and the Daman-i-Koh, and all through the Suleiman Mountains that fringe the right bank of the Indus, were full of a people of probable Aryan, Jăt, and Bactrian origin. that is to say semi-Aryan, with such Greek leaven as the long dominion of that race in Bactria may have imparted. Mingled with them were no doubt some of the early Tartar invaders of the Kushan period, though the stronger proclivities of Aryan stock seem to have eradicated physical traits. These races were all blended by some centuries of a non-exclusive Buddhism. It is not known how far the Hindu renaissance may have affected these semi-Aryans of the Afghan Hills, before the appeal of Islam stirred their hardy mountain minds and made their hearts desire to establish a Semite origin. Interspersed with these races in pockets were tribes of the Ben-i-Israel from Ghor and Kandahar, Turkish tribes who had come in with Alptigin and his successors at Ghuzni, and families, if not small clans, of Arab origin.

Among the Moslem invaders came all these peoples riding,

as horse in the train of the conquerors, with them came also the hordes of peoples of Oxus and trans-Oxus habitat belonging to one of the groups already referred to, described both here and in the world generally by the interchangeable name of Turk and Tartar. In addition to the actual forces of the invaders, the miscegenation wherever there were garrisons and the upbringing of the fruits of such miscegenation as Moslems, we know that all over the land, wherever the Moslem power gained dominion, there as in the Norman conquest of Saxon England, the barons and leaders, even down to the lesser officers received lands, and surrounded themselves with men-at-arms of their own religion.

North, south, east and west had this gone on in the centuries between the establishment of Qutb-ud-din Tughlak at Delhi at the beginning of the thirteenth century, and the coming of the Mogul Empire in the sixteenth, even as Cromwell settled his Scottish horse in Ireland.

All over the country then were there settlements of the Moslem barons, Turk, Afghan and Pathan, using these two latter terms to express the difference between the Ben-i-Israel and the men of the tribes of the Suleimans of more indigenous origin. Incidentally it may be said that the last term is often used indifferently for both peoples. Added to this as explained were the large number of local conversions, not only of Rajput clans *en masse*, but of the lesser local breeds who had no great stake in an arrogant Hinduism. This conversion was by no means always by force, but often by conviction, often for political reasons and protection. Where the foreigners settled there long remained patches of hardy warriors supporting the existing Moslem power, or too often turning to those other Moslem claimants, who by their constant rebellions, so helped to weaken the Moslem rule. There was often little enough love lost between the Moslem factions of Turkish ancestry and those of Pathan or Indian descent. The records of the day talk of the great rivalries at the Delhi courts between the Lords of Iran, and the Lords of Turan, the Moslems of Aryan or Persian blood and those of Turkish origin.

The settlers from the Afghan Hills especially those from what we now call the 'Frontier' were known as Rohillas, the Men of Roh or Ruh, the ancient name for those hills. The Province of Rohilkand, which lies between Delhi and the Himalaya is so called because most of the land-owners and followers were Rohillas. If you go among the peasantry along the borders of the State of the Nizam in the south, you will find that the Moslems in that State, especially if turbulent, are still known as Rohillas, a term in fact used by peaceful folk to denote any Moslem disturber of the peace. Throughout the land the Rohilla land-owners and their followers had no reputation as farmers and cultivators, a work that they left to their Hindu serfs and yeoman tenants.

For years the Rohilla settler would send, as a man of a Highland clan who has done well in Edinburgh London or Calcutta would send, for his young wild relatives to join him. His bodyguards would thus be reinforced by new stock, and if he were wise he would send, so far as his orthodox marriages were concerned, for daughters of the hardy mountain stock. It would seem that this practice came to an end both as to wives and henchmen when the Sikhs had closed the Punjab routes to the Rohilla and the Afghan, and when the creeping *Pax Brittanica* had brought the Moslem landlords to see reason and to plump for peace.

The foreign Moslem settlers in the land produced many sturdy soldiers, especially horsemen, in the early British days, a few of whom still retain their traditions and value, but the centuries in an enervating climate, and intermarriage within the land has produced, as it has done to the stock of Europe, a considerable falling away in energy, courage and the martial spirit, to the great regret of the old officers, who in times gone by, had seen their value. Those who read details of the Indian Mutiny will know many stories of how single horsemen among the rebels challenged young British officers to single combat in front of the opposing squadrons, and how varied was the issue of such encounters, while equally forward were loyal horsemen in supporting their British officers in similar action.

For good or for evil most of that spirit has passed before the enervating effect of peace on the Eastern martial traits. The converted Moslems of the lesser and clerkly breeds were rarely men of the sword, except in some passing phase of fanatical religious fury.

It is the converted Rajput clans of the North, who still retain their martial traits, who find a large portion of His Majesty's faithful Indian Army, and who help in many a Government job that needs a man, while from across the border the wild reiving clans are still eager to serve. Farther south alas, the Moslem is a shadow of his earlier self, save perhaps in the Dekhan, where the descendants of the conquerors still have heart and thew.

But of all these, and their modern equation, stock will be taken hereafter each in their place and time.

Chapter V

THE SACCA OF CHITOOR AND OTHER RAJPUT SAGAS

THE FIRST SACCA (A.D. 1303)—BABER CRUSHES THE RAJPUTS—THE SECOND SACCA (1533)—THE THIRD SACCA (1568)—SOME RAJPUT SAGAS: I. THE BRIDAL CORTEGE OF KORAM DEN—2. THE RAJPUTNI AND THE BEAR—3. THE RAJPUTS AND AURUNGZEBE—4. THE ANSWER OF QUEEN SUNJOTA.

The Drama of Chitoor

Among the many fascinating and pathetic stories of heroism and despair that are associated with the struggles of the Rajputs of Rajasthan with the conquerors from the North, there are none that surpass the annals of Chitoor, and the story of the Saccas. Sacca is the name for the immolation of the females of a beleaguered place, an immolation to save them from gracing the harems and even the lepanoirs of the conquerors, that inevitable fate of women in the warring East.

In the second century of our era, legend tells us that the first migrant of the solar race, the Surajbansi, came to Mewar and there founded an Aryan settlement by driving out some earlier race and ruler, who or what, hardly matters here. Before long the newcomers obtained possession of the rock of Chitoor on which no doubt was a fortress. Chitoor now stands on the great grey cliffs, close to the railway line to Bombay, a derelict and a warning. For many centuries its grey limestone walls and bastions formed the fortress capital of the Ranas of Mewar. For eight hundred years it held its proud position, but in the latter centuries it endured three terrible captures and sacks, and the last at the hands of Akbar, the greatest of the great Moguls, since which it has lain derelict like some giant ship's hull thrown high on the rocks. (See footnote to p. 87).

Long before Chitoor ever fell to Turkish foe it stood up to the early Arab invaders from Sind, and some of the first incursions of Mahmud of Ghuzni, a bulwark, and a strong place. Unfortunately the Rajputs must quarrel as bitterly among themselves as they resisted the invader, and sad to relate, clan jealousy at times made one lot accept aid from the common enemy.

Twice was Chitoor attacked by Alla-ud-din-Khilji, Emperor of Delhi, and this was due to two causes, Rajput raids and a skirt. Bhimsi, uncle of the then young Rana, had married the daughter of the Chief of Ceylon who had the soubriquet only given to the most beautiful of women, viz., 'Pudmini'. Alla-ud-din, investing Chitoor, demanded the rendition of Pudmini to his arms, as the terms of raising the siege. The refusal and fierce resistance induced him to mitigate his demands to a sight of the veiled and extraordinary beauty. Finally he was offered the sight reflected through mirrors and to this he assented. Trusting, as he knew he could, to the faith of a Rajput, he entered the fastness unguarded and duly enjoyed the sight of beauty in the mirrors. The Rajput Chief then accompanied the Tartar Emperor to the outer gates. Here, however, the faithless Tartar had prepared an ambush. Bhimsi was carried off, and his return was offered in exchange for Pudmini. It was now diamond cut diamond. The Rajputs represented that Pudmini should come properly escorted to be a Royal spouse. With her would be maids of honour, and many another lady would accompany her to bid her farewell. Strict were the precautions against curiosity violating the cortège of beauty. Seven hundred crimson curtained litters left the fort, and proceeded to the besiegers' camp. In each was one of the defenders of Chitoor with six armed soldiers disguised as litter bearers. The cortège was received in an enclosure of tent walls. Half an hour was allowed for the farewells between the Hindu Prince and his bride. Here again the Tartar had planned more treachery: Bhimsi was to be bilked and kept a prisoner. But no Pudmini and no maids descended from the litter. In lieu thereof the armed men who now sallied forth rescued the captive Bhimsi but as Alla was too well guarded for their vengeance, they had to content themselves with acting as rearguard to their chief who escaped on a swift horse. The devoted guard, history relates, were destroyed to a man. Alla-ud-din now attempted an assault, but was repulsed with heavy loss, and raised the siege awhile. Then he returned, better equipped, to recommence the siege anew. This time escape was impossible, sortie after sortie failed, and it only remained to die. No mercy was to be expected from the Tartars. Then was prepared the terrible rite of *Johur*, the giant burning, by which alone could the queens and all the women escape the Tartar lust. Beneath the fortress lay great caverns and in these vast fires had been prepared. The funeral pyre was lighted in the underground chambers and into this in procession walked the queens and all their wives and daughters who could by any counting be in danger. The beautiful Pudmini brought up the tail of the procession, and the doors were closed. The Rana's twelve-year son and a small party escaped through the enemy, that the line might endure. The Rana and the whole of the surviving chivalry now opened the gates and charged forth to sell their lives as dearly as they could. When the Tartars entered over their bodies, there was little of live flesh and blood for them to exult over. Thus fell for the first time in 1303,[1] the great Rajput stronghold.

But Chitoor was not alone in misfortune, for this Emperor of Delhi brought disaster on most of the Rajput principalities.

Baber Crushes the Rajputs

Before Chitoor was to be subjected to another Sacca the Rajputs were to suffer a crushing defeat at the hands of a new Tartar conqueror. The Lodi dynasty of Delhi was crumbling and all the unsettled elements were in arms, Moslem against Moslem and Rajput against all, including, alas, too often himself.

But a new master was on his way and in 1526, Baber, descendant of Timur the Lame, the world compeller, had made his way by stages to the ever-ready battle-field of India at Panipat. Baber, a man of courage, of humour, of enthusiasm and determination, thrice demanded from Ibrahim, the last of the Lodis, the throne that was once by conquest mighty Timur's. The Moslem forces of Ibrahim now met the fierce hard mountaineers and riders from the north on the famous field, Ibrahim was slain and his army scattered, and Baber marched to Delhi and thence to Agra. To him flocked the majority of the Moslem barons and soldiery, who but wanted to serve one who could hold India down and preserve the Moslem supremacy. But the chivalry of Rajasthan had arisen to shake off all vestige of Moslem authority headed by the Rana Sanga of Chitoor. With him rode all the Rajput princes and their clans, and all Rajputana rang with the thrill

[1] This is Ferishtas date, other authority says 1275.

of it. This was 1528, and Baber advanced from Agra against the patriot hosts. The Rajputs fell on this advanced guard marching carelessly, and 1,500 of his Tartars were destroyed while Baber himself was surrounded by the mounted hordes and pinned within his entrenched camp. After his manner his sins then fell heavily on him, and he repented mightily. This time he foreswore all liquor, and he was very fond of his cups after the custom of his race, whatever the Moslem law. These are the verses which he actually composed:

> " Oh my soul
> " How long wilt thou continue to take pleasure in sin,
> " Repentance is not unpalatable. Taste it."

Thus reinforced he broke up his camp, drove his foes before him and appeared before the actual Rajput camp a few miles in front of his own laager. A furious assault on the Tartars was then made bv the eager Rajputs which was their undoing. The Tartars, nothing dismayed, fought with some majesty, until one of the great chiefs prompted by some feud of jealousy went over to the Moslems. Then was the Rajput cause lost; long was the night of slaughter, heavy the tally of slain. Oodi Singh of Dongerpur with 200 of his clan, Rutna Singh of Saumbra with 300 of his Chunderwat swordsmen, Rai Mul Rahtore of Marwar and many another of the leading chiefs, with countless lesser barons and duine-vassals, and even a son of the last Lodi Dynasty, fighting with the Rajputs against the Tartars. Rana Sanga himself was carried off the field wounded and the beaten Rajput host made for the Mewatti hills, the Rana swearing that he would not return to his capital till victorious.

On the battle-field the triumphant Baber was piling up the usual trophy of the heads of his dead enemies and in tribute to his prowess for the Faith assumed the title of *Ghazi*, which his successors held until the last pantaloon puppet of the ancient kingdom lost in 1857 even the shreds of authority by turning on his benefactors at Delhi.

The Second Sacca (1533)

The defeat of the Rajputs at Kanua was enough for Baber. The Rajput menace was over for the present, and he had other fish to fry than run his head against the rock of Chitoor.

But there were other enemies of the Rajputs who would continue the struggle. Rajah or Rana Sanga was a forcible personality and had lived on war. He had lost an eye in a brawl with a brother, and an arm in action with the King of Delhi, and had long been a cripple since his leg had been broken by a cannon ball. Eighty wound scars from sword and lance he also bore on his body. He had not carried his life so successfully without making many enemies. Among other feats he had captured the Moslem King of Malwa, Muzaffer, in his own stronghold; he had also captured the famous fortress of Rinthunbur from Ali the Imperial general, and Islam was hot on his tracks and those of the Rajputs generally. Bikramajit, a son of the Rana, was now on the throne, his war-worn father having been gathered with his fathers of the Sun, and Bahadur King of Guzerat, took advantage of the weakening quarrels of the Rajputs then in progress to march on Chitoor. Bitter had been the Rajput dissensions. In the saying of the countryside *Poppa Bhai ki Raj* had supervened, Poppa being a princess of fable whose rule was proverbial for mismanagement. Bikramajit, brave enough if incompetent, hastened to meet Bahadur, and was severely defeated for his pains. Inside Chitoor was an infant son of Sanga, and there, burying the hatchet of dissension, the Rajputs hurried to defend the capital that was sacred above all things. Sacrificing everything, the most famous Rajput chiefs rallied to its defence.

The Moslems sat down before the fortress with a fine park of artillery, and with them it was said some European, probably Portuguese, gunners. A vast mine was sprung which brought down forty-five cubits of the rampart. Bravely did walls of flesh and blood hasten to fill the gap in the stone. The Queen-mother of the Rhatores, the noble Jowajir Bhai, herself led forth a sortie, clothed in mail, and was slain at the head of her clan. Still the besiegers gained ground. Then the infant child of Sanga was smuggled out, as was the heir in the last siege, to preserve the race, and since Chitoor can only be defended by royalty, Baghi, prince of Deoli, was crowned a temporary king. The great banner of Mewar flew out over his head, but in vain for the fate of Chitoor was again sealed as it had been two centuries before. Once more was the terrible *Johur* prepared. There was hardly time to get ready the pyre, so fast had the defenders fallen in the great breach that saltpetre had effected. But combustibles were heaped in the underground caverns and among the powder magazines, and the princess Kurnavaiti, mother of the prince, headed the martyrs' procession, as thirteen thousand women in the flower of their youth and beauty marched calm, triumphant and even exulting to the doom that was to defraud and disappoint the conquerors of their victims. Then were the great gates flung wide open as in ancient times, and the prince of Deoli charged forth at the head of the survivors, blind with fury and despair.

Not a man survived, and the triumphant Moslem conqueror looked on a terrible scene of desolation. Every clan had lost its chief, and 32,000 Rajputs are said to have lost their lives. This was the second Sacca of Chitoor in the year of Our Lord 1535 and of '*Sambat*' The Hindu Calendar, 1591. The deeds done and tragedies concerning it which the bards sing to this day, were legion.

And so the years rolled on, the Rajputs still in turmoil, and always in fratricidal war with their own kind, or strife of extermination with their Moslem neighbours. The story of how the infant Oody Singh was rescued to become a worthless scion, and bring down Mewar and Chitoor again need not be recounted. Suffice it to say that once more did Chitoor arise and once more was it to suffer *Sacca* and undergo *Johur* before it was to become a derelict, tragic ruin, at which even a Cook's tourist grows sad for a while.[1]

The Third Sacca (1568)

While the Rajputs continued their struggles and intrigues, the throne of Baber passed to his son Humayun, who after ten years of mismanagement and ill fortune had lost all that his father had gained, and finally, at the hands of the Afghan Sher Shah was driven forth a fugitive. More than once had he in incipient wisdom tended to help the Rajputs and lay the seed of reconciliation that afterwards his son Akbar was to ripen. During the period that Sher Shah held down the throne of Delhi, after the final defeat of Humayun, the Rajputs had been rigorously restrained within their own hills and some of their strongholds taken with concomitant massacre. In 1555 the tide turned and Humayun came back triumphant only to be killed by a fall from his horse the next year. His son Akbar succeeded to him at the age of fourteen and his armies defeated the Afghans on the field of Panipat. At eighteen, as related,

[1] Of late years, however, restored and repaired.

Akbar took the reins from his minister Bairam and started on the great career that was to bring his dynasty to a place among the world's greatest kingdoms. In 1566 all the Moslems had acknowledged him, and he was anxious to arrive at some better relations with the Rajputs. After a brief struggle most of the chiefs entered into alliance, Oody Singh alone, foolish and proud, defied the mighty Emperor, on which the Mogul sat down before Chitoor for the third and last seige, from which, however, the chief himself was absent.

Ferishta, the Moslem historian, records not, but local history states, that once was Akbar repulsed and compelled to abandon the siege by the determined defence which the Rana's concubine queen put up. But whatever the truth of that, in the twenty-fifth year of his age, and the seventh of his having assumed control, his vast army and siege train appeared before the grey cliffs and battlements that had seen it all so many times before. The site of the Royal *Ordu*[1] is shown to this day and the attacking trenches also remain. Once again the chiefs assembled to combat for their ancient capital though the Rana was not with them. Names are they still to conjure with in Rajasthan, but first and foremost among the heroes were Jai Mall of Bednor and Putta of Kailwa, both among the sixteen superior vassals of Mewar. The siege followed the usual course. Fierce were the stormings of the Tartars and Afghans, fiercer still the thrust and sortie of the defenders Within was all that the clan valued, all except their sovereign. Queens, princesses, and all the lesser women of rank and all the clansmen's families. Many a slip of a Rajput lass slung the buckler over the scarf and died in the breach. Salumbra fell at the gate of the Sun, and the sixteen year old Putta of Kailwa took his place.

[1] Camp.

His mother cast over him the saffron robe of the martyr, and then, that he should have no regard for the gentler side of his life, armed herself and gave his bride a lance, and descended the rock towards the foe. All Chitoor saw them fall and vowed a vow. The terrible *Johur* for the third time in history was prepared, and the garrison to the number of eight thousand donned the saffron robe, the *pan* of sacrifice —the *bhira*—was distributed, the women marched to the pyre and the gates of sortie and sacrifice were thrown open. Of what avail such valour against the countless hosts of the Mogul. All the heads of clans and all the allied chiefs fell, and seventeen hundred of the immediate kin of the prince. With them nine queens, five of their daughters and two infant sons perished, and Akbar like Alla-ud-din, or Bahadur, his predecessors in this barren victory, gazed from the head of the main gate on the slaughter and desolation he had brought about. But to him already planning an 'India' it was a shock and not a rejoicing. The greatness of the victory was gauged according to custom from the collars taken from chiefs of distinction; of such four and seventy and a half *mans* were garnered. A *man* is eight pounds.

Ever since, seventy-four and a half is an abhorred number in Rajputana, and is held *tilac* (accursed).

Oody Singh, the renegade, founded a new settlement at what is now the capital of Oodipur, and died at forty-four in great malodour, but leaving behind a vast progeny. Chitoor has to this day stood as a ruin, a haunt for the wild beast and the bittern, even its shrines and temples foresworn,—below it unheeding clatter the railway trains of the West (but see footnote p. 87).

SOME RAJPUT SAGAS

1. *The Bridal Cortège of Koramdevi*

The life story of Rajasthan, as has been said, lives in the memory of its people as do those of other Celtic races, and in the songs and stories of the bards. From mouth to mouth through the ages, like the Puranas, the Upanishads, and all the literature of the ancient world recorded long before the written cult, come the stories that have been handed down of memory often more accurately than careless or glossful copyists may write. Thus Rama and Krishna long before they became gods and incarnations were Kshattriya adventurers, leaders and heroes, the latter being in modern light parlance a 'bit of a lad', with a gift of the comether for every strapping dairymaid. Popular heroes in all times are recognized, and very properly so, as having at least some particle of the deity in their cosmos, men into whom the Kings of Orion have entered.

But we need not now go back to the hero-myth, but to those stout stories of medieval chivalry in Rajasthan of which the folk still love to hear. We shall be told of many more Saccas, when Rajput queens and curtain wives went to the *Johur* before less unholy foes than the hosts of the Turk. In the eternal civil war between cousin kings, the wives were prouder and often fiercer still, and scorned the bed of the conqueror, even when of their own blood.

The tale of the queens, however, is always a tale of faithful love and constancy, and is typical of the spirit of Hindu women, and their proud and patient outlook on life. Here is the story of the bride of Sadoo, son of Raningdeo Bhatti, lord of Poogal, a fief of Jeysulmere, as related by

Tod. Sadoo was a prince of raiders, the terror of the desert, harrying even to the Indus. It so happened that returning from a foray in typical Rajput style—and who said 'Scottish border'?—with captured horses and camels and sumpter mules, he passed through the dukedom of Manik Rao, the chief of the Rajput clan of the Mohils, whose rule extended, it is said, over close on 1,450 villages.

After the Rajputs' open way, Manik Rao bade the young baron tarry a while and sup. While so doing he attracted attention of the old chief's daughter, Koramdevi, who, masterful hot-blooded lass that she was, although betrothed to Irrinkowal the heir of the great Rahtore prince of Mundore, announced that she would renounce the prospect of a throne and marry the heir of Poogal.

The Mohil chief could not advise Sadoo to make a mortal enemy of the Rahtore bridegroom-elect by marrying his forward daughter, but how could Sadoo, a Rajput of spirit decline so commanding a favour, and the hand of so beautiful and highborn a lady. He promised to accept the Cocoanut, the symbol of betrothal, if sent to Poogal in Rajput form. In due time it came, the Rahtores were defied, and Sadoo espoused his bride with great ceremony at Aureent, the bride's home. Handsome was the dower of the Mohil princess, gems of high price, vessels of gold and silver, a golden bull and thirteen *dewadharis*, damsels 'of wisdom and penetration' to wait on their lady and share such trifle of her husband's affection as she could spare.

The slighted heir of Mundore was not however prepared to take the insult, the brazen flouting, placidly. With 4,000 of his Rahtore warriors Irrinkowal planted himself across the return path of the bridal cortège. Sadoo's father-in-law had offered him 4,000 Mohils as escort, but the laughing bridegroom, confident in his own 700 stout Bhatti clansmen, could not be persuaded to take more than fifty under his new brother-in-law, Megraj.

Sadoo and his bride halted to rest at Chondon, and there the Rahtores found him. The Rahtores brave and chivalrous however ruthless, scorned to fall on so small force with all their numbers, and a series of single combats ensued. Single combats passed to the engaging of larger bodies, and at length Sadoo mounted his horse, his bride watching from her chariot. As the struggle waged half of Sadoo's men had fallen, and six hundred of the Rahtores. Sadoo then bade his lass a last adieu, and she vowed that she would witness his deeds, and if he fell follow him in death. Irrinkowal, 'the Lotus of the Desert', awaited his successful rival in love, and at length they met to shower blow on helmet and shield as they circled on their high-bitted steeds. At last both fell to the ground, Sadoo dead, his rival in a swoon.

With the fall of the rivals and leaders the battle ceased, and the cause of it all, the fair Koramdevi, virgin-wife and widow all in one, prepared to follow her bridegroom, a grim and ruthless following, as grim as had been the strife. As the funeral pyre was ready Koramdevi called for a sword, and then, the story runs, struck off one arm "'For my father'. Saying 'such was his daughter'," she commanded the other to be struck off and given with the marriage jewels to the bard of the Mohils. Thus maimed she mounted the pyre, embraced her bridegroom with the poor stumps, and bade them apply the torch. To this day they show the 'Tank of Koramdevi', built in her honour.

That is the story, and from the accounts of the *saccas* and *suttees*, there is no reason to doubt it, so fierce and proud were these mistaken heroes and their women, with a ferocity, courage and pride so tense that could they have avoided quarrelling among themselves not all the Turks in Asia should have crossed the Indus twice. It is to the eternal disgrace of the Brahminical framework with its national claim, that it has ever failed to save, but has always sufficed to break the country of its pretensions.

2. *The Rajputni and the Bear*

Among the lesser stories of the womenkind, and their strength and courage, comes that of the Rajputni and the bear, as told by Zalim Singh, characteristic of the Rajpoot women. Taking the midday meal to her husband, a yeoman farmer at work on his fields, a Rajputni was attacked by a bear who advanced erect like Adamzad, 'the bear that walked like a man'. Uncertain whether the bear sought herself or the food the woman got behind the trunk of a tree, and the bear still erect, exhausted all his ingenuity to seize her but in vain. At last, however, the Rajputni, too weary to evade the brute longer, grasped his two paws with a grasp of iron from her fine-bred wrists. The short-necked bear roared with fear at being so tackled, and tried hard to seize her wrists but without success. While in this dilemma a foreign soldier, a *pardasi*, passed, en route to a neighbouring garrison. She called to him in a voice of great unconcern to come and give a hand for a time so that she might rest. He did so readily enough, but she had not gone a dozen yards before the soldier, finding he could hardly hold the bear, shouted to her to return. She however laughed and recommended perseverance, but soon returned with her husband and his matchlock so that the soldier was relieved. The story as told reads but as a piece of a normal day's work for a strapping woman.

3. *The Rajputs and Aurungzebe*

When conquered by Akbar as related, the Rajputs became the loyal servants of the Empire, serving the Mogul the length and breadth of India from the Hindu Kush to the Assam Hills, and it was not till the days of Aurungzebe that their chivalrous loyalty was ended. Bernier, the French physician with the emperor tells many stories of their prowess and self sacrifice. When this ungrateful son had planned to supplant and imprison his father Shah Jehan, the Rajputs stood for the Emperor, and a great battle between thirty thousand of them and the forces of Murad and Aurungzebe took place on the Narbudda. The vastly superior Moslem forces were too much for them, but when 10,000 Rajputs had fallen, the Rahtore Maharajah Jeswunt Singh drew off to his own capital with but 500 of his following surviving, and those mostly wounded. But his Queen, a daughter of Oodipur, would have none of him. She was not going to comfort and condole with one who could suffer defeat and live. She shut the gates of his castle against him, vowing that he was not her husband, and that the son-in-law of the great Rana could not have so mean a soul. In vain they told how he had scorned death a hundred times and fought till the remnant was forced from the field, bearing himself a charmed life. She but cried that they deceived her, he must be dead, and she bade the pyre be lit on which she too would burn. It was not till nine days later that her mother alone could persuade her that the Maharajah but lived to raise another army and fight Aurungzebe again—'a pattern' remarks Bernier 'of the courage of the women of the country'.

4. *The Answer of Queen Sunjota*

Once upon a time before the Rajputs were driven from Delhi, of which they were then the emperors and premier kings in Ind, the Chouhan Emperor carried off in triumph, the Princess of Kanauj, Sunjota by name. She had rejected the assembled princes at her father's court, and thrown the garland of marriage round the neck of her hero, and in his arms, it is related, abandoned herself to the wildest passion. Then she is to be seen taking part in a five days' combat between her father's and husband's forces, and after witnessing the overthrow of the former and the carnage of both armies, in her arms lulls her victorious husband to the neglect of all his kingly duties.

When however the Moslem came down from Ghuzni we are shown her driving him to the battle and inspiring him to fight till death, promising to join him in the mansions of the sun.

Sunjota must have been a remarkable and thrice fearless woman for the bards record her reply when the king left his warriors to consult with her as to the opposing of Mahmud of Ghuzni.

"Who asks woman for advice? The world deems their understanding shallow; even when truths issue from their lips, none listen thereto. Yet what is the world without woman? We have the forms of Sakhti with the fire of Siva; we are at once thieves and sanctuaries; we are the vessels of virtue and of vice—of knowledge and of ignorance. The man of wisdom, the astrologer, can from the books calculate the motion and course of the planets; but in the book of woman he is ignorant; this is not a saying of to-day, it has ever been so; our book has not been mastered, therefore to hide their ignorance, they say in woman there is no wisdom! Yet woman shares your joys and your sorrows. Even when you depart for the mansions of the sun, we part not. Hunger and thirst we cheerfully partake with you; we are as the lakes of which you are the swans; what are you when absent from our bosoms?"

Which whether spoken as it was close on a thousand years ago, whether spoken to-day, or when Babylon was at her zenith, is a very remarkable and effective swan-song. Alas! For swan-song it proved to be. Her Emperor was defeated, captured and put to death by Mahmud, and she, faithful to her vows, mounted the funeral pyre.

A RATHORE RAJPUT OF THE BIKANER CAMEL CORPS, (THE GANGA RISALA)

[Face page 96

CHAPTER VI

THE MAHRATTA STORY

ANCIENT MAHARASTHRA—THE MOSLEM KINGDOMS OF THE DEKHAN —SHIVAJI AND HIS HOUSE—THE STORY OF AFZUL KHAN—MAHRATTA AND MOGUL—THE LAST BATTLE OF PANIPAT—THE MOGUL RUIN AND THE MAHRATTAS—THE PINDARI HORROR.

ANCIENT MAHARASTHRA

THE story of the Mahrattas is intimately mixed up with the fall of the Turkish Empire of Delhi, as it is with the rise of the British, and this strange freebooting federation that tried to become an empire is not without fascination to all who love to watch the 'Wheel'. The Mahrattas to-day have an important niche in the defensive forces of the Empire, and in the World War the Mahratta corps in the Indian Army carried to a world-wide reputation the traditions of Shivaji Bhonsla.

The Mahrattas are certain folk of semi-Aryan extraction who own and cultivate the land of the coastal plains and hills north and south of Bombay, the spurs and valleys of the wall of the Western Ghats and the uplands known as the Deccan, more properly Dekhan, and the lower lands and jungles of the Konkan. Because some Aryan or Jăt strain had mingled with the earlier Dravidian or cognate race, because they were men of thews and hearts and because they were prepared to leave Buddhism and come back to the Brahmin fold, therefore they were admitted to have something, it is not quite clear what, of Rajput status. The term Mahratta must not be confused with those so-called 'Mahratta' Brahmins, the Brahmins of the Dekhan who have settled in Maharasthra, as the Mahratta land was known. They are Brahmins pure and simple, who perform Brahminical functions in that land, having come there from the north in the dark ages before time was counted, when the Aryan soldier forced his way through the jungles of Central India. As elsewhere, their numbers are far greater than the priesthood needs, and therefore they are numerous in lay occupations. The climate of the Dekhan, for some unknown reason, has intensified their brain power to an amazing extent. They furnished ministers and officials to the Mahratta states, high and low, judges and officials to the British Government, and they dominate in the clerical occupations of the Bombay Government. The coming of the British has in certain ways deprived them of their commanding offices, but in other directions has opened countless advantageous ways of life.

As intriguers and politicians of great acuteness their name is notorious throughout India, and in modern times as judges, lawyers, scientists, and financiers they hold a prominent position in Western India, but they are not racially Mahrattas.

This Aryan penetration of the South and West, as explained, is recorded in the countless Hindu legends and sagas and no man can deduce plain history therefrom. At the time when the sage Agastya bade the mountains grow less high, or in other words incited the Aryans to venture beyond the Aravallis, there is no doubt that the subjugation of Berar and the country about the River Godaveri was very thorough. While the languages farther south, Tamil, Telegu and Canarese are not Sanskrit languages, Mahratti certainly is. The various *Prakrits* are the dialects of the old Aryan tongue, of which the *Sanskrit* the 'polished' tongue remains standardized, from the moment it was memorialised and eventually written as a priestly and literary tongue. The homely human *prakrits* however have gone on developing and degenerating perhaps to suit the needs and psychology of the peoples of the countryside. The Mahratti is a peculiarly charming one with astoundingly poetic imagery in its everyday terms for 'nature's sweet familiar things'.

While the term Dekhan or Dakhan is the short of *Dakshini*, the 'right-hand' country as you face the rising sun, and hence the south, Maharasthra, is the land of the great Rathas or Rattas, put into Sanskrit form. Earlier records tell of this race Rattas, Rastikas, etc., and of missions from the north to their kingdoms. This southern and western country was a land of great kingdoms of antiquity, and great trade with the West. From the coast through the Ghats many trade routes cut their way up the scarred ravines that the rains have torn to the seas, and to this day on these stand great grey stone castles. Some were built by the earlier Moslem conquerors, some far older, the 'adulterine' castle that was the home of robber barons, others the official strongholds of the governors of the day. Eventually, they fell to the hands of the Mahratta chiefs, and from them to small British columns which tramped the Ghats with mountain trains, and pack mortars, till they too acknowledged the might of the 'Angrez' and the call of the *Pax Britannica*.

THE MOSLEM KINGDOMS OF THE DEKHAN

When the Moslem conquerors swept through the land it was not long before Afghan and Turkish leaders started dynasties in the West, subduing most existing powers Aryan, semi-Aryan and Dravidian. At the end of the thirteenth and commencement of the fourteenth century when the Khilji dynasty ruled at Delhi, the first invasion of the Dekhan took place, and Deogarh was captured. A generation later Muhammad Tughlagh, emperor of Delhi, subdued the greater part of the Dekhan and actually moved his entire capital and all its folks willy-nilly to Deogarh which he now named Doulatabad, 'The City of Dominion'.

The fortress of Doulatabad that was originally Deoghar is quite one of the most remarkable and romantic in India, not even excepting the great Rock of Gwalior. It stands on an isolated circular hill of which the circumference is 5,000 yards, and which has been scarped for the height of a hundred feet or so, so smooth that it is said neither a snake nor an ant could scale it.

The hill which towers several hundred feet above the scarp, and which has almost needlessly embattled walls and terraces, is entered by a dark spiral road, winding through the bowels of the rock, so dark that artificial light is needed, until it eventually emerges on to the inner terreplein. Apart from any gates the long tunnel thus formed is closed by a furnace and grating at the top, from which a charcoal fire emits heavy fumes to descend and make the passage deadly and impassable. The furnace and grating are still to be seen. Great cannon, with long Persian inscriptions carved thereon, still lie about the interior, while below a guard of the Nizam State Artillery keep uneventful guard, in the trappings of an earlier

British period, and boasting of names and clans from the frontier, from whose advent centuries earlier they count their descent. Below the rock are the ruined walls of the once capital city of a dynasty and of an empire.

It was not long before Afghan soldiers of fortune rebelled and set up kingdoms of their own. One Zaffir Khan, the menial of a Brahmin at Delhi named Gangu, gathered together all who hated the cruelties of which Tughlagh had been guilty. He made himself with their help, ruler of the Dekhan and assumed the name and title of Alah-ud-din, Hasan Gangu Bahmani, the latter word meaning Brahmin, and these strange cognomens he adopted because of his affection for his old master. The Bahmani Dominion was now extended to the Konkan and the sea on the west, and it lasted close on two centuries. By 1526, the Delhi Dominion under the Lodi dynasty was in its last throes. All over India its viceroys were in rebellion, and the independent Bahmani Kingdom, fell with it, breaking into five separate Moslem states, those of Ahmednagar (Nizam Shahi dynasty), Bijapur (Adil Shahi), Golconda (Qutb Shahi), and Bidar and Berar in both of which members of the Bahmani family were set up. To Delhi had now come Baber the Chagatai Turk to found the greatest rule of them all, the Mogul Empire.

The kingdoms into which the Bahmani had broken up had become hopelessly antagonistic one to another, wasting their substance in constant wars, and ere long the states of Bidar and Berar had been eaten up by Ahmednagar and Bijapur. Up till 1594 a powerful Hindu state, Vijianager, had succeeded in remaining in being, but it at last fell to Bijapur.

All the while the simple pastoral and agricultural Mahrattas had let the tide of invasion and conquest roll by. The daily village life continued, revenue was paid to him who could get it, and there were no signs of a Mahratta revival. But the countless wars between the Moslem states were the latter's undoing. The supply of Turks, Arabs, Moguls was not sufficient and the sturdier people of the country-side were called to the ranks. Thus there arose some military spirit and ideas in Mahrattadom. Even in the contending armies the Mahrattas were serving as mercenaries and they had plenty of feuds of their own to prosecute. In 1529 the Shah of Bijapur actually appointed a Mahratta Brahmin as his *peshwa* or prime minister.

It was during the sixteenth century that the Portuguese came to India and eventually shared with Bijapur and Ahmednagar what is now the Bombay Presidency. Before long we find them contributing some Portuguese artillerymen to the local quarrels.

Shivaji and his House

When Akbar came to the Mogul throne he speedily developed his policy of a combined India, though he felt compelled to take Ahmednagar which was defended for long by the great Queen Chand Bai. The Nizam Shahi dynasty, however, remained, with capital at Doulatabad and in 1620 when Malik Ambar was king of that state the modern Mahratta story may be said to have commenced. At that time Shahji Bhonsla a Mahratta country gentleman in the Muhammadan service, greatly distinguished himself in battle against the rebellious son and heir of the Mogul Emperor Shah Jehan. In 1629 after Shah Jehan had succeeded to the throne, his commander-in-chief in the Dekhan rebelled, inducing the Mahrattas to support him; but Shaji Bhonsla sided with the Emperor, for which he received a patent of nobility and a grant of estates. Other Mahrattas followed his example, and Lodi Shah Khan, the rebel com-commander, was killed.

The Moguls were now at war with the Moslem kingdoms of the Dekhan, which were brought to some sort of submission, the Nizam Shahi kingdom disappearing. In their wars with the Emperor and with themselves each side was encouraging the Mahratta nobles, both in their own quarrels and in their rebellions against Delhi.

Then it was that Shivaji, son of Shahji, came first as a Hindu champion with the desire to form a Hindu state.

In the middle of the seventeenth century Aurungzebe, the son of Shah Jehan, was made Viceroy of the Dekhan, and established his camp at Kirki near Doulatabad, which he now named Aurungabad.

Shahji was now in the service of the king of Bijapur and to him was born the famous Shivaji in the fort of Shivner, not far from Poona. While Aurungzebe was endeavouring to govern the Dekhan, the boy Shivaji was developing into the man that was to drive many of the nails into the Mogul coffin. Up and down the rugged ghats he wandered, noting the great fortresses that guarded the trading routes, or harboured the men-at-arms of the raiding barons. He noted how strong they were in themselves, how carelessly guarded by the Moslem garrisons. The adventurous lad summoned to himself, like Prince Hal of England a band of lads of spirit. He actually gained possession of the fort of Torna forty miles west of Poona high up on the mountains, and then offered to rent it from the Bijapur Government. In Torna of all places he discovered treasure.

His grandfather, ran the legend, the first Bhonsla to gather any of this world's goods, had received it from the goddess Bhavani, who had prophesied that one in the family should become a king, re-establish Maharasthra, and remove all 'who molested Brahmins or violated the temples of the gods'. It is to be noticed that it was always those who cherished Brahmins for whom great promises were made. When Shivaji found the treasure, he attributed the discovery to the protection of Bhavani, where some might have said he did, like merry Hal, but rob a banker or a Jew.

At any rate, he had now achieved his boyish ambition to be a *polygar*, the 'governor of a fort'. While this was in progress his father Shahji was a vassal of the Moslem Bijapur, and he explained his son's actions as but evidence of his assiduity for Government property in his hands. In prosecution of this duty Shivaji bought arms with his treasure and built himself another mountain eyry at Rajgarh, not far from Torna. Shivaji was thus embarked on a definite career of defiance, which could but have one end as soon as Bijapur should learn what was really doing, and he actually seized the fort of Chakun out in the plains some eighteen miles from Poona. Funds he now accumulated by retaining the revenues due to Bijapur for his father's estates. Later he gained one of the most powerful and magnificent of strongholds in which large masses of horse could be concealed. Bijapur for the moment, however, was strangely tolerant, content that Shaji remained at court while his son managed his estates. And while the Moslem slumbered the Hindu waxed powerful.

At last, two years later, Shivaji declared himself rebel by attacking and looting a convoy of Government treasure that was passing through the ghats below his eyry. As reprisals were now certain he secured ten of the forts that divided Dekhan from Konkan. This brought him into collision with the Sidis or Sayads of Janjira, who afterwards became the

Mogul admirals. Seeing that he might as well be hung for a sheep as a lamb, he captured Kalyan and took the Moslem Governor prisoner.

The Bijapur Government now threw the father into prison, as a hostage in some sort. Shahji appealed to Shah Jehan, who then took Shivaji into the Imperial Service, and obtained the release of his father from durance, though not from attendance at Bijapur.

While these events were in progress Aurungzebe was continuing his operations against the Moslem kingdoms of the Dekhan, but in 1658 hurried to Delhi to be at the bed-side of his father who was said to be dying. Shah Jehan, however, recovered, and his dutiful son who was *not* the heir, seized the throne and held his father eight years in subjection. Shivaji had offered to protect Aurungzebe's interests during the latter's return to Delhi, and was therefore allowed to put forward preposterous claims on certain Mogul estates. Aurungzebe who was now known by his Imperial title of Alămgir, returned to the Dekhan to prosecute his plans for reducing Dekhan kingdoms, whose rulers to his intense dislike held the Shiah rather than like himself professed the Orthodox form of Islam. How they fell before him is another story, but it is to be remembered that it was the destruction of these kingdoms, Golgonda and Bijapur especially, that was the cause of the growth of the Mahratta ulcer on the Mogul side. Because of his bigotry against his own folk that were not Orthodox he encouraged Shivaji to prey on them, little heeding what would eventuate therefrom.

Alămgir was forty years of age when he seized the throne and he was to spend the greater part of his long reign in trying to bring the Dekhan into the Mogul domain.

This period while Shivaji was rising to power, first by grace of and then in defiance of Delhi, is one of which many legends exist and many heroic deeds are sung. What the Bruce was to Scotland that is Shivaji to the Mahrattadom.

The Story of Afzul Khan

Among the many stories that are still sung at the fairs and told in the schools is that of the death of Afzul Khan, the commander-in-chief of the forces of Bijapur. It is not quite one that Western sentiment and sense of the suitable would choose to tell of their national hero, but then the story of the Jewish nation and the house of which even the Christ was born on earth, commences no better. It must be a strong race and story that dare commence with the dastardly deceit of its founder to his father Isaac, the blind patriarch, and the defrauding of the first born, and so it is with Shivaji.

The Bijapur Government had at last awoken to the fact that their legs were, in modern slang, being pulled by the Mahratta freebooter, and a well-appointed army under Afzul Khan, who vaunted of how he would bring in the Mahratta dead or alive, was sent against him. Shivaji had no intention of joining battle in the open, and withdrew to the mountain fastness of Pertabgarh, in the ghats not far from Poona. Mahratta-like, he could be as wily and treacherous as any situation might demand, and he sent offers of submission to the Afghan who halted at Wai and sent Pantoji Gopinath a Brahmin, to carry on the negotiations. Shivaji ordered the emissary to be well lodged and received and, visiting him at night, explained how he was commissioned by Sri Bhravani herself to free all Hindus, to protect kine and prosper all

Brahmins, and these arguments overcame the Moslems' Brahmin emissary.

Afzul was accordingly informed that it was the Bijapur army that Shivaji feared, but that he would accept the General's personal assurance and would surrender. The Afghan thus encouraged led his army into the mountains. Shivaji prepared for the meeting, blessed by his mother and 'shriven and shorn' by his own Brahmins, with a steel cap below his *puggaree*, and a mail shirt below his cotton coat, waited the arrival of Afzul Khan, but with the crooked Mahratta dagger up his sleeve and the terrible *waghnakh*, or 'tiger's claw' into which the fingers slipped . . . a favourite Mahratta weapon . . . in his right hand.

The meeting took place between the two armies, the mailed Moslems on one side, the wilder Mahratta clansmen on the other, and commenced with the customary embrace of ceremony. As the embrace went forward heart to heart, and hand over back, the *waghnakh* disembowelled the Moslem who was also stabbed with the dagger. Immediately the victim's head was cut off and held up, and instantly the Mahrattas, of whom numbers were concealed in the jungle, fell on the Moslem force hampered and confined in the narrow valley. It was routed and largely destroyed and its camp and baggage captured. Great was the fame that accrued to Shivaji by this timely act of treachery, and from this date 1659 the Mahrattas became a kingdom and something of a nation.

In vain did Bijapur storm and rave. Shivaji was established and was in collision with all and sundry, including incidentally the British, who had gained in 1661 the Island of Bombay by that wonderful dowry which Charles II had received with his Portuguese bride. The Mahratta was now able to maintain 50,000 foot and 7,000 horse.

Mahratta and Mogul

So long as Shivaji was useful in helping to destroy the Moslem kingdoms, Aurungzebe was well enough pleased, but when the former's newly found arrogance brought him into collision with the Imperial authority it was another matter.

When in collision with the Mogul, one of his exploits is as famous among the bards and in the countryside as his destruction of Afzul. High above Poona, and a dozen miles or so from it, stands on a steep massif the fortress of Singhar in which Shivaji had installed himself. Below in the plains the Mogul governor lay at Poona with his host around him. One night Shivaji descended and surrounding the governor's palace, slew his guard and his son, and was away to Singhar before he could be molested, signifying by big illuminations the deed that he had done.

The Mogul now sent a Hindu general against him, and Shivaji warned it is said by Bhavani, made submission, and co-operated with great valour with the Mogul troops against Bijapur. He was then invited to the Imperial court with his son Sambhaji, but showing resentment at something said he was placed in confinement whence however he escaped, and got back to his own land. In 1672 he defeated an Imperial army and it was not till 1682, two years after his death, that Aurungzebe took the field against his son with a magnificent if cumbrous army.

It was in 1674 that Shivaji, having assumed the title of Rajah, was openly crowned at Raigarh and declared himself independent of all and sundry, carrying on his wars with Emperor, Bijapur, and the Sidis and incidentally entering into treaty with the English till his death in 1680.

To Aurungzebe the conquest of the Dekhan had become an obsession and at the age of sixty-three he took the field to spend the last twenty-seven years of his life and reign in marching to and fro therein, and all the while he was so occupied, the traders of the West were consolidating their trading centres and wondering . . . wondering if the Mogul throne from which they received their grant was going to topple and wondering too as well they might . . if so what then?

In 1683 the Emperor took Ahmednagar surrounded with pomp and might . . . he that was so austere and frugal in his own life . . . inconceivable. In 1686 fell also Bijapur, and thus ended the brilliant *Adil Shahi* dynasty. A year later Golconda went the same way, and Alămgir had had his way, he had made a desert and called it peace.

Shivaji's son, Sambhaji, was not wanting in courage, but after the way of the East it was clogs to clogs in one generation, not three. Not for him the eager active alert adventurous life of his father. He was stupid in his diplomacy and had given himself up to the debauchery that comes so easily in an eastern court. The Mogul forces were spent after their long endeavours, but Sambhaji could not take advantage of it. In 1689 falling into Mogul hands, he was offered life coupled with Islam. Tauntingly refusing the apostate's boon, he was put to death with great cruelty.

While thinking little of their ruler the Mahrattas were infuriated at his death. His six years' old son was with his father at Delhi and was retained as a ward at court. Then followed a regency and fierce war with the Moguls till at last Alămgir himself died at Ahmednagar in 1707. Shahu, Sambhaji's son was at length allowed to return, whereon the kingdom of Shivaji broke into two jarring parts, that of Kohlapur and Satara, for Shivaji like Runjhit Singh in the nineteenth century could give no permanency to his building. By the middle of the eighteenth century Mahrattadom had developed in a curious way. The parent kingdom of Satara had become like so many of the Eastern kingdoms a puppet throne in the hands of a mayor of the palace who in this case, was the Peshwa or Prime Minister of the throne. How typical this seemed to Eastern minds is shown in the oriental game of chess. What we know as the most powerful piece, the Queen, is in Eastern language the '*Vizier*', the chief minister, who battles for and guards the useless king.

Four other Mahratta chiefs now rose to power, though not necessarily ruling a Mahratta people. They all but one remain to this day and retain the simple titles which illustrate the homeliness of their origin. They were the *Gaikwar* or cow-keeper of Baroda, *Holkar* who was originally a trooper from the village of Hol and who dominated Indore, the Raja of Berar with capital at Nagpur and usually spoken of as the *Bhonsla*, the family indeed to which Shivaji and all chiefs of his descent belonged. The fourth was *Sindia* the chief of Gwalior, known affectionately as the *Patel* or village headman. His territories eventually stretched to the Jumna. These four, with the Peshwa who controlled the actual state of Poona and Satara, composed the famous Mahratta confederacy, which as the years rolled on and the Mogul Empire crumbled, made a bid for the Empire of India and the headship of all the Hindus.

Their eventual compelling is part of the story of the British but up to that time may be continued here.

With the destruction of the Kingdoms of the Dekhan a Mogul Viceroy was appointed, an office which eventually fell into the hands of the famous Asaf Jah the Turk, whose actual name was Chin Khilji Khan, and whose titles were Asaf Jah and Nizam-ul-Mulk. He, it was who founded the present family of the Nizams of Hyderabad, the only Mogul governor who succeeded in remaining . . . remaining because his heirs when they had made their treaty with the rising British were wise enough to keep it.

The great movements and soldierings of the Dekhan are commemorated in popular verse by the ancient charter of the Brinjaras who carried grain for the armies.

> "*Rangan ka pani, chappar ka ghas.*
> *Din ka tin kun muaf*
> *Au jahan Azaf Jah ke ghore.*
> *Wahan Bhangi-Jhangi ke bail.*
>
> "Water and huts for the army,
> Three murders a day pardoned,
> Wherever Azaf Jah's cavalry are
> There shall be the Brinjara's pack cattle."

As the Peshwa grew in power, he and Azaf Jah were continually at loggerheads save when it suited them to combine against the Mogul at Delhi.

Alămgir was succeeded by an elderly son Muazzim who is known by two titles *Bahadur Shah* and *Shah Alăm*. It is the latter which fits the Imperial series, meaning 'King of the World' as *Alămgir* means 'World-grasper'.

We cannot follow here the decay of Mogul authority and quick-change palace murders which followed for a while on the death of Shah Alăm in 1712, but suffice it to say that the Mahratta confederacy grew more and more powerful and lawless, spreading with their hordes of horse and all over India and demanding the *Chouth*, a fourth of the revenue for themselves as their personal pickings. So far afield did they come, that at Calcutta far to the east and at Madras in the south, the merchant settlers protected themselves by a 'Mahratta Ditch' to bar entry to the environs of the cities. It was Baji Rao I the great Peshwa who built up this confederacy, and who gave to Holkar and the Gaikwars their fiefs, stolen, of course, from the Mogul. He died in 1740 and his mighty opponent Azaf Jah in 1748. Before either died, quarrelling India had seen another Turk, Nadir Shah from Persia capture Delhi. But he, seeing that he had stirred the whole of India to join for its protection, made off with all the riches and spoil that he could lift from Muhammad Shah his 'brother Turk'.[1]

From 1720 onwards the Mahrattas began a career which was to have eventually for its aims the actual domination of the Empire and finally the proclamation of a Mahratta scion as Emperor of India, a Hindu Empire once again. It was also to bring them to a terrible Waterloo.

By 1720 they first put in an appearance at Delhi with a rebellious viceroy of the Dekhan, and compelled their recognition from the Empire, such as it was.

Baji Rao was succeeded by his son Balaji Baji Rao, the original Nana Sahib, so that the Peshwa-ship had now become dynastic. But the Afghan Durani Empire had arisen and the Punjab was over-run and made an Afghan province. The Mahrattas appeared again at Delhi this time partly in their own interests as well as in that of India, and actually drove the Afghans, assisted by the Mogul armies, across the Indus, and this fulfilled a prophecy of Shivaji that one day their horses should water on the banks of that famous stream.[2] It was the last time, though Holkar tried it again as a fugitive before Lord Lake.

The Last Battle of Panipat

By 1760 the Mahrattas with all the flower of their chivalry, and many Moslems of the South appeared at Delhi, in a style and pomp of camp that rivalled that of the old time Moguls.

The Afghan was not long in returning again to his profitable Indian forays, re-asserting his sway over the Punjab and interfering with the affairs of Delhi. Many Indian

[1] See Chapter VII, p. 128. [2] See Chapter VII, p. 129.

Moslems indeed sought his assistance against the Mahratta domination of the Mogul throne. The Rohillas from their colony in Rohilkand especially craved his assistance as Moslem to Moslem and as Afghan to Afghan. So Ahmad Shah Durani, as he called himself, or Abdali, as he was called after his clan, marched once more down the road from Sirhind to Delhi town. In and about Delhi an immense Mahratta army had assembled, and it moved up the north road to the famous plain of Panipat some forty miles out of Delhi itself.

Shuda-sheo Rao, the Peshwa's cousin, known as '*The Bhao*' commanded the Mahratta armies, now far developed and over-civilized compared with the mountain rats of Shivaji's commandos. With him were Dattaji and Mahdoji Sindia, Mulhar Rao Holkar, and Wiswas Rao the Peshwa's son, who might have been Emperor of India. Govind Panth had even brought his Bandelas from Bundelkand, and with what was for the moment a national army, were Jāts from Bhurtpur and Rajputs as well as Mahratta chiefs from far and near. The Dekhan had sent an organized corps largely Moslem, under Ibrahim Khan *Gardi*, so called from his having commanded the French trained bodyguard at Hyderabad, and the fact that his corps was organized on that model. A vast park of artillery was drawn up in front of the flagstaff round which the Flag of the Confederacy the holy *Bhagwan Jhanda* was wrapped, and the camp and army was one to which the old cut and come again ways of Shivaji were quite impossible. Immobile as a whole it must win or die. It consisted of 30,000 good troops and 200 guns, with many thousands of the lesser stuff and countless followers, all hemmed in by the active Afghan horse who had usurped the old Mahratta irregular role.

It all availed nothing. After a midnight council, the Bhao resolved to fight, sending a last appeal to the Indian Moslem elements with the Afghan host to fight for India and not against it. With horses starving for forage, and the supply of food cut off, the Mahrattas sallied from their camp and fought the great fight by the Black Mango Tree, on the ancient battleground of Panipat, where Baber had defeated the Lodi Emperor, and where the fate of India had often been settled. Early in the morning the last rations had been eaten, and the troops assembled in no spirit to conjure victory. Faces smeared with ashes, turbans dishevelled, and hearts steeled for death but not for victory, the Pan-Hindu host went to its fate as many a Rajput gathering had done hundreds of years before, in the face of the implacable Turk of Ghuzni and his successors. It was but a Sacca of Chitoor in other setting, for there were many women with the camp. And so this astounding tragedy took place on the 17th January, 1761, what time Farmer George first came to the throne of England. We need not follow it. Gallantry, wild futile gallantry, was in ample evidence, but the same rot that has attended every attempt at a Pan-Hindu India had fallen on the Mahrattas.

Shouting *Hur Hur Huri!* and *Hur Hur Mahadeo!* they made their futile charges.

It was a desperate situation, and the Mahratta Chivalry fought with the courage and energy of despair, very nearly at one time gaining the day. The great yellow *Bhagwan Jhanda* was the rallying point, and round it the fiercest struggles took place.

But the charges of the fierce clansmen from the Afghan hills, Durani and Turk and Yusufzai, the reivers of the North, were too much for the Mahrattas who went down in one vast holocaust before the Afghan host.

The Bhao was slain, no one knows how, but his headless corpse was found on the field. Wiswas Rao the Peshwa's son fell, Jankoji Sindia was captured and slain next day, Mahdaji Rao Sindia escaped sore wounded after a long pursuit by Afghan troopers.

Rudyard Kipling tells something of the story in his stirring tragic verses, 'With Scindiah[1] to Delhi' and the story of the maid that rode at his saddle bow.

It is estimated that 200,000 fighting men and followers were killed. Ten thousand prisoners were put to death in cold blood next morning. All the younger women were taken off, the older slain . . . the camp had been full of women . . . wise Rajputs to do *Johur* rather than have it thus!

The story of this cruel battle is famous for the bankers' cryptic message, that went faster even than the electric message through India. This is how it ran "Two pearls have been dissolved, twenty-seven gold *mohrs* have been lost, and of the silver and copper the total cannot be caste up." The two hundred thousand were the silver and the copper.

The Mogul Ruin and the Mahrattas

Islam was restored, the rotten Mogul dominion was given another chance with the Rohillas, the cruel faithless Rohillas in charge, and Mahrattadom, less all its chivalry, sat down to lick its wounds for a generation. Such were the anvils hot with pain on which the fighting men of Maharasthra were forged. Gallant, futile in larger matters, staunch and enduring in lesser.

The story of the Mahrattas after the battle of Panipat becomes, to a great extent, the story of the British and their own mad aspiration, and will be recorded therein. Suffice it to say that within ten years of their defeat they had recovered sufficiently to make headway at Delhi. So difficult were conditions there before their return that the Mogul himself, Ali Johur, was a fugitive in Bengal, and eventually in 1765 received from the British the revenues of the districts of

[1] The older spelling in English.

Kora and Allahabad. When the Mahrattas had regained their influence at Delhi they proceeded to persuade the Emperor to return to their protection, taking with him Kora and Allahabad. It was a sad act for him. The Mahrattas eventually became the mayors of the palace, but in the great hurly-burly that followed the collapse of the central authority, Ali Johur, who had the magnificent title of Shah Alăm II, was blinded by the Rohillas, and with Sindia as Vizier, dwelt in a durance that had neither the show of dignity nor the semblance of comfort. From this condition he was rescued by Lord Lake in 1803, when there were 'none so poor as did him reverence'.

But with the great seizure of power in Guzerat and Malwa the Mahratta territories and forces were largely non-Mahratta in constitution, though chiefs and barons often led them. Mahrattadom and Mahratta armies were now but the same old Eastern armies that had always gone down before the ruthless valour of the North and the organization and fighting power of the West. The genuine Mahrattas who terrified and robbed India were scallywags on enduring ponies, armed with sword and matchlock and a long searching lance. They 'shot at the strong and slashed at the weak' from west to east of India and from the south till they struck the sturdier northern folk who would stand up for themselves. When the mountain rats emerged it was largely to join the predatory hordes and not the heavier organized forces of Malwa, who were foredoomed to a destruction that had overcome the more definitely Mahratta hosts at Panipat.

The Pindari Horror

The Mahratta States, especially that of Poona, were now in constant clash with the Nizam of the Dekhan, and at times with the British in Bombay and too often at war among themselves. Owing to the astounding crash of authority to which they had contributed, for they could not construct and cared for little but their illegal and illicit *Chouth*, there arose in Central India in the jungles and fastnesses of the Narbudda valley an astounding nest of land pirates, known as the Pindaris. Purely robber chiefs set up, and attracted to themselves all the masterless men and broken soldiery that had arisen on the world's disasters. Far worse and more inhuman than any Mahratta or Afghan they sallied forth each autumn to scour the land for hundreds of miles, loot and rape being their sole object. Merciless in their treatment of villagers, faithless in their observance of any agreements, this immense assemblage under several leaders, of all the equivalent cat-burglars, motor-snatchers and grabbers of the period, and everything that lawlessness and despair had thrown up in a masterless rudderless land, they called to high heaven for suppression. Outraged women, murdered children, pillaged coffers, were their sign-manual and to the eternal shame of the Mahratta chiefs they were not the least averse to turning the monsters of the Narbudda to their own purposes. The greatest task and relief that Britain has ever effected for the saving of humanity in general and India in particular was the extermination of these nests of all the evil ullage of broken kingdoms. And hardly a soul remembers it.

We are now coming to the hour of the big picture, the rise of the British, and how the men of the West were eagerly welcomed by the peasantry of the martial races as those who could restore peace and prosperity and decency to a sore outraged land; before that however, the strange film of the Sikh portent must be shown.

CHAPTER VII

THE STORY OF THE SIKHS

THE SIKHS—BABA NANAK—THE SIKH CANON—THE TENTH GURU—THE SIKHS AS A MILITANT BODY—MOGUL SIKH AND AFGHAN—THE RISE OF RUNJHIT SINGH.

THE SIKHS

IT is now possible to turn back in history for a brief outline of the early story of the Sikhs. Sikhism is a religion, not a race, and is theoretically at any rate as open to newcomers as is the faith of Islam. The story from the beginning is necessary if we are to understand this martial people, whose prowess first dispossessed the Afghans of their Indian premises, who under one filibustering young baron founded for his life, and for his life alone, a kingdom ruling at least five times their number of Moslems, who in sheer wantonness threw themselves against the British, and who then have made themselves for close on three generations one of the military pillars of the British raj. It is an astounding story, and one not to be parallelled in the history of any other dominion or of any other people.

To this day the whole of the Sikh peoples do not exceed three millions of all ages and both sexes, of whom perhaps two and a half million only live within the British province of the Punjab, the bulk of the remainder in the three Cis-Sutlej or 'Phulkian' states, feudatories as in varying degree are the other princes of India, by treaty specially protected by the British.

Sikhism, as just remarked, is a religion, and yet we find it politically expressed as a race. Races and religions may well go together, as in the case of the Jews, but the anomaly in the case of Sikhism is that it is a religion adopted by a small portion of one race, a few of various others, and yet must be classed as a people.

To follow it, we must begin with the first up-rising of the teacher whose humble following grew to such temporal power, and we must go back to the sixteenth century.

Baba Nanak

The story of Sikhism begins with the humble, kindly teacher Baba Nanak, who was probably a follower of another teacher of simple ways and kindly thoughts who is famous in Indian history, one Kabir, whose followers the Kabir-panthis still survive, though in no great numbers.

The sixteenth century was a very active period in religious thought and searchings in the world, the mediæval power of Rome in the West was breaking, and as just related, it was about the time of Martin Luther that Baba Nanak began to teach. It will be noticeable from even the short outline given here of the rise and wane and resurrection of Hinduism, how constant has been the stream of reformers, endeavouring to extract some gripping rule of life out of the tropical emanations that have sprung from obscure Vedic principles, Aryan imaginations and Dravidian fears. For the few that are on record, and the still fewer whose names have been mentioned here, there have been thousands whose names have gone out, or may be obscurely recorded in some quiet little mountain or jungle pocket. Why the teachings of one more than another 'caught on' is hard to say. Why Gautama should have led the millions and Mahavira only the thousands, is hard to explain, nor the fact of Buddhism having swept the land for centuries and died while the sect of Mahavira the *Jinna*[1] still remains.

Among then the rising and falling of reformers, it is not easy to say why Sikhism should have remained when the Kabirpanthis for instance are but a handful. But the reason probably lies in the story of the oppression by the Moguls that produced the Tenth Guru, and perhaps in the fact that the teaching was calculated to flourish in the sturdiness of that particular race among whom it incubated, the Jats between Delhi and the Ravi River. The cruel execution of the ninth Guru set the seal of success to Sikhism, and gives one more point to Talleyrand's remark to the young man who propounded his new religion, "It is a fine religion but . . . to start it you must be crucified."

Baba Nanak, who lived from 1469 to 1539, was a member of the Khatri caste, therefore a high caste Hindu, and was born and brought up on the banks of the Ravi near Lahore. After being married and having sons, he turned mendicant, affecting the society of *Sadhus*,[2] with whom he travelled far and wide, and visited most of the famous places of pilgrimage. Tradition says that he even went as far afield as Mecca. He was an ordinary orthodox Hindu, but was said to have picked up some of the ideas of the Sufis. Eventually he evolved his particular teaching, which aimed, like so many before it, at combining many faiths in the worship of the same God, whom all under different guises revered. He taught the Creator-spirit, outside whom all is *maya*, illusion. Salvation could be attained through a *Guru*, a leader, as a

[1] Jinna—The Conqueror. [2] Religious mendicants and holy recluses.

THE GRIP OF THE CHAGATAI TURK
Humayan's palace-fort in old Delhi, known as the *Purana Qila* (Old Fort), (A.D. 1530–40)

mediator between God and man. Through the *Guru*, reincarnation could be avoided and *karma* defeated. It is thought that Nanak must in his wanderings, although there is no record extant, have come into considerable contact with Christian teaching, so much does Christian thought figure in his 'way'. Besides the Christians in Travancore, there is a sect of friars, or *faqirs*, claiming conversion by St. Thomas in the North, who have the gospel of Matthew as well as the writings of Nanak. There is within the *Granth*[1] the following:

> " As great as Thou thyself art, so great is thy gift.
> Who having created the day, didst also create the night.'

Many *sloks*, i.e. couplets in the *Granth*, have Christian affinities. In fact it has been said, from an examination of the *Granth* from certain aspects, that Nanak taught nothing but the story of Christ from Birth to Ascension.

Sikhism under the Moguls

There was nothing at all in Nanak's teaching and pretensions to incur the enmity of any great rulers or religions, and his following should have been able to take the path of many other teachers of benevolence and piety. As has been mentioned, it is thought also that Nanak was inspired to take the role of teacher and reformer by the example and general teaching of Kabir. The Fifth Guru, Arjan, was an able man, who amassed some wealth and tried to blend the disciples into something of a race and a palatinate, and this first brought the sect into disfavour with the Moslem government. Arjan was probably put to death by the Moslems and his son Har Govindh succeeded him. In his hands the sect, hitherto a simple brotherhood began to take on military

[1] *The Sikh Scriptures.*

guise, and think about defending themselves. It was in the time of the Ninth Guru, Teg Bahadur, 1664–75, that trouble really rose with authority, and the Emperor Aurungzebe, who had so fiercely revived the almost dead practice of the persecution of non-Moslems, decided to exterminate the sect which had no doubt given provocation. Teg Bahadur was fierce, his visionaries unbending, and we who know something of the impossibility of bringing certain Indian visionaries to take a practical view of a practical world, may perhaps sympathize with the Moguls.

But the ways of Moguls with rebels are different from those of the British of recent years. Aurungzebe treated Teg Bahadur as England treated British gentlemen in rebellion, fifty years later. Tortured to death he was, drawn and quartered, and the pieces of his body exposed in the Chandni Chouk at Delhi, famous for ever as the scene of the tragedy, yet no one cares even to remember where the gentlemen of '45 met a similar death! When the Guru was put to death with such great cruelty, it was the rescue of his body by scavengers that brought licence to the poor and humble to become disciples.

It was Guru Teg Bahadur, says tradition, who before his death, standing on the roof of his prison told the Moguls "From the West will come my fair-skinned disciples wearing helmets, who shall avenge my death and utterly destroy my enemies." This story is much quoted by the Sikhs themselves, and has by some been taken to account for their instinctive enthusiasm in the support of the British.

The Tenth Guru

Teg Bahadur was succeeded by his son, Govindh, who from the age of fifteen years when his father died, brooded on that tragedy and the dispersion of the disciples. After much training and meditation he announced the appearance of a goddess (which we may, as already suggested, better interpret as a saint), who had directed a special initiation and baptism into an austerer form of the brotherhood. This he forthwith inaugurated, the story of how, does not matter here, the ceremony being known as 'taking the *Pahul*'. All the new disciples were to adopt the Rajput cognomen of *Singh* or 'Lion', and the *Singhs* were to be distinguished by the wearing of what is usually known as the 'Five' K's or *Kakkas* which are—

(1) The *Kes*, the uncut hair rolled in a knot on the head.
(2) The *Kachh*, a short drawers.
(3) The *Kirpan*, a steel dagger.
(4) The *Kara*, an iron bangle or quoit, a throwing missile.
(5) The *Kangh*, a small iron toothcomb, always worn in the hair.

Up to now the Nanakpanthis were but a Hindu sect, but the Tenth Guru had made their dress as distinctive as possible from Hindu or Moslem, and had now proclaimed measures to separate them finally from any touch with that communion. Caste was abolished, and the ranks of the brotherhood were thrown open to all comers, though unfortunately the caste instinct so deeply ingrained does still linger. The Jăts of the Punjab, sturdy and quarrelsome, flocked to the new brotherhood, and he soon had a force which enabled him to try conclusions, though not always successfully, with the forces at Delhi. He composed a code of law, the *Rahatnama*, for his *Singhs*, to be read in conjunction with the *Granth*.

Guru Govindh, says tradition, was murdered by a Pathan, in revenge, however, for his father's death at the Guru's hands. Before dying Govindh is reported to have said that no futrher Gurus were needed, and that he made over his brotherhood, the '*Khalsa*', or 'pure society' to God, and that henceforth the *Ad Granth* was to be the guide of his people. Therein he said would the Guru be found. It was thus three centuries after Baba Nanak taught, that Sikhism came into combined political and religious stability.

After this a bitter struggle between Sikh and Mogul continued, which contributed greatly to the downfall of the house of Timur.

THE SIKH CANON

The Sikh Canon is a small one. It consists of the two parts of the *Ad Granth*, the first, the *Japji* written by Baba Nanak, the second, explanations by subsequent Gurus of the extremely obscure, and often contradictory teachings of the *Japji*, and the *Daswin Badshahi*, or 'Tenth Government'. This was composed by Guru Govindh with a view to making his followers harder stuff than they would ever learn to be from the teachings of the *Japji*.

The teachings of the latter, confused though they are to follow, crystallize on the following—

> The fatherhood of God and all that fatherhood means.
> The brotherhood of man.
> The necessity of obedience to the inward voice divine.
> The unerring work of divine justice.
> The necessity of a divine teacher.
> The existence of a mediator and absolver of sin.
> The folly and evil of idolatry.

These seven points show what a long way Sikhism had travelled from Hinduism with its complicated obsessions, and even from *Bakhti* the Salvation cult. The law of the Singhs while embodying and accepting all these, are summed up so far as the faith of the warrior peasantry was concerned in these simple words.

Accept one baptism.
Worship one invisible God.
Let 'Hail Teacher!' be their watchword.
Of material things reverence steel alone.
Be ever prepared for war, eager to die in the war.
Maintain the five 'K's'.

In the precepts of Guru Govindh summarizing the *Japji*, it is written, "a Sikh should set his heart on God and on the name of God, on Charity and Purity."

Worship God every day.
Keep a place in the heart for the poor.
Give a tithe of all possessions.
He who professes holiness should act as such.
Avoid the lustful eye.
Offend none, for the Lord's sake.
Look for the advent of a spotless incarnation.

Indeed may it be said that Guru saw the conclusion of the whole matter "Fear God and keep his commandments," and yet there are those who would maintain that Sikhism is a Hindu sect!

The matter of Sikhs in the Army, and the British officer has been alluded to in Chapter I. Is it to be wondered that the British officer would foster such a faith among his soldiery?

The Sikhs as a Militant Body

Now were the humble band of simple pietists who had followed Baba Nanak changed indeed. The Jăt tribes about the Sutlej and the Ravi hastened to join the faith so simple in its tenets, so stirring in its appeal as the Sikhism of the Tenth Guru. No longer would they turn the cheek to the Moslem persecutor, and they began to group themselves by tribes and confederacies known as *misls*, and set themselves to form groups of villages and small baronies, all of which took a greater and a fiercer part in the growing struggle with the Mogul authorities. The Mogul Raj was beginning to totter, and the great road north from Delhi to Lahore, to Peshawur, and to Kabul was now disturbed by the constant attacks of the Sikhs on any Moslem parties and convoys that were weak enough to offer impunity.

In one of Govindh's battles with the Moguls his two eldest sons were killed, but his wife escaped with her two youngest children. Falling into the hands of the Moslems the two children were cruelly buried alive. Driven to bay himself in the fort of Chamkaur, he saw the last of his sons fall, and escaping by the deserts round Bhatinda eventually took shelter in a shrine in what is now Patiala, still known as the 'breathing place of the Guru'.

In 1707 a change for the better was to come, for in that year the powerful but old embittered Aurungzebe, the last of the Moguls to wield world power, died, and with him ended the extirpating hatred for everything that was not orthodox Moslem. Bahadur Shah, the elderly son and successor of Aurungzebe, sent for the Guru, who obeyed the call, and strangely enough accepted a command at the hands of the

[1] Muazzim, Bahadur Shah, Shah Alam.

Emperor. The reasons for this action are not on record, but we know that the Guru proceeded with troops into the Dekhan, and was there murdered at Nadreh on the Godavery, by the son of an Afghan horse-dealer, whom he had put to death. Where the Guru died has become a strange Sikh settlement and colony in the distant south. Thus in the old Mogul state of Hyderabad, and in his memory, there exists one of the holiest shrines of the Khalsa.

The military torch that Guru Govindh lit has never gone out, and the circumstances of the Mogul decay must be accepted as contributory thereto. Had not circumstances conspired to weaken all authority there is no likelihood that a sect that even now numbers scarcely three millions should have become if only for a lifetime, a sovereign people.

The Tenth Guru was the last teacher and religious leader; in his opinion with the teaching that he bequeathed, revelation was now complete. With the tenets and rules now established Sikhism was to go forward as a great military and religious body almost like a vast 'Order.'

Govindh's successor in political leadership was one Banda Bairagi, an ascetic who is said to have been a native of the Dekhan, who returned to the Punjab to carry on a guerrilla warfare with the Mogul. At length driven to bay at Gurdaspur in 1716 he was compelled to surrender, and the persecution of the Sikhs that followed was so terrible that almost for a whole generation nothing further is heard of the movement, which was driven underground. Banda himself was torn to pieces with hot pincers, a popular method among all torturers, and a hundred Sikhs a day were executed over some period. Eagerly the fanatics competed for the daily honour of martyrdom, and yet to some extent they were but reaping as they had sowed. It was not till they passed from pietism to politics that they clashed seriously with authority and they had themselves, as ruthless robbers and murderers, equally bitter deeds to their tally. But wherever the rights and wrongs of it, we shall now see them steadily combining with the other forces of disruption to pull down what had been one of the most gorgeous empires that the world has seen. And to follow the story of the rise of the Sikhs we must perforce glance at the fall of the Moguls, as we see it through the passing of the years.

Mogul, Sikh and Afghan

It was in 1738,[1] that a blow fell on India, which the internal weakness of the Empire had invited. Nadir Shah Quli, otherwise the 'Slave of Destiny', the Persian Turk who had acquired dominion after the downfall of the short Afghan conquest of Persia, proceeded to march to visit his 'cousin of Delhi', for the Mogul was equally a Turk. He arrived via Kabul, which was a part of India, in 1739, traversing the Punjab with little opposition from the Mogul forces, and duly camped outside the Delhi of Shah Jehan, the Delhi that we know to-day. The Sikhs by now acquiring some assurance after their earlier punishments, preyed impartially on both Mogul and Persian. Nadir Shah was by way of exacting from his cousin an enormous yet peaceably rendered tribute, had not a quarrel in the city resulted in a massacre of the Persians at the hands of Moguls and Indians exasperated by the invaders' assurance. A vast holocaust followed in revenge, and Delhi was left weeping amid piles of retributory skulls.

Then the Turk marched off, having secured a formal rendition of all Afghanistan and the districts bordering on

[1]See also chapter VI, page 113.

the Indus, taking with him the famous Peacock Throne from the Hall of Private Audience, and a vast booty and tribute totalling many millions sterling, but of which the accounts vary. Behind him the stripped Mogul throne was still less equipped to control the forces of disruption than before. By 1748 Nadir Shah met the inevitable fate of a man of his fierce disposition. He was murdered and his Afghan general Ahmad Shah, who was protecting with 10,000 horse a considerable portion of the Persian treasure, made himself ruler of the Afghan portion of the Persian Empire, including the districts on the Indus, which he proclaimed the Durani Empire, himself the *Dur-i-Duran* 'Pearl of the Age', and the true Afghan among his people *Duranis* the 'People of the Pearl'.

Ahmad Shah, a conqueror rather than a builder, among many activities on all his frontiers invaded India twenty-one times. His first inroad took him far south of Lahore, but defeated by the Imperial Forces at Sirhind he was forced back across the Indus. In 1758 the Mahrattas, who as told in another chapter were now trying to dominate the Empire, and the Sikh together drove out another Afghan inroad and they then as the prophecy ran actually 'watered their horses on the Indus'.

During this retreat and the general confusion resulting, one Jassa Singh, a Sikh, threw up a rough fort at Amritsar, under the very nose of the Mogul provincial capital of Lahore. This union, for a while, of Sikh and Mahratta had stirred Moslem opinion, and the Afghan settlers in Rohilkand brought down the Afghans to restore the Mogul and avenge the appearance of the Mahratta on the Indus.

Then was fought as described elsewhere that terrible battle of Panipat which destroyed for a generation the Mahratta influence in the north. The Afghan frontier was now established east of the Sutlej in the heart of the Jăt and growing Sikh country. Hardly had the victorious Afghan returned to his own mountains when the Sikhs rose and attacked his garrison at Sirhind. This brought the ubiquitous Afghans back, and the Sikhs who had greatly increased through Jăt adherence, now sustained a terrible defeat. So severe was the defeat and so terrible the slaughter that for generations after it was known as the *Ghalu Ghara*, the 'great disaster', and it took place some twenty miles south from Ludhiana. The newly built Sikh temples at Amritsar were destroyed, the sacred tank polluted with the blood of slaughtered cattle, and pyramids of the skulls of the Sikh victims erected.

South of the Sutlej, the ancient Jăt state of Phul had broken up into several principalities tributary of course to the Mogul, and in these states as on the Sutlej and the Ravi and in the Doab of Jullundhur, many had joined the new religion. Patiala then as now was among the premier of the Phulkian states, and with 20,000 Sikhs, Ala Singh the Patiala chief was taken prisoner.

Ahmad Shah however anxious for some settlement, conferred the title of Rajah on his prisoner Ala Singh, which intensely annoyed the latter's co-religionists, and he was compelled to be more than ever zealous as a partisan Sikh.

With the Afghans gone the Sikhs undaunted by their defeat, again in 1763 proceeded to attack Sirhind the obnoxious Moslem city where Govindh's children had been put to death. The Afghan governor met them outside, to be heavily defeated, and the city was taken, sacked and old scores repaid with a vengeance.

The story goes that the Sikhs who were said to number 40,000 scattered immediately, and galloped over the countryside throwing sword, scabbard or garment into the villages they passed through in token that they claimed them. The passive Indian villages cared little to whom they paid their revenue, Sikh or Moslem, provided the recipient did his share of the bargain by protecting them.

With Afghan Sikh and Jăt in Mogul territory, the prestige of the helpless Mogul machinery waned still further. The Sikh confederacies grew stronger and stronger, and were able to assemble at short notice hordes of mounted men, some indeed sufficiently well mounted to be worthy of the term 'horseman' and 'horse soldier'.

Year by year now representatives of the Sikh people would meet at Amritsar. Owning no common head, and by no means implicitly followed by the people of their groups, there was still a tacit spirit of solidarity not perhaps unlike that in the Mahratta confederacy in the west. A strong religious sense did animate these warlike, muscular Jăts and those from other tribes and races, who had also taken the *pahul.* The *Misls* or confederacies were now twelve in number, of whom some of the more important were:

The *Bhungis*, so called from a real or fancied fondness of its members for Bhang.

The *Nishanias*, who followed the standard bearers, the Nishan of the hunted armies.

The *Shaids* or Nihangs, the descendants of martyrs and zealots.

The *Ramgharia*, the people of the Ram Rowni or Fortress of God, named after Rama and built by Jassa Singh Ramgharia just referred to.

The *Phulkias*, from the family of Ala Singh and other chiefs, in the Phulkian states, and so forth.

All the *Misls* except the Phulkias belonged to the district north of the Sutlej still known as the Manjha. *Pari passu* with the *misls* but belonging to none of them grew up a peculiarly warlike, bumptious and independent set of militant *faqirs* who called themselves the *Akalis,* that is to say 'Immortals' or *Nihangs,* who led in almost every fight and are still a leading turbulent feature in the Punjab always ready to answer to the cry, genuine or otherwise, of the Sikh faith being in danger. In many a Sikh town and fair, bodies of this sect dressed in dark blue, wearing the sacred quoit and as many arms as the law will permit, will be seen perambulating with their exulting cry "*Wa Sri Guru*" or "*Sri Khalsa, ki jai*". "Victory to the Holy Khalsa or Holy Guru"! Many old soldiers join their ranks, and they are without doubt an anxiety in times of unrest.

The last half of the eighteenth century so far as Sikhism is concerned, is full of quarrels and fights between the *misls* themselves and their ambitious leaders. Even within the *misls*, quarrels were the order of the day as one man strove with another for the headship, a struggle and a quarrelling made easy by the natural dislike of all Sikhs of any form of vassaldom or feudalism, which in Rajput India came so naturally to the Aryan mind. As the years however rolled on, the stronger men in the larger *misls* began naturally enough to dominate, and it was said that "All that a Sikh chief asked from a follower in those days was a horse, a sword and a matchlock. All that a follower sought was protection and permission to plunder in the name of God and the Guru and under the banner of his chief and sirdar."[1] No highland chieftain or clansman could have asked for more in Bonnie Scotland, or in the marches of Wales. "Fame and success, that would bring all men at arms of prowess to his standard was the aim of every Sikh chieftain. Hard was the lot of the villagers among whom Afghan

[1] Cunninghame: *History of the Sikhs.*

invader and Sikh get-rich-quicker wandered at will, and no man could consider his land, his horse and his wife his own, unless he was strong enough to defend them. Every village was fortified, every neighbour was an enemy. It has also been said that while a Moslem or Imperial convoy appealed most to them, the Sikh was a bandit before he was a patriot. Yet while the Sikhs were undoubtedly robbers, and though cattle lifting was a honourable profession as it was on the Scottish border a few hundred years ago, their enthusiasm for their faith coupled with their hatred for Mussalmans, who had so long tramped them underfoot, gave them a certain dignity, and to their objects and expeditions an almost national interest."[1]

The Afghan Bogey

Before we come to the rise of the super-man Runjhit Singh it will not be out of place to see how dreaded was the Afghan name to Mogul Sikh and even British. Twenty-one times had Ahmad Shah Durani led his columns across the Punjab, and whether he came as foe or whether as was often the case as friend, the results were equally disastrous to the Moslem folk of the countryside. From the Sikh country to the Indus the people were chiefly Indian or settlers established on the land for many centuries. The long undisciplined columns of tribal Afghan and Pathans, Turks, Tatars, Mongols, Persians and what not, lived on the land equally ruthlessly whether friend or foe. For generations had mothers in the villages in the lands between the five rivers quieted unruly children by threats of the Afghan. Ahmad Shah had been succeeded by his unenter-

[1] Cunninghame: *History of the Sikhs.*

prising son Timur, entirely unworthy so far as personal character went of his enterprising namesake. He ruled by his father's prestige, and lost his lands on the confines in the process. To him succeeded his son Zaman Shah or Shah Zaman, 'King of the Ages,' and Zaman Shah aimed at invading India and recovering the Durani Empire in practice, which still in name reached to the Sutlej. All Northern India quailed at the rumour . . . the Mogul in the Mahratta hands once more; the Sikhs in their *misls* and the British in the Doab, who went so far as to establish a cantonment of observation at Anupshar not far from Meerut, in the 'nineties of the eighteenth century.

Sikh chiefs by now held the capital that was either Mogul by prescriptive right, or Afghan by conquest and treaty. In 1797 Zaman Shah first entered India again, but was recalled by troubles in the direction of Kandahar. Coming again next year, he had no difficulty in re-occupying Lahore, where there were plenty who preferred Afghan to Sikh rule, and once again the Afghan frontier was on the Sutlej. I have written elsewhere at some length[1] on what this Afghan threat meant, and how great it bulked. Tippu Sultan in the far south, again in trouble with the British, himself of Afghan origin, had called on Zaman Shah to come to his aid. The Rohillas, the Afghan colonists of Rohilkand, wanted neither Sikh nor Mahratta to prevail at the seat of the Mogul, and they too both sent to Zaman Shah and were prepared to join him. Napoleon already using every means to get at Britain was corresponding with Tippu and was discussing invasions of India through Afghanistan, and the British were preparing counter-moves in India, in Persia, and a little later in Afghanistan. It was no wonder therefore that the movements of Zaman Shah were watched with interest and

[1] In *Afghanistan from Darius to Amanulla*." (Bell & Sons).

JĂT SIKHS OF THE MALWA
Colour party of the 15th Sikhs (pre-war uniform)

apprehension in the Governor-General's camp. It is at this point that the young Runjhit Singh comes on the stage to place very unexpectedly a barrier on the Indus.

The Rise of Runjhit Singh

Among the Sikh chiefs who had come to some power and affluence in the last part of the eighteenth century was one Mula Singh of the Sukerchuckia *Misl*, to whom in 1780 was born a male child to be called Runjhit Singh. Bred in camp and brought up on a horse, the lad Runjhit became a daring leader before his twenties, and when Zaman Shah was in Lahore for the last time, the young man was presented to him. Anxious to make friends with the Sikhs the Afghan received him well, and because the Afghan guns could not be got across the Jhelum on the Emperor's return to the north-west, young Runjhit undertook to get the more accessible ones over (retaining the remainder!). In return for this service, Zaman Shah appointed him Governor of the Punjab in the Afghan interest.

Had the Afghan rule remained powerful and efficient, no doubt the young Sikh Governor would have continued faithful to his trust, but Zaman Shah was no world-compeller, events on his own borders were too much for him, and so far as India was concerned Afghan dominion was over. Great Britain was now to become the great healer of sores and restorer of order. The Mahrattas as already related were once more at Delhi, in pursuance of their old ambition to dominate the Mogul inheritance, but had foolishly chosen also to challenge the British as already related, and in 1803 was fought the Battle of Delhi. The British were now masters in the Jumna-Ganges Doab, the blinded Mogul Emperor a pensioner in their hands to be treated with dignity and consideration. Several thousand Sikhs had been in alliance with the Mahrattas in their opposition to the British, but had speedily retired to their own country.

But the struggle with the Mahrattas was not over, and Holkar now attacked the British. Finally pursued to the Sutlej by Lord Lake, he too, failing to get support from the Sikhs, was compelled to submit.

Runjhit Singh uninterrupted by his nominal master at Kabul had been consolidating his power and influence, and had actually gained Lahore itself from the Bhungi chiefs. When the British came north in pursuit of Holkar he is said to have visited their camp in disguise. Then apparently he formed the wise opinion that there was one thing he must never do and that was fall foul of this new and astounding power, and that there was more than a man's work before him in leading the Sikhs and dominating the Moslem Punjab, which moreover only longed for peace and freedom from Afghans at the hands of any strong man.

Gradually Runjhit Singn achieved the position he aimed at, by strategy and persuasion and force. Already the Punjab as far as the old Afghan fortress of Rohtas was in his hands, and except that the Phulkian Sikh chiefs succeeded in obtaining a guarantee of their status from the British who ordered hands off, the Sikhs of the other *misls* and confederacies acknowledged his chiefship. The Rajput chiefs of the hills were driven back whenever they invaded the plains. The Gurkhas endeavouring to conquer all the hills between Tibet and India were stayed by him on the Sutlej, before they were defeated and driven back to their own land by the British. In 1818 Multan was captured from the Afghans, and a little later Kashmir, long an Afghan province, Attock and eventually Peshawur itself followed. As early as 1813

Shah Shujah the refugee king of Kabul and younger brother of the now blinded Shah Zaman, was at Lahore, and Runjhit cozened from him the *Koh-i-Nur* diamond and also the famous Timur Ruby,[1] into his own jackdaw hands. The Sikh power crossed the Indus in the Derajat and carried the frontiers from which it demanded revenue, to where the British administrative border now lies, while Peshawar remained the scene of fierce struggles for its possession. By slaughter and gallows the Sikhs held the Peshawar Valley and their Khatri General Hari Singh, later killed at the battle of Jamrud, carried fire and sword and slaughter regardless of age and sex far up the Swat Valley amid the Graeco-Bactrian ruins.

The whole of the Punjab and the frontier provinces were thus in the masterful hands of Runjhit Singh by 1830. Because the Afghans and Sikhs could not come to a *modus vivendi*, because the whole world of modern trade was jeopardized by their quarrels, because the British wanted steamers and trade on the Indus, the British Government and Runjhit Singh engaged to restore the exiled Shah Shujah to his throne at Kabul. The story of the Afghan Wars that followed need not be enlarged on here, but we were now enabled to see something of the military power of the Sikhs at this time. The Governor-General, Lord Auckland, with the Army of the Indus, met Runjhit Singh with a large Sikh force at Ferozepore. Joint reviews, compliments and comparisons followed. For many years now Runjhit Singh had been modelling his reluctant Punjabis on the European model. French and Italian officers with an American or two, some English ex-officers from the Company's army, some European deserters from their Artillery and some Hindustani drill instructors who had served in the

[1] Now also in the British Crown.

Bengal Army, together produced a mighty line and a powerful artillery. A great kingdom it was, of its despotic kind, and to the Company it seemed a most efficient barrier against invasion from the north-west. It possessed however one great inherent defect, it was a one-man rule and Runjhit Singh had no effective heir to succeed him.

CHAPTER VIII

THE RISE OF THE BRITISH

THE EARLY EUROPEAN SETTLEMENTS—THE BRITISH AND THE FRENCH IN MADRAS—THE BRITISH IN BENGAL—PLASSEY AND BUXAR—WARREN HASTINGS—THE REGULATING ACT—THE MYSORE WARS—THE EARLY SEPOY ARMIES OF MADRAS—THE THIRD AND FOURTH MYSORE WARS—THE SECOND AND THIRD MAHRATTA WARS—THE FOURTH MAHRATTA WAR.

EARLY EUROPEAN SETTLEMENTS

IT is not yet possible to escape from sheer history before getting down to the races themselves as we know them in our own days, as they have served beside us in many campaigns and as we have seen representatives attending His Majesty here in Britain. We must trace in outline the rise of British dominion in India on the crumbling ruins of the greatest of the Moslem Empires, and the failure of the North to again swamp India, now defended by a greater than even Asoka, as a necessary sequel to the story of Sikh and Mahratta.

It is but common-place to state that the British for over a century were but traders and merchant adventurers, who carried on their business as tenants, and by permission, by Imperial *firman*, granted in due and ancient form by the Great Mogul. The point moreover worth remembering is this, that had that Turkish Empire endured, the British settlements at Calcutta and Bombay would have been but as the great far-Eastern Settlement in that other Tartar Empire, the International Settlement of Shanghai. . . . superb buildings, great quays and warehouses, great wealth, but sojourners by treaty and *firman* in another Empire's land. It was the crash of this Empire at Delhi, the dying out of the Tartar power to dominate and keep in order the vast structure which it had built up, that induced, nay compelled, a trading corporation to become an Empire, and act as the Crown of its own people, 'in commission.'

The coming of the West to the East in modern times was first possible when in May 1498 the famous Portuguese sailor, Vasco Da Gama, rounding the Cape of Good Hope arrived at Calicut. The enterprising Portuguese were not long in taking advantage of the discovery, for in the year 1500 their first trading fleet arrived at Calicut. It was not, however, till 1503 that they were able to overcome the jealousy of the Moslem traders, and establish a fortified trading station at Cochin, with a garrison of 150 Portuguese soldiers. It is not quite clear whether this was by the permission of local authority or in defiance thereof. In 1509 came Albuquerque as Governor and in 1510 he seized the harbour of Goa, and established what at one time promised to be a great empire. How and why it failed is outside this story. The adventurous British traders soon followed the Portuguese example, but it was not till a century later in the year 1600 that a British company of merchants for trading with the East was specially formed. In 1612, a British fleet defeated a much larger Portuguese one that had attacked them and sailed into Swally harbour, close to Surat. The prestige of their victory and the dislike that the ways of the Portuguese had induced, enabled the British to obtain permission from the Emperor Jehangir to establish trading stations, or factories, to use the old term, at Ahmedabad, Cambay and Surat. The next year a considerable naval and military expedition sent to exterminate them by the Viceroy of Goa was defeated. The British remained. In this same year King James the First had sent his ambassador, Sir Thomas Roe, to the Court of Jehangir whom he found at Agra after travelling via Surat and Burhampur. Magnificently entreated he accompanied the Great Mogul in a journey to the Dekhan, and concluded a friendly and valuable treaty.

In 1686 Job Charnock of Surat, under the *firman* of the Moslem Viceroy of Bengal, founded the first settlement at Calcutta, and two years later the Directors of the Company trading with the East Indies took that decision which sowed the first seeds of the British Empire in India. Previous to that the Directors had turned a deaf ear to any proposals from their agents to fortify or protect their settlements. They were traders trading under license and under protection of a great Eastern power—what need had they of forts and guards?—night watchman with cudgels was all that their affairs needed!

Well and good, but it was not well and good for long. The policy of Aurungzebe in subduing the Moslem kingdoms of the Dekhan had disturbed the whole country-side. The rule of the Mogul was ineffective and did not protect the traders. They were compelled to do it themselves, and then in 1688 came to a decision to erect fortifications round their premises and to organize what they hoped would be sufficient defenders. How these grew and grew as the condition of law and order deteriorated and the Delhi Government collapsed will be outlined.

While the British were making good their trade and coming to the fore-going decision, other European rivals than the Portuguese were entering the field. In 1664 after four previous unsuccessful attempts, of which the first was sixty years earlier, the first French trading establishment was started by M. Colbert and ten years later the Moslem State of Bijapur granted the French land on the Carnatic coast where was built Pondicherry 'The New City'. In the year that the British Directors had decided to fortify and become a power, the Mogul Viceroy of Bengal sanctioned the establishment of another French Settlement in India at Chandernagore on the Hooghly above Calcutta. In 1707 Aurungzebe, the last of the Moguls to be great, died, and on his death commenced the decay of the Empire of the Chagatai Turks, which soon became a rapid collapse.

The British and the French

With the decay of the Mogul authority there arose that new people, whose chief Shivaji, had already battled bitterly and by no means unsuccessfully with the Great Mogul. The rise of the Mahratta nation,[1] was another of the phenomena which forced the British on to their destiny as the masters and rulers of India. While the Mogul was failing and the Mahratta rising, the English and French settlements were waxing great, and the scene was being set for the struggle for the mastery in Southern India. In 1742 there arrived in India, as Governor of Pondicherry, Joseph Francois Dupleix, a patriot and a man with a vision. The aim of his life was to found a French Empire in India, and he was shrewd enough to see that to do that it would be necessary to get rid of the British. In 1740 war had broken out between France and Britain. The British were anxious to confine the war to Europe, but the arrival of a French fleet in 1746

[1] Chapter VI.

gave the opportunity that he was looking for. Forthwith Dupleix attacked and captured Madras, at a time when the great fortress of Fort St. George had not yet been constructed. The Nawab of Arcot, still the titular authority, who dreaded the possible rise of a French power, ordered its immediate restitution and attacked when his orders were not promptly complied with. The small French forces however, repulsed the vast, ill-organized array of the Nawab. This fight known to history as the Battle of S. Thome close to the famous St. Thomas's Mount, showed the Europeans the vast bluff that lay behind Eastern military pretensions, at any rate in the south. Driven from Madras the English defended themselves successfully at the smaller settlement of Fort St. David, Robert Clive being among the defenders. In 1748 peace between England and France was declared on the basis of restitution of all gains in India, and Madras once more flew the British flag. Now followed clever intrigues to assert French dominance, and the French with a claimant to the Nizam's throne at Hyderabad attacked the Nawab of Arcot and killed him, at the battle of Ambur. The Nizam summoned the English and Mahrattas to his assistance as soon as he was threatened by the French combine. A large Mogul and Mahratta army of these two allies with a few hundred English now fell on the French alliance, defeated it heavily, and placed a young nephew on the throne of the Nawab of Arcot. Intrigues and counter-wars which are too complicated to detail, resulted ere long in the young Nawab of Arcot being defeated, and a French force being installed at Hyderabad nominally to protect it. By 1751 French influence was supreme, the British holding little but their two factories at Madras and Fort St. David.

The Nawab of Arcot fled to Trichinopoly and it was

Clive who, having now come to the fore as soldier, devised the plan that was to save the Company's ally and bring the sepoy on to the field as a British soldier. He suggested to the Governor of Madras the daring plan of seizing Arcot while the usurping Chanda Sahib was besieging the young Nawab in Trichinopoly. With 200 Europeans and 300 sepoys, he surprised and seized the town and fort. Chanda Sahib sent 10,000 men to recover his capital, thus relieving greatly the pressure on Trichinopoly, but inducing the famous siege and defence of Arcot, with its well-known story of the sepoys who gave up their rations to the Europeans. After seven weeks a Mahratta chief Morari Rao, lost in admiration at the defence, arrived to the rescue of Clive with a force of 6,000 men, to which Madras itself was able to add a small contribution. Thus relieved Clive marched to the relief of Trichinopoly, was joined by Lawrence with another force and together they surrounded the besiegers, drove them to a small island and there forced the surrender of both Chanda Sahib's men and the French, the Indian chief having been murdered two days before.

British prestige now stood high and that of the French the reverse and from Arcot and Trichinopoly dates the rise of the British star.

Dupleix the man with a vision deserved better support than he got and in 1754 was recalled. After his recall the English and the French made peace in the East. It was not till 1758 that Count Lally arrived as successor to Dupleix, while Clive was absent in Bengal. France and England were at war again, and Lally was at this juncture besieging Madras, having taken Fort St. David, but when an English fleet arrived he gave up the siege. By next year the whole outlook had changed, England having made up her mind to support her merchants on more definite lines and sent

Sir Eyre Coote with Royal troops from England. In 1760 a decisive battle at Wandewash was fought between Eyre Coote and the French, in which the latter were severely defeated and their leader Bussy captured. In 1761 Coote even took Pondicherry and with it Count Lally. Though Pondicherry was eventually restored, that was in short the end of the French power in India, a power which better handled and supported would have changed the whole face of history.

The British in Bengal

The Eastern kaleidoscope must now be revolved in the direction of Bengal where, four years before the defeat of the Mahrattas by the Afghans in '61 and the French at Wandewash in 1760, great things had been happening. Three-quarters of a century earlier as related, Job Charnock had established by the Imperial *firman* the trading settlement at Calcutta. With the decision of the Directors to become a garrisoning and administering territorial authority British enterprise had done a great deal. Calcutta was now a wealthy station with a crowded ocean port, some miles up the river Hooghly. The Imperial Nawab, Imperial in name but independent in practice, Ali Verdi Khan, who had for years been concerned in preventing the Mahrattas from overrunning his territory, died in 1756, and he had nominated as his heir Suraj-ud-Doulat,[1] 'The Sun of Dominion', a young man of the worst parts. Ali Verdi Khan had dealt well, and generally reasonably with the British though he had made them pay heavily enough for protecting their settlements from the Mahrattas, or to use the spelling of the time the 'Morattoes'. The new Viceroy the Nawab of

[1] The Surajahdoulah of schoolroom histories.

Bengal who had great ideas of the wealth of the British settlement, and great hopes of filling his pockets therefrom, occupied and plundered their factory at Kassimbazaar and marched on Calcutta itself. The fort at Calcutta was a very different affair from the later Fort William, and in the palmy days of Ali Verdi Khan had been left to decay. The garrison consisted of but sixty European soldiers of no great efficiency. The Governor evacuated the place as far as possible, making the inhabitants retire to the shipping and himself moving to Fulta. On June 18th the Nawab bombarded the fort in which was Mr. Holwell a Member of the Council and 146 persons of both sexes, all the women not having been got off. Next morning they surrendered and there occurred the tragedy of the 'Black Hole',[1] or guardroom, from which Holwell and his twenty-three alone emerged, in which they had been crammed. The story is an outrageous one, but probably illustrates but the callousness of Eastern subordinates . . . as evidenced in our day by the tragedy of the Moplah prisoners and the satisfaction of the local folk thereat . . . as well as the inefficiency of Eastern routine, rather than fell design.

Clive, Governor of Fort St. David, after his exploits in Madras, was hurried up to retrieve the situation, with 900 Europeans and 1,500 Madras sepoys and with him sailed a squadron of the Royal Navy. Budge-Budge was retaken from the Nawab's forces at once, no less a person than Warren Hastings serving as a volunteer. Calcutta was easily recovered from the Nawab's troops who had never been handled by a trained enemy before, so that the Nawab sued for peace and agreed to make ample restitution for the damage he had inflicted. In fact it was obvious that had the Court of Directors with all their experience of disasters due to

[1] Black-hole—the old Army name for a dark cell.

military inefficiency before in Madras, not failed to arrange any security in Calcutta, the tragedy need not have happened.

PLASSEY AND BUXAR

With war between France and Europe, Clive and Watson turned the tables on the French by attacking Chandernagore above Calcutta. The Nawab, already plotting with the French against the English was greatly enraged, but Clive was in collusion with the large party in Bengal that hated the Nawab, who, to cut a long story short, advanced against the English with 35,000 Infantry of sorts, 15,000 *Rajwara* horse and a few French gunners. He massed his troops at Plassey close to Murshidabad while Clive with his 900 British and 2,500 Sepoys and 10 light guns was advancing against him. The former's knowledge of the worth of rajwara troops gained in Madras made him in no whit dismayed. The Nawab's troops were largely composed of the floating military population from many provinces who flocked round the various Viceroys, including many Moslems of Afghan and Turkish descent, barons with their retainers giving federal service, and a good many of the peasantry of Behar. The story of the battle of Plassey which was the foundation and charter of British dominion on the Bengal side of India, has too often been told to need retelling. The interesting item is the Nawab's guns served by French gunners in the European uniform of the period, mounted high above the crops on a moving platform erected over lashed bullock wagons. It was the rainy season and movement was a difficulty, but India was won by a British loss of 22 killed and 50 wounded, European and native. Clive made Mir Jafar who had with hesitation declared on his side, Nawab, and his son caught

Suraj-ud-doulat and put him to death. As a reward and as an act of sane policy Clive was appointed Governor of Bengal, while Mir Jafar gave the Company actual *zemindari*[1] rights over 880 square miles around Calcutta. Further, Clive's influence over Mir Jafar gave him virtual control but the latter ere long was involved in hostilities with the British for reasons beyond our present scope, and Mir Qasim his son-in-law took his place. Mir Qasim a stronger man than his predecessor, quarrelled with the British also and arrested the Resident at Patna with all British in the country. The British advanced on Patna and took Monghyr, where upon a file of the Mir's guard said to have been commanded by the renegade German Reinhart known as *Sombre* and *Somru*,[2] shot all the prisoners to the number of 148, including Mr. Ellis, the Resident. This massacre deliberate and not due to mere callousness as was the Black Hole, sealed the future of Bengal. Mir Qasim, now thoroughly frightened, fled to Lucknow, where was also the Emperor Shah Alăm II a refugee from the Mahrattas. The Emperor anxious to recover Bengal, together with Mir Qasim and the Nawab Vizier of Oudh advanced towards Patna weakened, and halted at Buxar. This gave the British time to overcome a mutiny, and meet what might be in truth called the Mogul Army at Buxar in October 1764. Then ensued another of those remarkable victories which with Wandewash and Plassey settled the future of India. The 50,000 Mogul troops were utterly defeated by Major Munro with the loss of 160 cannon. The British force numbered some 7,000 men odd with 20 guns, the largest force they had yet in the field in India, of which 867 were European and 918 cavalry. Shah Alăm now came in to the British to beg for terms, while the Nawab

[1] i.e. Landowning. *Zemin*=land,
[2] Whose widow the Begum Somru was so well known in later days.

Vizier who had hoped to be the arbiter was in full retreat. Allahabad was taken from him, and he was overtaken and defeated at Kalpi on the Jumna. Clive, now ennobled, came back to a second period of Governorship in time to settle the terms which were to follow the victory of Buxar. The Nawab Vizier was sent back to his kingdom paying a tribute and becoming an ally. The Emperor was given a tract made up of the districts of Kora and Allahabad as already related, in return for granting the Company the *diwany* or right to collect the revenue in Bengal, Behar and Orissa, while leaving the new Nawab, a son of Mir Jafar, on the throne in control of law and police. This was what is so often referred to as 'The Dual System'. The Emperor was given tribute of twenty-five lakhs in recognition of his suzerainty, but it was a system that could not last for long. With the Mogul and Oudh armies settled for the while, Lord Clive was now free to enter into his great work reforming the administration and thus to lay the foundation for the most humane and benevolent civil service that the world has ever seen. Through it for a century and a half Great Britain, to her own serious loss, has sent the pick of her schools and colleges, to help piece together the fragments of what once had been the Empire of Asoka and in modern times the ruthless domain of the Afghan and the Turk.

Warren Hastings

We must soon turn south again to watch the struggle against a new enemy and also to see the Mahrattas striving to their own undoing. But before doing so we should see the great Warren Hastings on his uneasy throne and how it became necessary to curb the cruel Rohilla barons. Clive's second governorship ended in 1767 and for a while Bengal was able to go ahead without any great trials. In 1772, however, there came to power a second great statesman, in the person of Mr. Warren Hastings one of the Company's administrators, after a highly successful career. The Dual Government in Bengal had failed, and without Clive's strong hand the old abuses and irregularities of the Company's servants returned. The Nawab's Government failed hopelessly in his matter of order and justice, and in 1770 famine and disease had brought the land to great straits. The administration was now actually taken over by the Company and the service placed on the high-grade footing that Clive had aimed at, but it was no easy task. As related, Shah Alăm tempted by the Mahrattas by promises of a revived Empire returned to Delhi and attempted to add the districts entrusted to him to his own nominal dominion. But it was impossible to allow the Mahrattas to have these territories which adjoined Oudh, and Hastings therefore occupied the fortress of Allahabad himself, and stated that the Company would control the territory in question. As the Mogul had left British protection of his own accord, the allowance of twenty-five lakhs was discontinued. The occupation of the Allahabad and Kora districts protected Oudh from the west, and it was necessary to protect her also from the threats and intrigues of the Mahrattas and the incursions of the entirely unscrupulous Afghan-descended Rohillas. This resulted in the war between Oudh and Rohilkand in which a brigade of Bengal troops participated and in which the Rohillas were defeated. It is difficult to say what status the Rohillas had, except as subjects of Delhi who defied Delhi's authority. The attack on Mr. Hastings for this policy was entirely unjustified, for by no means was it possible to consider the Rohilla chiefs and their comparatively few fellow colonists as anything but unscrupulous opportunists who oppressed as much as was economic their Hindu tenants and peasantry. Rohilkand was then added to Oudh, and British troops were lent to maintain the Vizier against his neighbours, the beginning of what was later to be called the 'Subsidiary System'.

THE REGULATING ACT

By 1773 the Company's finances were in such a state owing to the many disturbances and the magnitude of their undertaking, that they had to apply to the British Government for assistance. This was only accorded on terms. Those terms included the appointment of a Governor-General, aided by a Council to be appointed from Home. The story of the cantankerous and futile personalities selected for that purpose is one of the great blurs on the early British administration of India. They first distinguished themselves by entirely upsetting the arrangements with the son of the Nawab Vizier on the latter's death, and their mischievous actions were legion.

We cannot here enter further into all that happened, the story of Nunkomar, the duel with the wretched Mr. Francis nor the events which led up to the outbreak at Benares, when Hastings escaped with a small following from the attack on his escort, and from which the popular rhyme descriptive of the hurried flight of the Governor-Generals party was derived.

Ghore par howdah, hathi par zeen
Jaldi chagya Warren Hasteen

"Howdah on horse and saddle on elephant.
Hurriedly fled the great Warren Hastings."

[1] Also sung of Colonel 'Monseen's' retreat before Holka in 1804.

In spite of this constant frustration Hastings' reign was fraught with the most important results in the matter of good government and wise statesmanship, and it was not till 1783 after eleven years in the saddle as Governor of Bengal, for ten of which he was also Governor-General, that Warren Hastings laid down his appointment.

The Mysore Wars

While Clive was making history in Bengal, the Madras Government did little to live up to the victory gained for it at Wandewash, and a period of gross incompetence in administration and policy followed. The year following that battle, a new power had arisen in the person of Haider Ali, a mercenary of Afghan descent in the service of the Rajah of Mysore who seized his master's throne and under the title of Sultan of Mysore gathered to his aid every Afghan, Turkish and Arab soldier of fortune in southern India. Enriching himself by the plunder of his neighbours he raised a powerful army to the dismay of all.

We must, however, skip over the various treaties with and intrigues between the British, Haiderabad and the Mahrattas, to whom the new Sultan was by no means welcome. In 1766 commenced the *First* Mysore War between Haider and the British which lasted three years. Haider had persuaded the Nizam to break his treaties and join him. The British commander gained brilliant victories which the folly of the Madras Government made of no avail and a peace was accepted on Haider's terms which included an alliance. He then attacked the Mahrattas and was soundly beaten, the British refusing assistance to their new ally's arrogance as they had not been consulted as to the war making.

In 1775 broke out the *First* Mahratta War, when the British in Bombay supported Raghoba the deposed regent at Poona. While Hastings' ill-advised Council condemned the action of the Bombay Government, Hastings saw that they must be supported, and a force was sent under Colonel Goddard right across India. The war had several vicissitudes including the astounding pusillanimity which led a Bombay Column to the disgraceful convention of Wargaum, the leaders being beaten and the troops not. Goddard, after his march across India of 300 miles in twenty days in the month of February 1779, retrieved this disaster by successes in Guzerat, and an amazing incident occurred when another small force under Captain Popham, took the Rock of Gwalior and the famous fortress thereon. Thus generally the British prestige and hope of peace in India were enhanced by the war. The fierce restless Haider, however, could not let things alone and the *Second* Mysore War (1780–1784) commenced with his pouring into the Carnatic carrying fire and sword to the outskirts of Madras itself. Sir Hector Munro, no longer the alert hero of Buxar, was defeated, one of his columns being severely handled and its commander Colonel Baillie captured, and it needed the despatch of troops by Hastings under Sir Eyre Coote from Bengal to restore the situation. Haider now sustained three smashing defeats, of which Porto Novo and Sholingarh are the more famous. Coote returned owing to disagreement with the Governor, the war dragged on, the French now tried to resuscitate their influence, a French squadron under Admiral Suffren succeeding in landing 3,000 French soldiers. Haider died, Tippu, his son, succeeded, and actually captured a British force in Mangalore under General Matthews. Hastings again sent Coote, now an old man, with full powers, but he died two days after landing, and ere long the Madras Government made a humiliating peace with Tippu, producing a situation that could not long endure. Thus in 1784 ended the Second War.

In 1786 came Lord Cornwallis, the famous soldier, as successor, and under him Tippu was to receive the first real blow that was to restrain his outrageous attempt to become Emperor of Southern India.

The Early Sepoy Armies

Although reference has been made to the sepoys with whom Clive and Coote and Munro first carried the *Pax Britannica*, the story of their evolution has not yet been told, nor how the early armed watchmen grew into an army of soldiers. It was not till 1746 on the Madras side that the nondescript armed retainers first were formed into companies of sepoys, and European soldiers were raised from sailors and adventurers of all races, some even being specially enlisted in Switzerland. It was in Madras indeed, whose fate was to become first involved in the necessity for defence, that the idea of the Indian sepoy was first evolved. Between 1746 and 1758 only eleven companies of sepoys were raised and most of these accompanied Clive to Bengal after the Black Hole. The Madrassi as then known was of no military account and these early soldiers were Kaffirs from overseas, Arabs, Rajputs from Hindustan, and even slaves bought in Madagascar. It was not till 1758 that a battalion even was formed, and cavalry had not then been thought of. It was not till the same year that certain European gun-crews were entertained and the famous Madras Artillery thus inaugurated, but the second siege of Madras in that year also resulted in the pushing of military organization a substantial step further. Five battalions were now formed which by 1767 had increased to sixteen, and the great Line of the Coast Army was further on its way. In 1754 had come the first Royal unit to India, the 39th Foot, who bear the motto '*Primus in Indis*', and with them Stringer Lawrence, Forde, Eyre Coote and Hector Munro, all to be famous in the annals of the Company's Wars.

It was not till 1772 after the Second Mysore War had commenced that the sepoys were clothed, first clothed in scarlet it is said, because there was a lot of that coloured cloth in the Company's godowns. Later the moral effect was realized and it remained as a policy. As the prophet Nahum has it 'Lo! the valiant men are in scarlet' and it was now that the Line in scarlet jackets, shako-like puggarees and white cross belts, began to attain its moral force. The actual periods of the growth of the Coast Army divide into five epochs each responsible for greater evolution; they have been put as follows:

1746 to the First Mysore War in 1769.
1769 to the Second Mysore War ending in 1784.
1785 to the Third Mysore War ending in 1792.
1792 to the Fourth Mysore War, the Capture of Seringapatam and death of Tippu in 1799.
1800 to 1820, the period of the Second and Third and Fourth Mahratta Wars.

The officer cadre during the second period was much improved, and it now began to model itself in dress and custom on the British Army also. The scallywag and adventurer class from which the Company took its earliest officers had long disappeared. The cadet system in England, which ended in Addiscombe and Baraset, was beginning.

After the Second Mysore War four cavalry regiments were raised which by the end of the Third War had increased to eight, and the battalions now stood at no fewer than thirty-four, with three battalions of Madras Europeans and a highly organized artillery, and by 1807 the battalions were increased to fifty. It was indeed in the period of the Third Mysore War when Lord Cornwallis, whose army was known as the Grand Army and with which were several Royal corps, introduced the precision and disciplined ways of Europe, that the real Madras Army came into being.

The rank and file were still largely of the mercenary type, that is to say the Afghan- and Turk-descended invaders, and or else the outcaste Hindus and Christians, and a useful hardbitten force they had become. As the force grew, the *chetty*, that is to say the cultivator, began to be enlisted, but it was not till the 'Brahminization' of the Army, to be described later, began, that the Hindu cultivator became the principal constituent.

The Third and Fourth Mysore Wars

The Third Mysore War was of the greatest importance to India and deserves more detailed attention. Tippu was even more implacable than his father, and aimed only at combinations which should drive the British into the sea, and unite Islam against them. He was stimulated in this by the numerous French officers still serving the various courts, some from the original French cadres, others refugees from the French revolution seeking a livelihood. The Hindu kingdoms were equally victims of Tippu's intolerance, and he was by nature endowed with a peculiarly cruel and bloodthirsty disposition. Kanara and Coorg were overrun and converted at the sword's point. It was said that 2,000 Brahmins died by their own hand, to escape him and the *Qoran*. Just as the Moplals destroyed or forcibly circumcised the Brahmins and Hindus around them during the recent Moplah risings, so did Tippu and his merry men treat the very races whom he should have aspired to cherish. This had the advantage to the British of cementing a friendship with the Mahrattas, who were furious at the ill-treatment of the Hindus by Tippu. The assumption of the title of *Badshah*, only the right of the Delhi Emperors, also enraged the Nizam, so that he and the Mahrattas declared war on Tippu. Tippu however, was too much for them, and he now boasted the destruction of 8,000 Hindu temples. Indeed had the times of the early Pathan and Turk invasions of the North now come to pass in the South.

It was not long then before the British were compelled by his action to join Nizam and Mahratta in humbling Tippu, but the Madras Government as usual, started badly. Then it was Lord Cornwallis, as already related, came and with him some Bengal troops, but difficulties of transport and supplies resulted in opening reverses. It was not till January 1792 that the Grand Army, the finest yet seen in India, appeared before the immensely strong fortress of Seringapatam, accompanied by a small Mahratta force and some worthless Nizami troops. As the outworks were carried Tippu craved for terms, which were granted, but Lord Cornwallis was to stand no more trifling. Tippu was to restore Coorg to its own rajah, give up certain districts to the British and pay thirty crores of rupees as indemnity, while giving up his two sons as hostages. This final scene as well as those of the siege is well portrayed by Martens in a well known series of pictures. In 1793 Lord Cornwallis left India after seven years of hard work, in which he had completed Clive's and Hastings' work of modelling the Civil Service. An amiable but not very effective successor who endeavoured to avoid all interference with quarrelling neighbours succeeded in the person of Sir John Shore who was in 1798 replaced by one of the most brilliant servants that the Empire has ever had, or who has ever served India. Lord Mornington, afterwards the Marquis Wellesley, was the brother of the Duke of Wellington and was endued with as much character and foresight as his younger brother.

As soon as he had mastered the situation he realized that the strange Mahratta confederacy, fully recovered by now from its disaster at Panipat, was quite determined to try conclusions with the British for the mastery of India. Sindia was holding the Mogul seat of power with the blind puppet Emperor Shah Alăm II in his hands. Peace and humanity, prosperity and trade demanded that wars should cease, that there should be a paramount power in India, to whom the public good was a matter of concern. Neither Mahratta with their fixed idea of spoil, nor Tippu the fiery proseletyser with the knife of circumcision, nor the Sikhs in the North or the Nawab Vizier of Oudh in the East could possibly fill that role. He saw clearly that the Mahratta federation must go, and that each Mahratta state and every other state must be confined within its own boundaries in tributary alliance with a paramount power. The autumnal *mulk-geri*, the sallying forth to remove your neighbours land-mark, must cease. And he set about to make it so, the peoples of India through their sons that they sent to the British Army and the British service generally, who saw that it was good, eagerly assisting. Indeed at all times even in the dire days of the Indian Mutiny it was the eager help of the mass of the people that have put and keep the British as the only possible paramount power.

The outlook was by no means re-assuring, the French deprived of their territorial role were working by other means. During the more foolish days of Sir John Shore's Government, French influence had become paramount once more at the courts of the Nizam, of Tippu and of Sindia the Mahratta, who had been steadily pursuing a policy of aggrandisement, and whose agent Perron threatened the British frontier on the Ganges. Napoleon Bonaparte was corresponding with Tippu and a French general with officers and a few volunteers had actually joined him. Tippu himself had called on Zaman Shah the Afghan ruler in Kabul to come to his assistance and that of Islam, and the Afghan had entered the Punjab. The times called for action and Tippu Bahshah, who had not learnt his lesson nor was keeping his treaties, was obviously the first to bring to reason. The Governor-General who had landed in April was not long in gripping what threatened to be a crisis, and in getting his blows in first. At Hyderabad a French contingent of sepoys was a dangerous and unnecessary item. It was transformed by a *coup d'état* into an English one. Tippu was called on to stay his hand, keep his engagements and send away his French. On his declining, the Governor-General went to Madras to assist in implementing the large Army of King's and Company's troops, which was being assembled under General Harris, the local Commander-in-Chief. Troops came from Bombay by sea, and a Mahratta and Nizam's force also were directed on Mysore. Tippu first struck far afield and fought two containing battles with ill success, and then the armies closed on Seringapatam, terribly hampered though they were by poor transport and want of roads through the ghats, and at times in straits for food.

How Seringapatam was stormed is a story too well known to need further detail. The romantic incident was that of

General Baird who once spent four bitter years in a Mysore dungeon, leading the storming. As the Mysoreans murdered at the last moment any British prisoners in their hands, the enraged troops gave no quarter; Tippu by now a madman, was slain with vast hosts of his men in a great *cul-de-sac* in the fortress.

The Madras sepoy had much distinguished himself, and Arthur Wellesley was now sent off with a body drawn from them to chase the ruthless Mahratta freebooter Doondiah Wah, with the result that Mysore and all its neighbourhood saw peace and ruth. The old Hindu state of Mysore which Haider had engulfed was restored and the Nizam and the Mahrattas were assigned tracts that more properly belonged to them. Distinguished as the Madras soldiery had been, the personnel was largely still from the half-Turk and Afghan Moslems, and the Pariahs, and no great attempt yet had been made to enlist the *chetty* referred to.

The Second and Third Mahratta Wars

The Mahratta chiefs who made up the confederacy had little power of adhesion, and as when the Rajput quarrels admitted Turk and Afghan, were often engaged not only in intrigues against each other but in hostilities, Sindia and Holkar about this time having fought a pitched battle outside Poona with European adventurers commanding corps on both sides. By now all the princes of India had seen the efficacy of Western military ways and had endeavoured to copy them. Sindia especially had a large French trained army, which the Count de Boigne had raised, with a regular cadet service and all the trappings of the Company. M. Perron had lately succeeded to its command, and had been

THE SURRENDER OF PONDICHERRY TO COOTE, 1761
From a picture by the French Military Artist, N. Dupray

[*Face page* 160

assigned the revenue of the Doab between Ganges and Jumna for its support with the old Mogul fortress and capital of Agra as its headquarters. Sindia with all these resources at his disposal was anxious to try conclusions with the Company once and for all.

Now begins the final story of the Mahrattas, that we left off after the second coming to Delhi and the enticing of Shah Alăm II to the Mahratta trap there. We need not trace the combinations which induced the British to take the part of their ally Baji Rao at Poona when threatened by Sindia.

Suffice it here to say that two armies moved against Sindia. Lord Mornington had the great advantage of a young and leading soldier as the Commander-in-Chief in Bengal, General Gerald Lake, the *Lik Sahib* of his triumphant soldiery. General Lake led the Grand Army from the vicinity of Allahabad, while Major-General Arthur Wellesley led that of the Dekhan, and with the latter marched also the troops of the Peshwa, and of the Nizam. A great series of victories ensued, notably those of Assaye on the west and Laswari on the north-east. Agra was captured, Delhi taken and the French trained troops with their officers defeated. At Argaum Arthur Wellesley beat the troops of both Sindia and the Bhonsla, i.e. the Mahratta rajah of Berar. The two were magnificent campaigns. The Sepoy Army of Bengal had followed the example of Madras, and consisted of a splendid Line enlisted from much the same types as in the Coast Army, but including a good deal of the peasantry and messenger classes of Behar and Bengal. Indeed the glamour of the swaggering Oudh Rajput had already taken hold of the Bengal officers, for an Army Order of 1797 points out that these are the men who deserted so frequently and that more use is to be made of the men from 'our own provinces'.

At Delhi the blind Shah Alăm II was rescued from filth and durance and restored to comfort and dignity by General Lake, on whom the highest title of the ancient Mogul Empire was conferred by the old puppet, a puppet whose imperial name however was still one of prestige and reverence.

Sindia and the Bhonsla were now beaten to terms and entered into due treaty with the paramount power. Sindia having abided by this treaty like the Nizam, remains to this day, a premier chief in India. At the end of 1803 the British armies went into cantonments as best they could, but all was not yet peace. Jeswunt Rao Holkar, the enemy of Sindia and prince of Indore a fierce ambitious uncertain character, held aloof from Sindia and the Bhonsla, and not till the war was over did he appear on the scene in arms and inaugurate that Third Mahratta War, which is often in men's minds tacked on to the Second but which was quite distinct. Colonel Monson set forth from Agra in the hot season of 1804 to meet the inroading Holkar, and through sheer bad soldiering and want of foresight suffered a disastrous defeat which rang triumphantly through all that part of India that longed for the destruction of the British. Holkar swung north and tried to capture Delhi, which put up, under Burns and Ochterlony, a celebrated defence. Lord Lake took the field, again, and with a large force of cavalry, Light Dragoons and Indians chased Holkar up and down the land, finally overtaking him on the Sutlej where he had gone to try to raise the Sikhs. Holkar's infantry were destroyed at the battle of Deig and the war so far as that prince went was over. Unfortunately Lake endeavoured with scanty artillery to storm the Jăt fortress of Bhurtpur, the Rajah having broken his engagements and joined Holkar. Four times hurled back with very heavy loss, he was obliged to make terms, though Bhurtpur gave up Holkar. A Bombay force had joined the

Grand Army before Bhurtpur, and here we have this delightful story of the "*Untoo Goorgas*" afore-said. The strange *prakrit* of the Mahratta troops amused the Bengal Army who dubbed them this name imitative of the uncouth tongue, but so much was it resented that an Army Order forbade its use.

The repulses before Bhurtpur plus the defeat of Monson sadly battered the gilt off our prestige, which was not really restored till Bhurtpur fell to Lord Combermere in 1826.

That, however, is another story. The Mahratta chiefs, handsomely beaten, had each and all to go into their legitimate territorial box, with such alleviations to the chiefs of Rajputana whose territories they had seized, as seemed just to the Governor-General, now the Marquis Wellesley. Poona was already an ally, Sindia, the Bhonsla, Holkar and the Gaikwar now became so, and, except the Peshwa at Poona, as they became so have they remained. The Delhi Territories became British, the Cis-Sutlej or Phulkian Sikh Chiefs also became allies, protected as they desired from absorption by Runjhit Singh. The larger tributary or allied states accepted a 'Subsidiary' British force to protect them if their neighbours attacked again, and agreed to maintain also a 'contingent' that would help maintain the peace of the Indian Empire, a just and statesmanlike arrangement in view of the strange shifting catch-as-catch-can conditions which the Mogul crash had left behind.

Since these arrangements India has changed little except that the impossible state of Oudh, evil beyond belief, compelled the paramount power—the power that reigned in place of the Mogul and with Mogul prestige and heirship—to annexe it, after trying for fifty years to avoid doing so. In the north a curious chain of circumstances compelled us also, much against our will to assume in due course the burden of the Punjab.

The Fourth Mahratta War

It might have been thought that Assaye, Laswaree, Deig and Argaum would have been enough for the Confederacy, especially since the knowledge of British might on the continent of Europe and the crowning victory of Waterloo must have been well known. But the Company, upset at the strain of the long war, and the British Government fatally shortsighted as usual, proceeded to try and be rid of much that Wellesley had won for them. Aged Cornwallis came out again to cancel and to economize, but died almost immediately. Sir George Barlow, an Indian official of inferior type, ruled for two years, and then came Lord Minto who from the years from 1807 to 1813 struggled to get back what Barlow had let go. The pacification of thrice lawless Bundelkand was his great work and the sending of important missions to Kabul to Sind and to Teheran. In 1814 came another distinguished soldier Francis Rawdon, Lord Moira, and later the Marquis Hastings. The Nepal War[1] which was not all to our credit was the first anxiety, and then came the terrible question of the Pindaris, whose conduct already described called to high Heaven for vengeance. Hastings summoned the Mahratta allies to assist in their repression. But already the Peshwa and the Bhonsla were planning mischief and were themselves deeply involved with the Pindaris. Sindia, by the wise handling of his political agents, was fortunately for himself, kept clear. The Peshwa was handsomely defeated at Kirkee and Poona, and the Bhonsla at Sitabaldi and Nagpur, both after treacherous attacks on the Residents at their court and the British Subsidiary Force which protected them.

[1] See Chapter X.

The scene before the battle of Kirkee was described by an eye-witness when the immense forces of the Peshwa horse, foot and artillery, elephants and standards, poured out of Poona is like the 'bore coming up the Severn' and swirled round the little British force on the plains of Kirkee, while the beautiful British Residency went up in flames. In the afternoon sun the slanting rays fell on the golden temple tops of the hill temple of Parbatti which still dominates the landscape and used to be known to the British soldier as 'the Brass Castle', and where the pusillanimous Peshwa offered up prayers for the force he was too timorous to lead. Among those who fell leading a cavalry charge on a British square was the Mahratta Gokla who commanded the Peshwa's horse, but who in the previous war, when the Peshwa was our ally, had been the admired friend of Wellesley and those British officers who knew him, and who regretted that he should have so lost his life.

A week or so later occurred another incident famous still and much treasured by the 102nd Bombay Grenadiers, to use the name they held till the World War. A small force of Indian soldiers marching from Sirur to Poona to join the Subsidiary Force, was fallen on by the whole Mahratta army at the little mud village of Koregaon, and only after a prolonged defence of the utmost gallantry was rescued. It was one of those fights which so illustrate the affection and admiration with which those people of India who knew the British regarded the officers who led them, their service and their power.

On the hill of Sitabaldi close to Nagpur, similar dramatic scenes were being enacted, and a small force of Bengal sepoys and cavalry were defending themselves against huge surging hosts of Mahrattas and Arabs. A detachment of the 6th Light Cavalry led by young Hearsey, afterwards the famous Indian General, made a series of most daring charges at which all the world of the day marvelled.

With the Peshwa and the Bhonsla finally dealt with, it was the turn of Holkar, who was putting all his westernised troops into the field in support of his friends the Pindari horrors . . . and it was his turn to be handsomely drubbed at the battle of Mehidpore in Malwa. After this a great network of columns crowded in to destroy and chase up and down the country till exterminated, the whole of the Pindari pests. The war began in 1817, and it was well into 1819 before all was over. When finished it was the finest piece of work for humanity and ruth that the world had yet seen. The Peshwa, faithless and irreconcilable, was deposed and his territories annexed, the line of Shivaji at Satara was restored to some small temporal power, and the Bhonsla and Holkar duly cribbed, set back on their thrones. That ended once and for all Mahratta attempts to dispute the crown of India with the British, yet all the five chiefs except the Peshwa remained. As the years rolled on the want of an heir led to the annexation of Nagpur, but Sindiah, Holkar and the Gaikwar remain to this day among the premier ruling princes of India.

As this is the finale of the Mahratta story, it may be said that except among the directing personnel, and that often Dekhani Brahmin, the Mahrattas as a race were not conspicuous as members of the modern Mahratta armies and it has remained for the British to find them out as staunch and gallant rank and file, to forget them for a while, and then to find them in the World War better and stauncher than ever.

Two more conflicts with Mahratta forces in some sort were to take place. One was the destruction in 1843 by Lord Gough of the remnant of the French-trained Mahratta standing army, in a curious outbreak against its own Government to be described in the next chapter. The Mahratta himself, however, was in no great evidence in the ranks of the batteries and battalions destroyed at Maharajpore and Punniar. The other in 1844, was a dragging, badly managed campaign against rebellious elements in the Southern Mahratta country. Far the most serious in its possibilities was the attempt of Tantia Topi, the confederate of the Nana of the Mutiny days, when the rebellion had been crushed in Oudh and the mutineers defeated, to raise the *Bhagwan Jhanda* in Central India and stir the whole Mahratta race and interests to national rebellion. Happily prompt military action by all concerned stamped out a conflagration which was never really lit, or which did but smoulder, but which 'put the wind up' authority in India to an extent that has now been forgotten.

CHAPTER IX

THE ARMIES OF JOHN COMPANY

THE GROWTH OF THE PRESIDENCY ARMIES—AFTER LAKE AND WELLESLEY—THE BRAHMINIZATION OF THE ARMY—THE FIVE WARS OF QUEEN VICTORIA—SIND AND GWALIOR.

THE GROWTH OF THE PRESIDENCY ARMIES

IT is not necessary to trace further how the Company's forces first developed; that has been done in outline in the chapter on the rise of the British power, but the modern story of the martial races is their absorption into the army, or their struggles against that army. It may here be remarked that the martial races that put up a stout fight, or whose rulers endeavoured to drive out the British, such as the Mahrattas, the Gurkhas and the Sikhs, and who got most handsomely beaten for their pains, are just those which serve the Crown most loyally and affectively. As the night-watchmen in the godowns were first armed and then grouped into companies, the companies grew to battalions, class, caste or race were no great moment. The first men to hand who had the 'guts' to bear arms were those first employed. In all parts of India there was a miscellaneous class of men who carried important messages, or hired themselves out as guards to protect the caravans of the merchants, as the country grew more lawless, and these, naturally, were suitable in their time. In Madras the native Christians who had no prejudices and Pariahs or sturdy outcaste tribes soon proved, with a tot of rum in their stomachs and a Brown Bess on their shoulders, to be no mean opponent to the *Rajwara*[1] troops, and dacoits who might be opposed to them. In Calcutta the enmity of the Nawab of Bengal, and in Madras the rise of the French made it necessary to evolve something better than companies of guards. By the middle of the second half of the eighteenth century, a great army was beginning in Bengal and Bombay similar to that in Madras, and a growing artillery was coming into being. Generals and staffs and more royal troops had followed the 39th Foot, and the Royal Army was the pattern to be followed by that of the Company. The eighteenth century had seen the British Army constantly employed on the Continent, and always with success. From Marlborough's days, for forty years, the British soldier had come to renown, and was looked upon as the best model to follow, and therefore it was not surprising that the complete model of the British line came to be adopted. The actual clothing of the men in scarlet has been described and how thus clothed they were often mistaken for Europeans and dreaded, which made the custom universal. Thus the Line of the three Presidential Armies became modelled on the British line, and from having puggarees tied on, came to copy first the three cornered cocked hat, and then the shako, at last even came to wearing a leather one. It is to be remembered that each Presidency was separated for at least two hundred years from the others, by hundreds of miles of trackless jungles or of independent states, and for many years had even no common Governor-General, and therefore no co-ordinated policy. They were entirely separate countries, dealing with widely different peoples. Their armies there-

[1]Belonging to a *Raj* or Indian State.

fore were in many ways different, though from time to time the Company issued regulations governing the main organization with a view to making them similar in their broad lines. Yet different they remained for many generations, and it was not indeed till Lord Kitchener's day that the last trace of the separate armies disappeared and the numbering was combined.

The summoning of Europeans by the independent princes to model their armies on Western lines, and the struggles with the French, compelled the Company to still further regularize and develop its forces, and as related, it was found that a line of scarlet and shako clad troops, of which perhaps a fifth might be European, undoubtedly presented a commanding appearance. An enemy could not see where the line was European and where native, and was perplexed accordingly.

The success of the British armies in the Napoleonic period still further emphasized the importance of the British model, and we now see the armies of the three Presidencies copying the dress and equipment of the British line in every particular. The native battalions even had their Grenadier companies in bearskins, and their rifle companies in green like the British Line, and officers, both horse and foot, followed slavishly the dress regulations of the later Georgian periods, regardless of climatic suitability.

The Brahminization of the Army

After the Third Mahratta War when the Madras Army had achieved great distinction under Arthur Wellesley, not even transcended by the Bengal troops under Lord Lake himself, there began a period bitterly referred to by some of the older officers as 'the Brahminization' of the Army. In the account of the early Madras armies just given, the presence of the old mercenary type, the descendants of the foreigner, the *Villayatis*, (the word being our old friend 'Blighty'), viz., Pathans, Arabs, Turks, Afghans, Moslem negroes, and Mekranis, is referred to. All these races had for many generations flocked to the great Moslem Kingdoms of the Dekhan, as they even to-day are still attracted to the Nizam's capital of Hyderabad which Tippu's and Haider's courts must in some sort have resembled. The other class was as just said the Pariah with rum in his belly, and Brown Bess on his shoulder. Splendid soldiers as these made against the ill-disciplined hosts of the Indian princes, hardy and cheerful under difficulties, lead and disciplined by the British officer, still they undoubtedly did not redound to the eventual credit of the British Government. They were not a national army or militia. If the British were to govern India—for the Indians and with the good will of the Indians, as became the determination of the Company as soon as it realized that it must become a temporal and sovereign power—its army should have better roots among the people. Then the fiat went forth that the real folk of the country-side, the yeoman peasantry and the landowners, were to be encouraged to soldier in the Company's ranks, wherever man of heart and thew could be found. In the Carnatic this meant recruiting the Tamil and the Telegu *chetty*[1], from whom in time a body of estimable young men filled the ranks for three-quarters of a century, but filled them at a time when the army had got over its great trials. The Mysore and Mahratta Wars were over. There remained after the re-constitution had begun, only the Fourth Mahratta War, which was also the Pindari War. During it the officers

[1] Cultivator.

of the Armies of the Dekhan are loud in their dismay. What had come to the Madras Army? Where were the cheery hardy soldiers that Arthur Wellesley had marched so hard and done so much with? The Madras Army as a whole did not cover itself with glory in this last Mahratta War, and it was Bombay and Bengal, and, above all, Thomas Atkins who took the palm. But that was in the transition. A few years later the Madras Army would certainly have done well against Mahrattas, Mewatis and Pindaris. It was only the fierce Arab that seemed to form the '*pièce de résistance*' both of Mahratta and Pindari forces, that few Indian soldiers could face. Whether the so called Arab was entirely Arab or whether he was Pathan and Mekrani as well, is hard to ascertain. The same gentlemen survived in Malwa so late as 1857, and generally were tough customers. Indeed the toughest customers at Delhi and Lucknow in 1857 were not as usually supposed the mutineer sepoy but the Ghilzais and other Afghans who visit India in the cold weather, and who hearing of coming trouble stayed behind to see the fun. The term Brahminization in this connection but means 'high caste' as distinct from low and outcaste people.

In the Bengal Army, the 'grenadiering' of the Line was popular enough and ere long the Bengal Army was almost entirely composed of the tall Hindustani sepoys from Oudh and Behar, Rajputs and actual Brahmins, the Oudh Brahmin making a fine soldier, or Moslems of the same provinces, either Turks and men of Afghan origin or '*Sheikhs*', men of good clans who had been converted. This Army stood with a strength of 74 battalions and 12 regiments of regular cavalry, the infantry in shakos, coatees and cross belts like the Victorian line, the tall sepoys with their moustachios and curled whiskers being most martial to look upon. The cavalry were in French grey with the equipment of Light

Dragoons, and in addition there were many irregular corps of horse and foot.

But with all this regularity and solidarity, the army was losing its grip of fighting and soldiering. A rot was setting in, discipline was not what it had been. There was enough active employment to keep it in order, but something was wrong in Bengal. Too much admiration, too many 'kiss-mammy' ideas at headquarters, something of the lesser spirit of Victorian sentiment, had spoilt this machine towards the end of the first half of last century.

The capture of Bhurtpur in 1826, the capture which wiped out the slur of Lord Lake's failure in 1805, was the last occasion when this great army was at its best. On the other hand the Army of Madras which numbered 52 battalions and 8 cavalry corps was now in a better state; it had tapped the right class of young peasant of good caste. Bombay with its 30 odd battalions did not trouble its head about grenadiers and kept to its humbler and very alert soldiery, and its principle of selection. In Bengal promotion of Indian ranks went solely by seniority. The Subahdars were often men of seventy.

After Lake and Wellesley

How eagerly the sepoy flocked to the Company's service, both the mercenaries' descendants, the low caste men, and now the high caste yeomen, is one of the glories of the British memories. The officers who led from the front, the officers who saw that food and pay were regular, the Company that liberally rewarded its soldiers, all made a happy and romantic story. In the villages the red-coated soldier on leave was highly regarded, and his stories eagerly listened to. There is a book *From Sepoy to Subahdar*, being the life of

Subahdar Sitaram, which is the most fascinating of stories. It first appeared in the 'sixties, and is redolent of all that the officer and sepoy were to each other, and of the complete trust and comradeship. Sitaram tells of his uncle, a sergeant, coming to his village and promising when he was old enough to take him and ask the colonel to enlist him, and how the *perohit*, the family priest, came in to be consulted and had approved. There is one typical and charming trait that runs through it. One of the sahibs had captured Sitaram's admiration and heart. Barampeel *Sahib*, 'My Barampeel *Sahib*' (believed to be a Dalrymple) is always being quoted, almost as a *chela* would quote his Guru, and it is still so as many of us know. Then there was the quaint human complaint as old as the hills, that I have still so often heard. Sitaram laments as he grows older that 'the sahibs to-day are not as the old sahibs', and as *Punch* has truly said, they never were. It is all part of that glorious camaraderie which takes the British officer to serve with the Indian army, in dull, sun-baked frontier stations, where the amenities of life are nil, and only the joy of service remains, or where jungle and heat make life a purgatory, where the ordinary regimental routine and the long days on the rifle ranges have nothing to relieve them. Now and again a scarlet and gold ceremony gives a little psychological glamour to what is else a hard enough life. Even where the large concentrations of troops makes life an exciting whirl, the long, long months of summer drag out the heart and health. It is endurable because of the life with the men, a camaraderie that Indian politicians and even our own ignorant hot-air merchants would give their eyes to destroy, forgetting how the roof comes down on their own head with the pillars.

The wisdom of some of Lord Kitchener's entourage succeeded in getting Sitaram's story, originally written in

Hindi, translated into the various languages that the military officer needs to know, and had it made the text book for vernacular reading. As it contained the first and the last word of what the sepoy really thinks, the value of this step was immense. Since the World War some foolish educationalist has managed to get it abolished. Those who read sucked in with the language a knowledge of India which was of immense value, and a good deal of history. It was also published in English as part of the same series, and is fascinating reading for those who would mark and learn.

And so the great armies of the three Presidencies were wound into the administration and the heart of the country and into the service of Britain, and before the greatest of them all blew up in quite unnecessary tragedy, a considerable portion of the armies was to go through a period of great strain and gain much distinction, which must now be outlined.

THE FIVE VICTORIAN WARS: AFGHANISTAN

The first decade of the reign of Queen Victoria was to see a remarkable series of wars in India, so much so that the Bengal Army, and to a lesser extent that of Bombay, had no rest. It may be said that all these series of wars were for the purpose of recovering for India proper the territories and dominion that were hers during the Mogul Empire. These wars were—

- The First Afghan War, which was in reality two wars (1839–42).
- The Conquest of Sind, in other words the bringing back of Sind into the fold (1843).

The Gwalior Campaign, being the outbreak of the old French-trained Army of Sindiah against authority (1843).

The First Sikh War known as 'The Sutlej Campaign' 1845–6.

The Second Sikh War known as 'The Punjab Campaign' 1848–9.

Down in southern Indian there was the lesser campaign in 1844, referred to in the present chapter, in which the Madras and Bombay Armies were involved, known as the Southern Mahratta War, in which the great hill fortress Panalla was besieged. Now these wars took the Bengal Army away from its own country for a long time, always a hardship to soldiers who own land, and who want to supervise or perhaps assist in its cultivation during their leave.

The first half of the Afghan War, undertaken as the result of the famous Tripartite Treaty between the British, the Sikhs and the ex-King of Afghanistan, though full of hardship was a brilliant success. It was not in reality a war, it was undertaken in what were believed to be the interests of Afghanistan and India, and in accordance with the wishes of many Afghans. The Shah was escorted by his own contingent, raised as he had raised it before in Northern India, but now commanded by British officers of the Company's service rather than as before by Eurasians and nondescripts. The Army of the Indus marched from Ferozepore, where it assembled, down to Sind where, by treaty the Baluchi Amirs handed over the crossing and the town of Bakkur for the time being. There it was joined by a Bombay column and a huge unwieldy force entirely unorganized for service in such a terrain, lumbered up to Kandahar. Thence it passed on to the ancient city and citadel of Ghuzni, which was brilliantly stormed, and this was the only action save for scraps with tribal marauders. In 1839 the Army under Sir John Keane entered Kabul, and Shah Shujah sat on the throne of his fathers. All the while the British lived as allies in an ally's country and indeed fraternized with the hard-riding sporting Afghan quality very readily, as something quite different from the somewhat sombre personnel of India.

The story of the two years in which the new king failed to make good, the military vacillation and the unauthorized withdrawal with the disasters that followed, are well known and need not be dwelt on at length. Eventually General Pollock took a grip of the twittering ill-disciplined sepoy troops at Peshawar, and finally reinforced, forced them through the Khaiber and brought aid to the defenders of Jellalabad, who had actually relieved themselves by a victory under the walls. Four thousand Bengal sepoys had been destroyed by frost and snow rather than by the enemy, with followers innumerable. During the advance of the avenging army, as during the previous two years, the Bengal sepoy and equally he of Bombay, who remained near Kandahar, had been infinitely better men than the Afghan. Despite their coatees and their white cross-belts, they could chase him over any mountain and stand up to any rush of swordsmen. It was not till the senior British officers of the Kabul force lost their grip and their nerve and pulled the army down with them, that the Bengal sepoy went down in the cruel frost and snow to which he should not have been exposed. Tails that curl over the back can as easily uncurl when circumstances are bad. It was not to be wondered at that Pollock found the sepoy feet at Peshawar after the destruction of Elphinstone's force in the Khurd Kabul Pass, icy cold.

The disasters were amply retrieved when Pollock forced the passes from Peshawar, and Nott came up from Kandahar and the two met and snarled at each other in Kabul, and the British and Indian soldiers were paramount once again. The British drums and fifes sounded reveille and retreat once again in the Kabul valley, the European prisoners and English ladies were recovered and the troops marched out. Unhappily the staff work of the Army was atrocious and the two generals ignorant beyond modern belief of such matters, so that on the way home the Khaiberees took 'entirely unnecessary tea' with the columns. But Atkins and Jack Sepoy were supreme, crowning the heights and piquetting with *élan* and confidence. One pathetic thoughtless scandal did occur. The bazaars of Kabul were full of footless beggars who had once been Bengal sepoys and their followers, and the arrangements to get them home were nil. It is not to be wondered at that the prestige of the British, and the spirit of the Bengal Army were badly shaken by the whole futile, unnecessarily feeble, carrying out of a policy that had much to recommend it. All this while the Punjab, be it remembered, was not British, and Runjhit Singh, our ally, had died in the early days of the venture. Two points are worth remembering for all time. The 44th Foot of those days was notorious for its supercilious attitude towards the Indian Army, both the Company's officers and the sepoy. There was none of the camaraderie important in peace, essential in war, and the bones of the 44th with three battalions of Bengal sepoys still whiten the hill side in the Khurd Kabul Pass! The 13th Foot on the contrary was equally famous for the opposite attitude, and together they and the 36th Bengal Native Infantry, held the crumbling walls of Jellalabad even after an earthquake had brought them down to heaps of rubble. To this day they are spoken of where deeds of valour are remembered as the 'illustrious garrison', the happy phrase of the Governor-General. Farther, when the two regiments marched back across the bridge of boats on the Sutlej and through the triumphal arches into British India, before they went their ways, the high caste 36th Native Infantry entertained the whole of the 13th to a meal. It was spread on an earthwork dug by themselves, their guest's feet in trenches on either side, the *demblaie* forming a table. May such camaraderie ever flourish!

SIND AND GWALIOR

The horror of Afghanistan and the disasters of 1841 had penetrated far down into India, and the curling tail of the Army now became draggled, despite the victories and the real triumphs of the avengers. The fact was that the officer cadre was horrorstruck that it should be possible for the unpractical mentalities of certain politicians to tear a great people from its base and rock of self reliance, just as we are paralysed in modern times to see soft false sentiments combining to destroy us, and no one able to call halt!

Then there came to India an old, war-battered, perverse, but understanding, old soldier of the Napoleonic wars in the person of Major-General Sir Charles Napier, appointed to a comparatively small command, that of the Poona Division. His staunch heart that beat at one with Arthur Wellesley, Duke of Wellington, fiercely grieved that a British Army should have its tail down and that Indian hearts inside the scarlet tunic that had withstood the French so stoutly should be dumb-cowered in that dress. He would have none of it. Officers who talked unguardedly and disparagingly of the Army were badly bitten by this fierce long-haired, hawk-eyed, bearded old man. He tackled the heresy that was being quoted to account for the Afghan disasters, and which was calculated to still further lower vitality, viz., the superiority of the Afghan musket, the long-barrelled *jezail*, over the Brown Bess, the love and the mistress of the British Army. His knowledge of the theory and science of musketry, then a sealed book to the majority of regimental officers, saw at once the fallacy, saw that it was not a matter of superiority but of trajectory, that a *jezail* high up on the mountain side would naturally have a long range whereas a musket fired from below and pointing up could not have the same range . . . further that a *jezail* below, would be just as badly off as a musket in competition with a *jezail* a few hundred feet above. He organized demonstrations on the rifle ranges which showed the musket every bit as good, nay, a better weapon than the *jezail*. The Indian soldier looked on eagerly and took heart of grace. Here was a man to conjure with them. Then after the disasters and ineptitudes of Brigadier England in the Bolan Pass, Sir Charles Napier was sent to take command in Sind, and conduct the final withdrawal of Nott's details and England's force from Southern Afghanistan, when the former had marched North to India via Kabul and Peshawur. It was a ticklish job, and was done thanks to Outram, the political officer, and Napier's general control. But it was not done well, because the staff did not know their job. Then Sir Charles was ordered to take full control in Sind, with Major Outram as the political officer under his orders, and not as in Afghanistan as representing the supreme government directing the soldiery. The whole of India vibrated with the stories of the false positions that this latter conception of a political officer's status had brought soldiers to. Sir Charles would have none of it. He found the Amirs of Sind were not abiding by their engagements. Especially were they collecting from the hills large numbers of fierce Baluchi tribesmen instead of discussing with him and Major Outram the question of the treaty. The demands made on the Amirs were not excessive, and were practically those necessary to a reasonably civilized existence. The Amirs were either vassals of Kabul or of Delhi, and the pretence that they could set up as an independent power without attending to the ordinary requirements of their neighbours was untenable in the opinion of the Governor-General. Outram had with some success kept them from turning on us while the disasters in Afghanistan were taking place, and the picturesque side of these fierce old hidalgos appealed to him. He would not admit that tens of thousands of armed hillmen were being collected, or that the chiefs had hostile intentions. The officers of the British force, and the natives of India believed that the Amirs did intend to 'Kabul' Sir Charles's small force, and he was fully determined not to be trapped by the folly and optimism of political officers. Public opinion and the experiences of Afghanistan supported him. Whether or no the Amirs did contemplate an attack on the British must remain a matter of opinion, but Sir Charles was right and Outram wrong so far as the suspicious fact that unknown to the political officers, tens of thousands of hill Baluchis and Pathans had been collected and these prepared to surround Sir Charles as his force, little more than two brigades, moved down to Hyderabad. Then occurred two of the fiercest battles that the British army has ever been called on to fight, those of Meeanee and Hyderabad, or Dubba. The 22nd Foot and the sepoys of Bombay and Bengal involved, fought five times their number of swordsmen at the bayonet's point on the banks of high mud cliffs of a watercourse, and triumphed. The prestige of the victories was enormous, and the Governor-General, Lord Ellenborough, annexed that district of dust and mud watered by a few flood-time canals, in which an industrious Hindu and Moslem peasantry had been shockingly ruled by Baluchi conquerors from the hills, arrivals as a matter of fact of but two or three generations earlier. To all that British rule has done, comes now the astounding coping stone of the Lloyd Barrage which will put the whole of the snow waters of the Indus over millions of acres of arid or partially irrigated land. Napier ruled the country in a few brilliant years of shirt-sleeve government, that paved the way of an unhappy land to a more normal system. The Baluchis cribbed within their own hills, are now among the most orderly of the martial races, and Sind is one of the jewels in the Indian crown.

Under Napier's strong personal stimulant the Bengal sepoys regained their good qualities, and when the Sikh Wars came he was able to lead a strong force up the Sutlej to the support of Sir Hugh Gough at Lahore.

Soon after the Bombay and Bengal regiments were fighting desperately in the severe heat of Sind, two divisions of the Bengal Army found themselves unexpectedly called on to take the field in the following cold season. These troops however enjoyed the comfort of manœuvre scales and a delightful season of the year. The story runs thus.

In 1842–3 there was trouble in the state of Gwalior where had ruled Sindia, the Mahratta chief, who since 1803 had abided by the terms of his treaty with Lord Wellesley. But Junkoje Rao was dead, and the state was in turmoil as to who should hold the reins of regency for the young Rajah. The old Gwalior Army trained by the French was far too big for its present needs. With no wars to fight, it had become a power in the state, and was taking sides in politics. Lord Ellenborough looking for a peaceful solution of serious internal trouble, collected two considerable British forces on the frontiers ostensibly for military manœuvres. As the Mahratta army now claimed to settle the domestic controversy these two forces under the supreme command of Sir Hugh Gough, moved on Gwalior, and the Governor-General himself marched with the latter's column. The Gwalior Army disposed itself across the two roads to the capital. The British Army ordered to sweep them aside when the situation proved that force was necessary, attacked and had to its considerable surprise to fight two fierce pitched battles at Maharajpore and Punniar. The brunt of the fighting was borne by the European troops, but the Bengal sepoy took his share and casualties were severe, the Mahratta artillery being heavy and resolutely served. It was the last of the battles of internal India apart from the struggles of the Mutiny. They had not been wanted and were only necessitated by the pretensions of the masterless Gwalior army. The latter now thoroughly broken was re-organized on much smaller lines, and the existing Contingent was enlarged and made to maintain order within the state. It is probable that the unruly mutinous state of the Sikh army at this time, to be described in the next chapter, was a considerable factor in the behaviour of the Gwalior troops. It was known also that those disaffected towards the British both in the Punjab and in the Mahratta states were working to combine both peoples in a final struggle against the inevitable march north of the red line on the map.

The next two unwanted wars of this period were the two Sikh wars, the 'Sutlej' and the 'Punjab' campaigns. How unwanted they were the ensuing pages will show and how they brought to the Indian Army that mass and mixture of glorious races which have so conduced to the fame of Northern India, as a breeding place for men.

Chapter X

THE GURKHA STORY

THE RISE OF THE DYNASTY OF GURKHA—THE GURKHA INVASIONS OF BRITISH INDIA—THE FIRST ASSEMBLING OF THE BRITISH ARMY—THE SECOND CAMPAIGN—THE RACES OF NEPAL—THE GURKHA REGIMENTS TO-DAY.

The Rise of the Dynasty of Gurkha

The Gurkha soldier is so famous and popular a constituent of His Majesty's Indian Forces, that the story of his race and the more recent history thereof is as worthy of a chapter to itself as that of Maharasthra. The people whom we talk of as Gurkhas are the people of the ancient kingdom of Gurkha, who are of many races, tribes and clans. They are here placed last in the marshalling, because they alone of the soldiers of the King-Emperor are technically foreigners . . . folk outside India, and the rule of John Company or the British Crown, close and staunch allies though they be. Indians in the major sense however they are. The country of Gurkha or Nepal runs for over 500 miles on the hitherside of the great Himalaya, from the plains of the British border to the unmarked, uninhabited borderline of Tibet, right in the very centre of the Northern Frontier of British India. All along the border from the Pamirs downward, there are many such states, and all but this one acknowledge to a greater or less extent their

THE SUBAHDAR MAJOR OF THE 2/2 GURKHAS IN 1912.
A GURUNG BY TRIBE

[Face page 184

oneness with the British Indian Empire, as they did that of the India of the Moguls.

This Nepal is famous in history because it was at Kapilavastu therein that Gautama Sidattha was born as related, son of a petty Rajput prince. Through the isolated passes, somewhere and somehow, Tibetan Mongoloid races in the distant past occupied the hill country, enslaving perhaps some aboriginal tribes. Up from the plains of India, also at some distant date, before Alexander of Macedon had come out of Khorassan, and before the Buddha had taught, Aryan tribes swarming down the Ganges valley and ever pushing up rivers and passes that led to a land worth having, had impinged on, subdued and mingled with the Mongoloid folk from Tibet. Aryan kingdoms and baronies had been carved at the sword's point. Brahmins and Kshattriyas had bred freely both from their own stock and that of the tribes. When the great rebuilding of Hindu India began, and the reforming of the castes already described, the half-bred races of Nepal in return for accepting the Brahmin and Rajput denomination, were themselves admitted into the Rajput clan tables. Independent as hill men are, freely saturated with Buddhism, they have little of a reverence for caste prejudices and distinctions, and here Buddhism and Hinduism meet as easily as already described in this period on the revival of caste. The ancient Khas race, who were the dominant semi-Aryans, once again assumed the sacred thread as Rajput or cognate races, and no doubt allied themselves to the Rahtore rule at Kanauj.

In the sixteenth century there was established at the town and in the principality of Gorakha or Goorkha,[1] a virile dynasty which gradually increased its influence over its neighbours by fierce hostilities, but it was not till 1749

[1] Which we now spell Gurkha.

that there came to the throne thereof at the age of twelve a dynamic personality of the reigning house, one Prithwi Narayan, who established the famous house of Gurkha.

At the age of seventeen, Prithwi Narayan invaded the Nepalese territory of King Jayaprakasa. Both sides had foreign mercenaries from India as well as their own troops; after a battle of great slaughter, Prithwi barely escaped with his life to his own country. That resilient personality soon recovered from his first failure, steadily increased his dominion over his neighbours and subsidiaries, and nineteen years later took Katmandu, the capital of his old opponent, Jayaprakasa. Installed at Katmandu, 55 miles from Gorakha, Prithwi defeated a large force sent by the Moslem Nawab of Murshidabad to help his friend Jayaprakasa, and 5,000 Nagas bent on a similar errand. By now his dominion was widespread in most of the Nepal basins. Prithwi Narayan died in 1775, but his dynasty continued to extend its influence, though seriously defeated in 1792 by a Chinese army which penetrated to within 25 miles of Katmandu. Definite relations with the British were now imminent for this year Lord Cornwallis, the Governor-General of India, entered into a commercial treaty with the Gurkhas, as the ruling race was now called.

The principal peoples acknowledging the sovereignty of this Rajput rule were the Mongolian tribes of Magar and Gurung, and the more Aryan tribes and races of the Khas and the Thakur.

The Gurkha Invasions of British India

The dynasty that Rajah Prithwi Narayan left behind was now master of the greater part of the habitable basins of

Nepal, and made ample use of the warlike tribes that admitted the control of the various semi-Rajput chieftains. To such regimes, new fields to conquer are as the salt of life, and the Rajah of Gurkha cast his eyes on the tracts that belonged to the lapsing territories of the Great Mogul, without realizing that a greater star than ever stood over at Delhi was rising in the East.

Regardless of the shadows of coming events the Gurkhas over-ran the hill territories to the north of Nepal, and gradually passed up to the Sutlej where they were at war with the Rajput princes in Kangra, and were even prepared to try issue with the growing power of the Sikhs. The hill districts of Kumaon and Garhwal groaned under their iron heels, as did the less virile chiefs in the Simla Hills. The chieftains who were at all likely to dispute their rule were ruthlessly exterminated, and to this day in Kumaon or Garhwal, any arbitrary action, any attempt to obtain unjust dues illicits the retort of memory "*Ho! Ho! Gurkha Raj phir agya*", "Oh-ho! the Gurkha regime is back again", and yet though it is the best part of a century and a quarter, still the bitter taste remains, a taste that might well remain in other quarters of India of similar oppressions that the British have lifted.

As political hints and remonstrances failed to produce restraint, and the Gurkha inroads into actual British India grew more provocative, culminating in an attack on and destruction of a British police force, the patience of Lord Moira, the Governor-General, who was later the Marquis of Hastings, gave out. He formally, after due warning, declared war on the Gurkha king, and started on what was to prove a long and arduous campaign—arduous because of the nature of the foe, long because of the inefficiency of the elderly commanders selected, and the inferiority of some of the Company's troops employed. The 'War with Nepal' began in 1814 and lasted till 1816, and was as serious as the wars with Tippu Sultan, and had it not been the years of the close of the Peninsular Campaign, of the War with America, of the thrills of the Hundred Days, and the victory of Waterloo, it would have attracted far more attention in Europe. The first thing to realize is that the Gurkha invasion of India proper was on a front of several hundred miles, and Gurkha forces were established with strong points from the Simla Hills (to use an entirely modern name), far down to Dehra Dun, Almora, and the road to Katmandu.

The First Assembling of the British Armies

The British campaign was very definitely an offensive one, that aimed at clearing out the invaders from all the hill tracts recently over-run, and consisted in the first stage of four definite forces, each termed a division, though varying considerably in strength, and being really forces of all arms, without any divisional organization as the term is usually understood.

The 1st Division, under Major-General Marley, was to assemble at Dinapore and seize the pass at Makwanpur as a preliminary to an advance on Katmandu (6,000 men).

The 2nd Division under Major-General Wood was to assemble at Benares and move on the Bhutwal pass, and thence advance also on Katmandu (3,500 men).

The 3rd Division under the famous Major-General Gillespie, of Vellore and Java fame, was to march from Meerut on Dehra Dun and clear Garhwal (3,500 men).

The 4th Division, under Major-General Ochterlony, was to leave the frontier station of Loodhiana on the Sutlej, where it kept watch and ward on Sikhs and Afghans, and move up the river, and operate against the Gurkhas in Belaspur and east of the Sutlej.

The supreme command was exercised from Calcutta. It is not necessary to go into the details of the fighting that occurred. The 1st and 2nd Divisions advanced to the frontier, met with some minor reverses, and footled for a year, their commanders giving the most miserable exhibition of the efficacy of aged nonentities.

The opening of the campaign was singularly inauspicious, save in the north. The 1st and 2nd Divisions both advanced due north over a hundred miles, in the early autumn of 1814. General Wood met with a slight reverse, led his force back to Bettiah and disappeared. His successor did little better, and, when the unhealthy season commenced, withdrew to cantonments.

The 2nd Division advanced over a hundred miles, and left Gorakhpur on the 13th December, reaching the foot of the Bhutwal pass on the 31st. After making reasonable plans to attack the pass in front and by turning movement, General Marley marched into an ambush and was severely handled. He now halted and proceeded to demand more guns. When a battering train arrived half-hearted attempts to advance were made, but by May '15 the division was back at Gorakhpur. Contemporary opinion was loud in condemning the feebleness of the ineffective seniority-promoted commanders, and the bad staff work.

The 3rd Division from Meerut started for the Dun heartily enough, and occupied Dehra. On October 31st a force of 2,700 men attacked the little Gurkha fort of Kalunga.[1] The small Gurkha garrison fought desperately, and the British were repulsed with heavy loss, General

[1] Kalunga is the Gurkha term for fort.

Gillespie himself being killed in leading an assault that threatened to stick. General Martindell now assumed command, a second assault was also repulsed with heavy loss, and then the remnant of the Gurkha defenders cut their way out to the number of 90, leaving their works piled high with dead and dying, including some of their women.

It is related how during the cannonade of the fort a Gurkha soldier walked out waving a handkerchief, was allowed to approach, and proved to be a man with a shattered jaw craving attention. When cured in a British hospital he returned to his own force. Indeed many are the stories of chivalrous conduct in which the Gurkhas vied with the British.

Eventually this division pressed on to the siege of the stronghold of Jaitak, overlooking the town of Nahan. It has been said that the British attack hereon, which culminated in a severe reverse, was but typical of scenes which many of us have known in modern mountain warfare. An approach by an arduous night march two days after Xmas '14, and an initial success, was followed by an impasse and a turning movement. A decision to withdraw late in the day had the result so often seen to-day on the frontier when the retreating troops were hotly pursued by the hillmen, who inflicted severe losses, totalling close on 400 men. A two months' wait which ensued, saw the arrival of a siege train, but to the surprise of the troops the bombardment was not followed by assault, although a formal siege was pressed to close quarters. Two months were devoted to bombardment only, when the garrison of 1,500 were allowed to march out with the honours of war, a thousand women and children with them.

In the north the 4th Division under Major-General Ochterlony alone told a different tale, meeting with complete success. This astute commander was concerned with the effect that any reverse might have on the Sikhs across his frontier and proceeded to advance with considerable caution. No rash advance and reverses occurred, fort after fort was carried, and by April the stronghold of Malaun was stormed, and what are now the Simla Hills occupied.

While these successes were in progress in the two northern columns, the Governor-General anxious to compensate for the follies and failures of the two southern columns, decided to strike at Kumaon which he was most anxious to rid of Gurkha domination, and from which it was known that most of the regular Gurkha troops had been withdrawn. He decided to experiment in a new direction, and authorised the celebrated Indian soldier of fortune Colonel Gardiner, with Captain Hyder Jung Hearsey to organise an irregular force from the Rohilla yeomanry and chiefs in Rohilkand, which lay between the scene of operations of two southern divisions and the operations in the north. Colonel Gardiner with 2,500 Rohillas was to advance from Kashipur up the Kosi river, and Hearsey with 1,500 from Pilibhit up the Kali, eventually to capture Almora. By March Gardiner's force augmented by more levies had driven the Gurkhas from the hill that is now known as Ranikhet, but Hearsey who had entered eastern Kumaon, after occupying Champawat close to the genuine Nepal border was attacked by the best of the Gurkha generals, by name Hadtidal, defeated and himself taken prisoner.

Lord Hastings however recognized the importance of Gardiner's success and had assembled a force under Lt.-Col. Jasper Nicholls of the 14th Foot, [1] consisting of two and a half battalions of Bengal Infantry and some European Artillery, to go to his support. By April Nicholls had joined Gardiner and taking command of the whole force of 5,000 men,

[1] Afterward General Sir Jasper Nicholls, Commander in Chief in India.

proceeded to invest Almora after several skirmishes. Surrounded, bombarded, and attacked whenever they gave a chance, by the end of April the Gurkhas surrendered at discretion, agreeing to the entire abandonment of Kumaon, and were allowed to march out with their arms. On all these occasions both here and in the north numbers of the Gurkha troops came over to the British, and from them were formed the Corps long famous by their local names, and now part of the Line of the Indian Army, whose stories will be told hereafter.

The Second Campaign, '15–16

With the successes of Ochterlony, Nicholls and Gardiner, and the operations of Martindell, the first campaign came to an end, and the Gurkha Government proposed peace. As however it was not prepared to accept the British terms, the successful and judgmatic Ochterlony was brought down to the south, there to prepare an advance with 20,000 men into the fastnesses of Nepal and threaten Katmandu.

On the 16th of February Ochterlony reached the border to find himself confronted by a stockaded position of great strength. There was little to gain by running his head against so obvious a barrier, and selecting another route he succeeded in reaching the Makwanpur pass within twenty miles of the Gurkha capital.

This was enough to convince the Gurkha Raj that their day was come and that they must make friends with the enemy at their gates. Eventually was signed the Treaty of Segowlie, by which Briton and Gurkha have become abiding friends and allies to their mutual advantage and military glory.

Many were the fruits thereof graitfying to Britain. In 1848 the Gurkhas offered help for the Second Sikh War. In 1857 the Prime Minister, Jang Bahadur, led a fine force to support Sir Colin Campbell in the capture of Lucknow, and the suppression of the rebellion that followed the Mutiny of the Bengal Army. Since 1857 they have freely allowed an increasing number of their subjects to enlist in the British Indian Army. In the Great War of 1914 not only did the Gurkha regiments in the British Service carry the Union Jack to Flanders, to Jerusalem and to Mosul, but actual Nepalese troops entered India as allies to supplement the attenuated garrisons of the North-west Frontier, depleted by withdrawals of the other theatres of war.

The Races of Nepal

The formation of the mountains of Nepal, and the ranges that spring from the massif of the Himalaya, divide the country into four upland divisions in addition to the low-lying malarious Terai that takes the drainage of the hills between Nepal and British India. The divisions are Western, Central and Eastern Nepal, and cut through the centre the separate hill-girt Nepal valley that leads to Katmandu.

A brief mention has been made of the Aryanization, of or better, the Aryan infusion among, the ancient Tartar and aboriginal folk of the mountains and of how a veneer of Hinduism has set sufficiently lightly on the tribes in the Rajputment of India described, to admit many into the warrior castes of India. The highest military caste is the Thakur to which the ruling family belong, who are an Aryan Rajput folk, and though not numerous so far as enlistment goes, make admirable soldiers. The races of Nepal are many, of which the

Thakur, the large semi-Aryan Khas race, the Magar and the Gurung are the true Gurkhas, to whom the term *Gurkhali* can be really applied, but the more aboriginal Newar, and Sunwar, and the races of Eastern Nepal, generally known by their main group names as Limbus and Rais, may nowadays be well included in the general description Gurkha. In fact it is almost impossible, for the European at any rate, to distinguish any difference in the equally Tartar appearance of Magar, Gurung, Limbo, Rai or Sunwar.

The slightly Hinduized Tartars, the Magar and Gurung tribes, have long been the most popular in the Army, chiefly perhaps because our officers were better acquainted with them, but as the demand for more Nepalese troops in India increased, the net was thrown wide, and Limbus and Rais and the Khas are held in almost equal esteem. The Limbo and Rai groups together form the Kiranti group of clans, and their country of Eastern Nepal is known as the Kiranti country. The original habitat of Magar and Gurung though now more widely spread, was the country west of the Nepal valley. They are it is said but Hindu by custom, and they certainly exhibit that close touch with Buddhism which must have been so much the case in India itself in the centuries already described when the land was returning to Hinduism. Indeed a Lama or a Brahmin is summoned indifferently to officiate at family feasts in Eastern Nepal. The Magar and Gurung women have had so much commerce with the Hindu Khas, that there are many variations of Khas breeds and mixtures.

The Magar country is nearer India than the Gurung tracts both of which are in Central Nepal, the Magars being nearer Gorakhpur, and running up into Western Nepal just above the lower country. In the centre of Western Nepal north of the Magars is an isolated Gurung colony.

The Tartar races of Nepal are short, thickset men, and in accordance with the 'rifle' spirit of the British Service smallness if combined with strength is no bar. The Nepal Army itself likes bigger men, and some of the Nepalese regiments get an average of 5ft. 9in. which is far above the height of the sturdy little tykes whom we associate with the name Gurkha. The Khas Gurkha however is a taller man, with his greater admixture of Aryan blood. Speaking generally it may be said that the bulk of the Gurkha tribes are in no great sympathy with the races of India, and in the Army would far rather associate with the European soldier than with other Indian troops. This especially dates from intimate association of the 60th Rifles and the Sirmoor Battalion, now the 2nd Gurkhas, during the siege of Delhi in 1857, a connection which has been very close ever since. But it was equally in evidence at the siege of Bhurtpur in 1826, when the 59th Foot and they were close friends.

The Gurkha Regiments To-day

The increase and development of the separate Gurkha line within the Indian Army is an interesting subject. It has already been stated that, as has so often been done by the British elsewhere, the prisoners of war in the campaign of 1814–16 eagerly enlisted into four rifle battalions specially organized to employ them. The rifle kit of the British Army was adopted for officers and to some extent for the men. These four Corps were the Malaun Battalion (now the 1st Gurkhas), the Sirmoor Battalion (now the 2nd), the Nusseree Battalion (now the 3rd) and the Kumaon Battalion (now the 4th). These battalions were all given permanent locations along the lower hills of the Himalaya, and to enable the men to settle, to bring their women and to form Gurkha colonies, these stations were peculiar and separate for each corps. The Kumaon and the Malaun Battalions were located in the Punjab Hills, the Nusseree Battalion in the Simla Hills and the Sirmoor Battalion at Dehra Dun.

The story of the Nusseree Battalion is of interest. In 1850 there was a considerable amount of sedition and indiscipline among the Bengal troops over the matter of how long the active service batta should be continued to the corps serving in the now annexed and cantoned Punjab. The Governor-General was away recruiting his health in the far south of India, and inaccessible. Sir Charles Napier, the Commander-in-Chief, proceeded to Wazirbad, then a cantonment in the Punjab and the centre of the trouble. He forthwith disbanded the whole of the 66th Bengal Native Infantry at fort Govindgarh which had been specially ill-behaved, and took into the Line the Nusseree Battalion, lock, stock and barrel. There was a terrible "*hooha*" at this very wise proceeding. The Government of India in the Military department were afraid of the Bengal sepoy, the Finance pointed out that Gurkhas drew starvation pay, and could not possibly have the rates of the Linesman. Sir Charles stood to his guns, but his action had been unnecessarily irregular, and Lord Dalhousie, instead of thanking him for a prompt action in a crisis when he himself was inaccessible, felt compelled to censure. The 66th remained Gurkha and part of the Line, survived of course the Mutiny, and were re-numbered the 9th Bengal Infantry. From this position they eventually were transferred to the Gurkha line in modern times as the 9th Gurkha Rifles. A new Nusseree battalion was raised known as the "extra" Nusseree Battalion, and was stationed at Jutogh in the Simla Hills. Just as the Mutiny broke out, it, in the throes of an eccentric pay grievance, also went through a mild form of mutiny frightening the residents of Simla into fits. It returned to its duty in a few days and did good work in keeping open the Punjab road, ultimately becoming the 1st/3rd Gurkha Rifles. The story is a rather intriguing one for those who can see the romance in the inner history of regiments.

One other of the Gurkha corps has a special interest of the past, viz., the 5th Gurkhas, which while being in the Gurkha line, has a second affinity in that it was a part of that Irregular force that was raised from the Sikh armies. For long there had been Gurkhas with the forces of Runjhit Singh, so that they came to be perpetuated where one would not expect to have found them.

The continued strain on the Indian Army as its frontier liabilities and external responsibilities increased, gradually demanded an increase in the Gurkha regiments, and the 6th and 7th of two battalions each were raised. The 42nd, 43rd and 44th, originally the Assam and Sylhet Light Infantry localized in Assam, which has a host of wild tribes on its Himalayan frontiers, always had Gurkhas and such like men in its ranks. They too were eventually brought into the Gurkha line as the 8th and 10th Gurkha Rifles. A battalion of the 10th had already been raised as the 1st Burma Rifles for service in the Shan states and this came to India to join the family. The result has been that twenty battalions of the little men in rifle green and Kilmarnock caps are cantoned often by themselves in the Himalayas, with the exception of the 7th who made arid Baluchistan their own,. They live always in the same place, save when doing some tour of frontier service and garrison. Purposely the Indian Government have allowed them to become a cult, a service apart.

They have attracted some of the very best types of British officers, who have exercised the Anglo-Saxon parish principles to the full. With rifle, bugle and highland pipe they live in their little Himalayan stations, it had almost been said "the world forgetting and by the world forgot." That however is not quite fair, for they are extremely efficient and entirely *corps d'elite.* A brigade of the little men in their rifle green or in their modern khaki is a pleasant sight to see. To dine in the officers' mess when the pipes come in and the Tartar pipe-major takes his tot of whiskey and wishes "*Slanthe*" to all, is to feel that Britain really does inspire. The rest of the Army looks on them with happy amusement and is always ready to pull the legs of the officers when they "*gurk*", to use the Army slang, too freely, and many amusing stories are cherished.

It is the pretty conceit of the British officers of Gurkha Corps to resent the term sepoy being applied to their men. They must always be "riflemen" and the Army smilingly acquiesces. Among the many stories of the kind is one of a British Gurkha officer bursting into the circle at a camp fire after a hard day's soldiering, exclaiming loudly at the inefficiency of the staff. "Look at this, did you ever see such a shame! After all the work we've done. Here's an order authorizing an issue of rum, but look at it, it says rum for British ranks, rum for Indian ranks and none for 'our little fellows'." The war services ever since those days of formation at Malaun and Almora, nearly a century and a quarter ago, have been more than distinguished and the stories of sacrifice and devotion are legion.

The twenty battalions are not the only home for Gurkha soldiers in India. The famous Guides take a company for their proficiency in the jungle, and some five thousand are taken by the military police for service on the Assam and

Burmese frontiers while the Jammu and Kashmir Army, by an old custom, as old as that of Gurkhas in the Sikh service, has one or two battalions with Gurkha companies, and at one time wholly composed of the little men.

Their soldierly qualities and simple ways endear them to those who soldier with them, and they can live up to the acme of the British cachet for smartness and turn out, while they will play happily at drilling each other for hours at a time. Their lack of interest in Brahminical holiness and in anti-British intrigue and hatred, is the despair of those subtle brains who fish in troubled waters, and who would sow discord at any price. Yet the old principle of *saepe cadendo* is always at work, and has to be watched.

The distinguished service of the Gurkhas in the World War will be referred to later.

One interesting feature of the Gurkha Corps is the problem of the 'line boy,' the boy born and bred in the lines and in the colonies. If born of a Ghurka mother he has for one generation at least most of the warlike traits of his father. Sucking in the regiment tradition he makes an extremely smart soldier. Opinion rather goes in cycles as to the wisdom of encouraging him, or of going back fresh to the Tartar matrix. The Governmental policy of encouraging Gurkha colonies near the regimental stations does to a certain extent postulate their employment. With the cuteness of the line life may also come undesirable petty villainy. They are certainly most valuable as signallers, and technicians as well as in the quarter-master's branch. Sir Charles Reid who commanded the 2nd at Delhi always said that out of the twenty-five Orders of Merit gained by the regiment twelve were gained by line boys, i.e. men brought up in the regiment, and at Aliwal and Sobraon in the Sutlej campaign five out of seven were gained by such.

In days gone by line boys were a pretty feature, in Madras and Bombay regiments. So many boys born in the lines, were enlisted as 'boys' and in the full dress of the corps were drilled and used as messengers, and eventually transferred to the ranks. But here again the question of their courage and hardness arose as compared with the wilder recruit from the land, and it is always to be remembered that the first duty of a soldier is to fight.

Chapter XI

HOW THE PUNJAB BECAME BRITISH AND THE BENGAL ARMY MUTINIED

AFTER RUNJHIT SINGH—ANARCHY IN THE PUNJAB—THE EXECUTION BY ARMY SOVIETS—THE SIKH ARMY ENTERS BRITISH INDIA—SOBRAON AND AFTER—THE SECOND SIKH WAR—THE MUTINY OF THE BENGAL ARMY.

It is now time to return to the story of the Punjab and the Sikhs and how they rushed on their fate, a fate from which the British tried hard to save them.

When the famous Tripartite Treaty was signed that brought the Afghan policy on to the stage, Runjhit Singh was failing. In his later years he had given way to extreme debauchery and the Sikh court was an astounding scene of relaxation and immorality. Despite his wives and many concubines the number of his children was small, and he had none to whom his great state could be consigned. Long before the collapse of the Afghan policy, a collapse that he was said ardently to desire, he died at Lahore at the comparatively early age of 59, shortly after the British occupation of Kandahar, and before the capture of Ghuzni and the forcing of the Khaiber by his own troops, put the seal of apparent success on the Kabul venture.

Cunningham thus sums up his career: "Runjhit Singh found the Punjab a prey to the factions of its chiefs, pressed by the Afghans and Mahrattas, and ready to submit to

British supremacy. He consolidated the numerous petty states into kingdom, he wrested from Kabul the fairest of its provinces, and he gave the potent English no cause for interference. He found the military array of his country a mass of horsemen, brave indeed, but ignorant of war as an art, and he left it mustering 50,000 disciplined soldiers, 50,000 well armed yeomanry and militia, and more than 300 cannon for the field. His rule was founded on the feelings of a people, but it involved the joint action of the necessary principles of military order and territorial extension and when a limit had been set to Sikh dominion and his own commanding genius was no more, the vital spirit of his race began to consume itself in domestic contention."

When he was Lord Auckland's host at Lahore and Amritsar his strength was gone, his utterance was difficult, and he had lost his power of speech and grasp of affairs. Before his death the three Rajput brothers from Jammu had usurped most of the functions of Government. The story of these Dogra brothers, Gulab Singh, Dhyan Singh and Suchet Singh is a strange one, and it still echoes in the troubles that have been going on in Kashmir in 1931–2. Gulab Singh commanded a large army of Rajputs from the Jammu hills and the other brothers were great at court.

It was Dhyan Singh who accompanied a litter said to contain the dying Maharajah round a great review of the troops, it was Dhyan Singh who was most assiduous in his attentions to his failing master and it was Dhyan Singh who declared the almost imbecile Kharrak Singh, the eldest son, as successor and himself as Wazir. At the cremation of the Maharajah's body there was a mighty holocaust of wives and concubines on the funeral pyre, an atrocity, which the Army insisted on, and of which the story is told with bated breath to this day, though by no means every wife, unfortunately for the country, went to the tragic pyre.

Sher Singh another reputed son urged his superior merits on the Governor-General, a striking tribute to the position now held in India by the paramount power, but the Governor-General informed the Resident that Kharrak Singh would be acknowledged. The son of Kharrak Singh, Nao Nihal Singh a lad of eighteen, showed considerable promise and was averse to the influence of the Jammu Brothers.

On November the 5th, 1840, the Maharajah Kharrak Singh died of drink, and that very same day also the young Nao Nihal Singh returning from his father's funeral pyre was killed by the falling of the gateway as he rode under. With him was also killed a son of Gulab Singh of Jammu, though the Jammu Brothers generally were held to have planned the accident. Had Nao Nihal Singh lived the whole history of the Punjab, and also of Afghanistan, might have been very different.

Anarchy in the Punjab

A period of astounding anarchy and drama was now to ensue. The good-natured voluptuary and putative son of Runjhit Singh, Shere Singh appeared to the British to be the only possibly successor to the Sikh throne and he duly received their support. The situation was complicated by Mai Chand Kaur, the widow of Kharrak Singh, declaring that Nao Nihal Singh's widow was pregnant and that she would act as regent till the happy event should have taken place. Most of the army supported Shere Singh, who besieged Lahore. Eventually the Mai though treated with dignity and generosity was ousted and Shere Singh prevailed, but he could not control his army, which now proceeded to expel Runjhit Singh's European officers, one of the best an Englishman, being cruelly murdered. The Army thought it had many grievances and created astounding disturbances. The Sikh Governor of Kashmir was killed, old General Avitabile at Peshawur even contemplated flight to Afghanistan, and the merchants clamoured for British protection. All this time parties of British were moving backwards and forwards between the Sutlej and Kabul, through Sikh territory but avoiding the disturbed capital. Early in 1842 the Governor-General and a large British force assembled at Ferozepore to meet and support the British troops returning from Afghanistan, and this being over, Shere Singh had the Punjab to himself and a rough ride he found it. In June 1842 the Mai had been slippered to death by her own women and popular belief attributed responsibility for the deed to the Maharajah. This was but a prelude to an orgy of murders in which the Army factions and Sikh leaders had their parts.

Sirdar Ajeet Singh of the powerful Sindan-wallah family was now the Maharajah's boon companion, and in September '43, having persuaded Shere Singh to inspect some levies shot him while doing so, at the same time Sirdar Lehna Singh of the same family shot Shere Singh's son Pertab Singh. They then joined the Wazir Dhyan Singh, the Jammu chief, and proceeded together to place a new king on the throne. But Dhyan Singh's time had now come, for Ajeet Singh separating him from his friends shot him too. They however neglected to kill Hari Singh the Wazir's son, while the Army, which was prepared for the death of the Maharajah, was not so for that of Dhyan Singh. This meant that the murderers were not to escape justice for Hira Singh called on the troops to avenge his father's death, whereon they entered the citadel and put to death in their turn both Ajeet and Lehna Singh.

Then it was that the little Dhulip Singh the son of the concubine the Rani Jindan, whom as has been said, Runjhit Singh's vanity had admitted as his begotten son, was declared Maharajah and Hira Singh inducted to that high, and in this disturbed and headstrong capital usually fatal, office of Wazir. For the moment the young chief was all powerful, and the estates of the assassin chiefs were escheated and their dwellings destroyed. Two other sirdars said to have been concerned in the murders were also put to death.

Hira Singh wise in his generation, raised the pay of the soldiery by two and a half rupees a month and remained on the crest of the wave of army favour. His period of office was stormy, for other illegitimate sons of Runjhit Singh, Kashmira and Peshawara Singh, raised rebellions. Further the third of the Jammu brothers Rajah Suchet Singh now marched on Lahore jealous of the power in his nephew's hands, and in the belief that he too was an army favourite. He had, however miscalculated, for in March '44 he was attacked on approaching Lahore and after defending himself in a ruined building was also slain. Attar Singh the last of the Sindan-wallah family with the young Kashmira Singh, was also killed shortly after and Peshawara Singh fled across the British border. Hira Singh's time to fall from his giddy pinnacle was also approaching. He was not a man of very great parts and was largely prompted by his confidant the Pundit, Julla, a Kashmiri Brahmin, while an intriguer for the Wazirship was at hand in the person of one Jowahir Singh, brother to the Rani Jindan, and uncle of the little Maharajah. Hira Singh and the Pundit seeing that their reign of power was over, on December

21st, 1844, fled towards Jammu, were pursued by the army, and put to death.

The Execution by Army Soviets

While this orgy of strife and murder was tearing the kingdom of Runjhit Singh to pieces, the Sikh Army was becoming more and more the master of the situation. There had arisen the most complete Soviet system within the army whereby each regiment was dominated by its elected '*punch*', or council of five. The officers of the corps carried on their duties by sufferance of the *punches* which were supreme and controlled everything but the daily military routine. The *punches* or *punchayats* met in general assembly to decide the line of action to be followed by the Army as a whole.

Meanwhile the able governor of the Multan province was murdered for some trivial reason, and Peshawara Singh having left British territory was in rebellion at Sialkot. Captured, however, in the fort there Jowahir Singh, the new Wazir, put him to death too. But as Peshawara was a child of the old Maharajah, this act annoyed the Army, who summoned the Wazir to appear before them. This summons Jowahir Singh who had often contemplated flight to the English with the Maharajah was obliged to obey. The *punchayats* had decided on his death, and though on September 21st, 1845, the Wazir in his apprehension appeared before the troops assembled on the Plain of Mian Mir, seated on an elephant with a bodyguard, the infant Maharajah and much treasure at his side, it served him in no stead. As his elephant slowly approached the centre of the parade, the wretched Wazir proceeded to address the Army, making lavish promises of gifts to all the leaders. He was sternly bade to be silent, and to give up the child, who was removed to a tent hard by. A party of soldiers then advanced and shot him seated on his howdah.

He was burned on a funeral pyre that evening, on which the exultant ferocious soldiery insisted that his wives and concubines should burn in *Suttee* with him, probably the last of those terrible sacrifices to be made in public in India. This last scene of horror, the finale of the orgy of murders, accompanied through the years by the complete abandonment of all sense of morals and decency, hurried Sikhdom to its doom.

It is to be remembered that all this occurred in quite recent times, during the reign of Queen Victoria, and is perhaps typical of the disorder in which an uncontrolled Indian state can project itself.

There was now, naturally enough, some lack of candidates for the Wazirship, the Rani Jindan and the Army punchayats carrying on alone. By November, however, the Rani caused her paramour Rajah Lal Singh to be elected Wazir, and Sirdar Tej Singh was confirmed as Commander-in-Chief. The first thing needful, however, if their power and position were to remain, was obvious enough. The Army must be brought to its senses and the only people who could do that were the serried ranks of the great neighbouring power paramount.

The Sikh Army Enters British India

The Sikh Army therefore, stirred by the leaders of the Khalsa to its undoing, was encouraged to spend itself as the lesser evil, against the bayonets of the British, and it was not averse to the suggestion. For some time the British authorities had been aware that some such inroad might take place.

Unfortunately, the retrenchments after the Afghan Wars of three years earlier, had left the British Indian Army entirely bare of any transport. The force could only be moved and fed by means of such unorganized civil transport, officially known as 'carriage' as the civil authorities and contractors could get together. When in December 1845 the Sikh Troops poured across the Sutlej, the army itself under Sir Hugh Gough, was expecting the event, but was without the needed 'carriage'. Nevertheless it hurried up to the north as best it could, where, on the banks of that river the British cantonment of Ferozepore with a force of all arms was in some danger. The first collision took place between 16,000 British-Indian troops, and 30,000 Sikhs. It was an encounter battle, the British forces being at rest and cooking at Mudki after a long approach march. The men sprang to arms in their bivouacs, formed a front and attacked the Sikh Army, achieving victory but with heavy losses, the Commander-in-Chief, Sir Hugh Gough, being in command, accompanied by the Governor-General Sir Henry Hardinge. Seventeen Sikh guns were left on the field and the British pushed on towards Ferozepore, only to find larger Sikh forces entrenched athwart their line of advance. Then occurred the hard fought two days' battle of Ferozeshah in which the combined force of the Commander-in-Chief and Sir John Littler from Ferozepore during a night of great anxiety amid terrible scenes of carnage, stood their ground. In the morning the Sikhs were driven off and their whole camp captured, but the British losses were enormous, largely owing to the very light metal of the British guns which alone it had been possible to bring up. Sir Hugh Gough advanced his army to the vicinity of Ferozepore, and then waited for a far heavier artillery which had been summoned. Until it arrived he did not feel competent to attack the very heavy park with the Sikh forces, who served their guns with both skill and determination. Their gunners, it was said, always fought with a bottle of fiery spirit lashed to their waists, and invariably died at their posts by the guns.

The Sikhs had retired across the Sutlej to refit, but appeared again on the south side towards the end of January 1846, and made for Ludhiana, but were defeated at Aliwal by a detachment of the British army under Sir Harry Smith. Driven across once more they then made for the fords and islands of the Sobraon, or the two Sobras, crossed in force close to Ferozepore and entrenched themselves within heavy earthworks with much artillery. On February 10th, the re-united British forces, whose heavy artillery and trains of ammunition had arrived, proceeded to attack, and after the most desperate bayonet encounter captured the trenches and their cannon, and drove the Sikhs into the river, smashing with their artillery fire the bridge of boats crowded with fugitives.

That was the end of it and a few days later the British Army entered the capital of Lahore, there to dictate the terms. Part of the Punjab known as the Jullundur Doab was annexed, Kashmir and Jammu were detached, but the main Punjab kingdom was to remain governed during the minority of the little Dhulip Singh by a Council of State of which the British Resident at their court, Sir Henry Lawrence, was to be the guiding spirit. It was a very generous attempt to preserve the Sikh kingdom and it only failed of the direct volition of the Sikhs themselves. Sir Henry was able to borrow to assist the Sikh Durbar in the matter of reconstruction the most remarkable galaxy of young enthusiastic officers that probably has ever been got together for one purpose. By them the Sikh revenues and administration were in process of regeneration, when the silver cord was loosed.

The Second Sikh War

The Sikh people or rather the Sikh military classes and old army Soviets were not content to let well alone. Under the beneficent guidance of Sir Henry Lawrence, the best friend ever a race had, the Durbar and its officials were being taught a system of government that Runjhit Singh had quite failed to inaugurate.

Here and there in the districts, Englishmen were training Punjabis in revenue and police work that would endure. The Punjab for generations had been shattered by Afghan invasions, and the rebuilding was no easy matter. In the spring of 1846 the young Prince Dhulip Singh had been replaced on his throne, without the fear of the overbearing mutinous Army. Sobraon had broken that spirit, but there was still a large portion of the Army who had not been through that wholesome if terrible chastening. The Army spirit was not prepared to go back from the astounding position it had arrogated to itself, and it was once more to try its fortune. The trouble began in this way. Two years after the settlement, one Mool Raj, Diwan or Governor of the province of Multan, had been called on by his own Government on the advice of Sir George Clerk,[1] early in 1848, to submit his administration and revenue accounts. Mool Raj rather than do this, asked to be relieved of his appointment. A new governor was appointed and proceeded to Multan accompanied by a Gurkha battalion of the Sikh Army. With him were Mr. Vans Agnew as adviser on behalf of the Durbar and British Resident, and Lieutenant Anderson who accompanied the troops. Mool Raj who had never expected to be taken at his word, after making a show of

[1] Then acting for Sir Henry Lawrence who was on sick leave.

meeting his successor caused the British officers to be attacked in the streets, and when wounded surrounded and destroyed in the Eedgah garden where they were encamped. Mool Raj then joined by any Sikh troops and local sirdars, resumed charge of his province, occupied the fort of Multan and declared himself in rebellion against all and sundry. It was a distinct challenge to his own Government but still more to the British power behind it. The actual murder of the two British officers was an entirely unnecessary act which put him out of court.[1]

At Lahore was a British brigade under Brigadier Wish. But the hot season had set in, Multan was several hundred miles distant, and the British authorities hesitated to take prompt action. It was for the Durbar with its own troops to set about the tackling of their own rebel. We need not follow the many recriminations which accompany the criticism of the British action. What that Government wished to avoid was another Sikh War. The Sikhs should, if possible, bring their own folk into line. However that might have been, one of the most distinguished of the young soldier-civilians with Sir Henry's staff, one Herbert Edwardes, was on that part of the frontier known as the Derajat across the Indus from Multan. He immediately moved on Multan with a number of tribal levies who had summoned from the *Daman-i-koh*, the skirts of the frontier mountains, under certain famous chiefs men of the frontier marches—Babers, Gandapurs, Khatti Kels and the Sadozai and Alisherzai settlers from Afghanistan—and with them some Sikh troops under Colonel Cortland, an officer in the Sikh Service.

Inspired by the energy and commanding character of the young Edwardes, these hastily gathered and ill-trained

[1] How far he planned these murders, or how far his followers got out of hand, is a moot point.

troops with a few cranky old cannon fought two pitched battles with the rebel Sikhs, who endeavoured to bar his advance on Multan, and who were joined by more Sikh troops for the second. The engagements, and they were almost battles, of Kineyree and Sadosam, were fought in the extreme heat of the early Multan summer, and were complete victories. Thus inspired, Edwardes announced that given the engineer officer Major Napier he would take Multan. As a matter of fact a Lieutenant Lake was leading the troops of the Bahawalpur State to his support, from further down the rivers and with these Edwardes actually advanced to Multan, the strongest fortress in Northern India. Seeing that Edwardes had taken so brilliant a part, the British Government had decided late in August, despite the hot season, to send the brigade from Lahore under Brigadier Wish and ordered General Shere Singh commanding a large force of Sikhs also to move on the rebel city, which was now surrounded. In the meantime the delay in moving British troops had had its inevitable result. Chatter Singh, the father of Shere Singh, had brought out against the British, all the Sikh troops on the Afghan frontier in Hazara and at Pindi, and Shere Singh marched off from the siege of Multan to join him. The British were now faced with another Sikh War to fight. Wish was ordered to withdraw from the active siege till he could be reinforced from Sind, while Sir Hugh Gough took the field and began to collect an army at Lahore, the Sikh armies assembling on the far bank of the Chinab.

We need not follow the campaign closely—its famous soldier's battle of Chillianwallah and the 'crowning mercy of Goojerat' are still household words. Indeed at the time of writing[1] there has just died in the west of England troop-

[1] March, 1932.

sergeant-major John Stratford, aged 104, who was with his regiment at both those battles including the rather disastrous affair of Ramnagar on the banks of the Chinab. Chillianwallah was fought late in a winter's afternoon of January 1849, an encounter battle, when the British settling down for the night at the village of Chillianwallah were fired on by Sikh guns in the heavy scrub hard by. The Chief, whose cavalry had evidently done little to probe the fog of war, ordered an attack, lest his camp be bombarded all night. A desperate hand-to-hand battle ensued. The Sikhs were drawn up in line in a country thick with thorn bush. They were beaten by the European troops for the most part, the bulk of the Bengal troops showing no great zest. But the guns captured could not be secured, the Chief would not bivouac on the field, and many of the British wounded were left out to be slaughtered and cruelly mutilated. One little British drummer-boy was taken and slain, and the wounded often stripped, and while alive drawn backwards and forwards through a thorn bush.

Next morning the battle-field was cleared up, but the Sikhs had re-possessed themselves in the night of several of the guns they had lost. The armies now sat down to watch each other, and Lord Gough to wait for the Bengal and Bombay troops who had just taken Multan.

The battle had been fought close to where Alexander had beaten King Porus as already related. Ere long the Sikhs suddenly broke away from the front of Lord Gough and made for the Chinab in the hope probably of getting more into touch with the actual Sikh country which lay to the south-east. Gough followed and there was fought the comparatively easily won and well fought battle of Goojerat, in full view of the magnificent wall of snow that separates Jammu from Kashmir. Lord Gough had now, as at Sobraon, got his heavy guns up and had something more suitable to meet the heavy Sikh guns than his ubiquitous horse artillery and his light field batteries.

Two incidents here are worth mentioning. One, the surrender of the whole Sikh army a few days later, throwing down their arms in heaps before the British line, and then receiving a rupee and a blanket to go home with, a treatment that produced the enthusiastic content with their conquerors which still lasts. When the war had begun Lord Dalhousie, the recently arrived Governor-General, had said in Calcutta as he left for Lahore:

"Unwarned by precedent, uninfluenced by example, the Sikh nation has called for war, and on my word, Sir, they shall have it with a vengeance."

And have it they did, to this last spectacular scene of surrender, when the undaunted Sikh and Moslems of the Sikh Army threw down their weapons, before the long scarlet line that presented arms to them, salaamed to the Commander-in-Chief, and stalked off the field sadder and wiser, beaten but not disgraced.[1]

As for the Bengal sepoy he did not cover himself with renown. In fact he had not the 'guts' sufficient to fight the Sikh. Some of the battalions did well under brilliant leading, the bulk were not so fortunate. It has been said with some force that perhaps the downing of the last Indian kingdom and one with some trace of Hinduism was not to their liking. That may be. Lord Hardinge who went through the First Sikh War with the army said that the sepoy seemed to him to be like the Portuguese whom the British had re-organized in the Peninsular War, and to have their good and their bad days. Some days they would fight, others they would not. One has heard the same said of *Jean Baptiste* in the Great

[1] This scene is depicted on the reverse of the medal for the Punjab campaign.

War. But whatever it was they did undoubtedly form the bulk of the line that beat the Sikhs,[1] and so it was.

The other incident was the pursuit of the Afghans to the frontier, when hard-riding Sir Walter Gilbert led the mounted troops and the horse artillery hell-for-leather up the Punjab, after a contingent of 5,000 Afghans under Sirdar Akram Khan,[2] who had come of all things to help the Sikhs, and who were present at Goojerat. Sir Walter just missed them at Attock, where they fired the bridge of boats as he came up—but he crossed and hustled them 'like dogs' as the Sikhs said, through the Khaiber. It is an incident long forgotten and yet troop-sergeant-major Stratford aforesaid had taken part in it, in 1849, and had lived to remember it and let us hope rejoice, till the year of Our Lord 1932, ere there came to him from Sergeant Death the order, as the old song has it, 'Pile your arms! Pile your arms! Pile your arms!' It is a matter of history that the British public were as frightened at the garbled accounts of Chillianwallah as they were with the foolish statements about Jutland. The Indian Empire had however, been shaken, and the Duke of Wellington appealed to 'old Fagin' otherwise Sir Charles Napier to go out. "If you don't, I must," he said. In the meantime Sir Hugh had won Goojerat in fine style and the war was over when Napier arrived.[3]

[1] Curiously enough I came across an interesting side-light recently. I had mentioned to Sir Michael O'Dwyer that the Indian Regiments of the company's Army had nominally twenty-four British officers, and though many of the seniors would be away there was always a host of young officers doing training who would go into the field. "Ah" said he, "that explains what has always puzzled me. I once asked an old Sikh who had been in the Sikh War, how it was the Hindustani troops beat the trained Sikhs. 'Sahib' he said, 'It was the *chota sahibs*, the young officers.' I never quite followed that, now I see." There were lots of daring boys with the Bengal regiments who led and insisted. There is something romantic about these 'Chota sahibs,' the boys just from school and college, and in those days they went out at 16.

[2] Son of the Amir Dost Muhammad.

[3] Then a curious incident happened, long forgotten, which I give because it will interest those who know Simla intensely. The hot season was in full

Lord Dalhousie now annexed the Punjab, for there was no alternative, so the red line moved up to the Afghan foothills practically to where it now lies.

Hardly had the Sikhs and Muhammadan soldiery left the Sikh ranks when they hurried to enlist in the British Army. Cavalry, infantry, and artillery were to be raised at once for the defence of the frontier, the Bengal Army was to take a percentage in every unit and military police were required on all sides. The Sikh and the *Chota Sahib* were now to become fast friends—the men who had lashed themselves to their guns and who fought with spirit bottles tied to their wrists—the men who had stood up fair to the bayonets of the British battalions the thousand marching as one, and who let the round shot from the British guns crash through their ranks. Now with the hilts of their swords presented to their conquerors, they were going to serve them better than ever they had served themselves or the Mogul.

How they flocked from every village eight years later, Sikhs and Moslem and how they filled the ranks of countless new corps when the Bengal Army mutined eight years later, is a story now to be shortly told.

The Mutiny of the Bengal Army

We have now passed through the scenes of history, and spun the reel of the cinema rapidly to get a glimpse at the past that alone controls the present, and must always remain with us, as inseparable a man's shadow. And we have come into that decade which saw the greatest of all tragedies, the

blast when Sir Charles arrived, and took over command at Simla. It was too hot to let old Lord Gough and Lady Gough wander down through the heat by *dak gharry* to Calcutta, so they stayed on at Simla as guests of the Viceroy for several months, a rather embarrassing situation.

Mutiny of the mass, almost the whole, of the units of that great Bengal Army which had served the Crown and the Company so faithfully, and which enjoyed the affection and confidence of the British officers and their families as much as and in some respects even more than is the case to-day.

For reasons many, and none of them effective, the somewhat pampered Bengal Army in which caste had been allowed to become a tyrant, mutinied and often massacred its officers and Europeans generally, with every sort of painful atrocity. In this work they were more than seconded by the disreputable portion of the population, but rarely by the reputable. Where there were no troops, there was seldom rebellion. The mass of the country side hastened to give 'the masters' their support, as soon as it was realized that they were masters of themselves and worthy of support. The same phenomenon is before us now when the Viceroy and the National Government have called the Congress bluff and pricked the Ghandi bubble. The mass of the country side and all that spells commonsense and good feeling at once rallied.

In 1857 most remarkable was the response of the Punjab which was largely garrisoned by the Bengal Line, as supercilious and arrogant towards the Sikhs as it was in itself inefficient as a fighting machine. The Sikh and Punjabis generally owed many a grudge to the mercenaries of Hindustan who had monopolized the glorious military service of the Crown (for the Crown and the Company were in reality identical at bottom). The actual Sikh soldiers recently enlisted into the Bengal Line were segregated from the rest in the disarmed regiments, and if they had been carried away in those corps that had mutinied were encouraged to return. As more and more irregular corps were required, more and more did the men of the Punjab flock to the British colours. On the frontier itself the prestige of our disarming the Bengal regiments and blowing mutineers from the guns, brought the men of the border, eager to serve men who could be men, and incidentally offered a rebel Delhi to capture and perhaps loot. Regiment after regiment both the permanent corps of the Frontier Irregular Force and the new corps, poured down to the storming of Delhi and to the capture of Lucknow. In fact the Mutiny of the Hindustani troops was largely suppressed by the Punjabi soldiery, and when the reconstruction came, no longer was the old soldier class of Hindustan to predominate. The monopoly was broken and the job was to go largely to the Punjabi and the Gurkha.

And so it has remained to this day, and as the years have passed a large portion of the corps of the old Coast Army have also given their colours with the honours gained under Clive and Coote, to the custody of the Punjabi. To what actual extent, and to which of the races of the Punjab, will be explained later.

Despite the horrors done by the mutineers, there were a considerable number of faithful and self sacrificing men of the old Army. Almost every corps went, the plotters had seen to that, but there was a modicum that did not go. The great instance is of course, the number of the men of the regiments of the Lucknow garrison who stayed with the British and took part in the defence of the Residency, later gathered into a new corps known as The Regiment of Lucknow. It is not too much to say that had there been more Henry Lawrence's and more defensible centres there would have been far more rallying of the loyal who were carried away by the storm.

However, that may be, suffice it now to say that the Sikh, the Dogra, the Punjabi Moslem and the Pathan hurried to bury their swords in the carcases of the 'Dogs of Hind'.

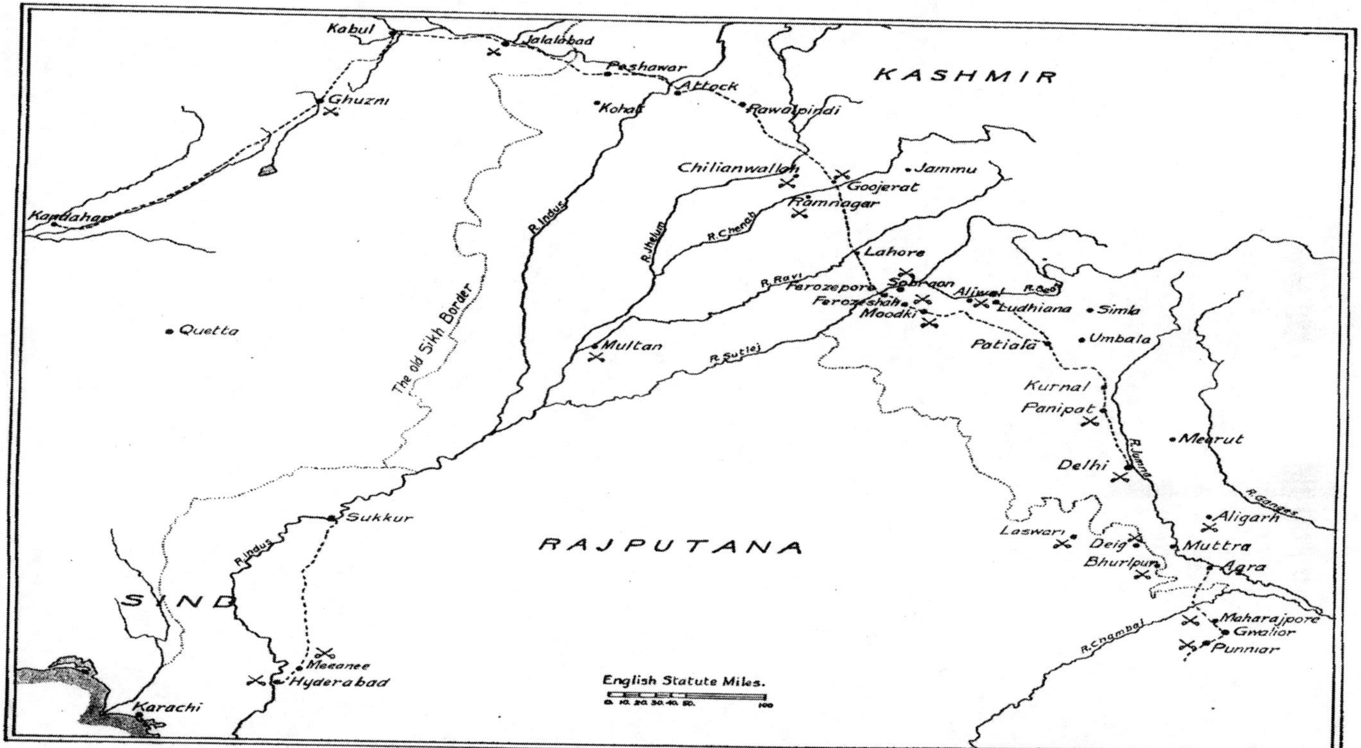

SKETCH MAP OF NORTHERN INDIA TO ILLUSTRATE THE CAMPAIGNS OF LORD LAKE, LORD GOUGH AND SIR CHARLES NAPIER

[Face page 218

Further to these reasons we may add the fact that the Punjab being full of picked young administrators selected by merit alone, of whom many were soldiers, there was energy and determination everywhere. The young men in the disarmed regiments, especially those of character were selected to organize the new levies, and a brilliant job most of them made of it.

Not only was a considerable cadre of artillerymen found from the old cannoniers of the Khalsa, sent south also but the great discovery of the *Muzbi* was made, those sweeper castes allowed into Sikhism, who were made into impromptu pioneers for the siege of Delhi. They have continued to serve in three regular pioneer corps ever since,[1] so much so that the World War saw the title 'Royal' bestowed on one of them. Thus did the tragedy of 1857 open up a much fuller knowledge of the worth of the martial classes of the Punjab.

[1] Alas, since writing, selected for disbandment in view of changed conditions.

Chapter XII

THE INDIAN ARMY, 1860–1914

THE REFORMING OF THE INDIAN ARMY—THE MODERN COMPONENTS—THE FRONTIER AND AFGHANISTAN—THE LONG WARS OF THE 'NINETIES—THE ARMY OF LORD KITCHENER—THE ARMY OF THE GREAT WAR—THE ARMY INDIANIZATION PROBLEM BEFORE THE WAR—THE SOLDIERS OF THE INDIAN STATES.

The Reforming of the Indian Army

Before turning to the picture of the martial races as we know them now, it will help us to interpret the conditions of to-day, if we glance at the forcing house where the cultivations are specially studied viz. the Indian Army in its modern evolution, from the end of the Mutiny to the strain of the World War. It is in the Army that the better traditions of the virile villages are maintained, and that the foundations of good citizenship are laid.

The Mutiny ended the old system of a regular Indian Army, Infantry, Cavalry and Artillery, dressed and clothed like the pre-Crimean Army of Great Britain and modelled generally on the Queen's Service so far as exteriors went, but a brotherhood in itself worshipping the ways of caste and somewhat dead to the ways of war and the habits of efficiency. Further the old hereditary infantry class, who had so long, like the cat, served the house rather than the master, had destroyed its own career. No longer were the Rajputs of Oudh and the Brahmin farmers to have a comparative monopoly in the ranks of the Bengal Army. The Bombay and the Coast Army had remained faithful to them and the races who had come down from the north to destroy their old enemies the Hindustani, were to succeed to the mantle and to pride of place. Many grieved that it should be so, or rather grieved that a people who had so long served the Crown, even if the Crown was in commission, should have so torn the old bonds of comradeship and fidelity and even affection.

However, military opinion was quite made up. The Regular System was to go. The irregular system had stood the shock better than the 'Regular', the old Indian sirdars had brilliantly led their men against the mutineers, therefore in future there should be few British officers in a corps, above all the Punjabi the frontiersman and the staunch Gurkha should have a much larger place in the ranks.

That was all very well, but as time rolled on two things happened in the last half of the nineteenth century. First the problem of war altered. The tribesmen of the frontier as met in the great uprising about Ambeyla in 1863, proved that the Indian soldier must be of the very pick of the races if he was to face the new foes. The Second Afghan War still further emphasized this fact. Further the appearance of Russia on what was virtually the frontiers of India, again impressed on all the lessons of Ambeyla and Kabul. The best of the races were needed in the ranks and more British officers to get the men to face their foes.

From this resulted a far more careful study of the races of the North and those of South and West who could supply any lads of grit and courage. In the early days on the frontier a few clans and groups in the Punjab easily furnished the quotas required, the views of Commanding Officers were conservative; why search far afield when your regimental connection found you enough good stuff for your purpose? The march of the generations soon showed also that the *Pax Britannica* had undermined the old martial spirit in the southern races.

What passed for natural courage had been little more than a spirit of self-defence born of fierce necessity. With two generations of kindly British cotton-wool, it was going or had gone, and as the enemies at the gates grew more formidable, so the men grew less effective for their purpose, drill they never so neatly.

From this knowledge a great study of the subject came to be made, of how to preserve and extend the Indian Army so that it should serve its purpose for protecting India, and how to group the well known martial races so as to get the best effect from them. It was generally found that grouping the races by companies, produced magnificent rivalry, while the skirmishing and mountaineering qualities of the frontierman stimulated and were also balanced by the solid fighting power of the less imaginative Sikh, and so forth.

A good many methods had to be tried before finality of grouping was arrived at, and then the casualties of the Great War, and the problem of maintaining regiments at establishment in the face of constant losses, still further affected the manner of grouping, so as to make drafts more easily absorbable in war-shattered cadres.

The Modern Components

This outline of the reconstruction that followed on the tragedy of '57, brings us now to the hard practical facts of to-day, and the composition of the force that maintains India from her troubles both within and without, backed be it always remembered by some 65,000 British troops, and backed be it also said in mutual confidence and camaraderie. In studying the changing conditions of India's military problem, it should be noticed that the coming of the change at a period marked by the Mutiny was but incidental. The change and advance of all methods of transportation and engineering that was opening up in the last century happened to be taking place about this time.

In the account which has been given of the forging of the Indian races as we know them to-day, the making of Rajputdom has been dwelt on at some length, and it has been shown that under various guises and names the martial races almost without exception, come from some branch or derivative of the great peoples of Northern India who we know as Rajputs and Jats.

With the reconstruction which gave to the Punjabi, the military birthright hitherto accorded to the Hindustani, the classes from whom the new Bengal Army was to be drawn were:—

(1) Tribesmen from the N.W. Frontier both within and without the border.

(2) The cultivating classes from the Punjab Plain, viz.,
Sikhs.
Muhammadans.
Hindu Rajputs from the Punjab Hills known as Dogras.

(3) Certain of the classes of Hindustan as listened in the old army but to a far lesser extent.

(4) Men of Nepal and the adjoining hills, viz.,
Gurkhas, Garhwalis, Kumaonis.

(5) The Madras and Bombay Armies as before, the former with its Tamil and Telegu peasantry, its Pariah classes and Christians, and the Moslem descendants of Afghan, Turk and Arab settlers. The latter with its Mahrattas, and Dekhani Moslems of descent similar to those in Madras.

Very soon after the Army had been re-grouped, the series of wars just referred to began, which showed how sadly the older races had lost their fighting power and how much more formidable were the new foes and the modern armaments. This experience resulted in regiments being steadily re-constituted with men of Northern races. The campaigns in Burma resulted in many Madras regiments being converted to Punjabi, and this process once begun has continued ever since till now the Madras element has practically gone.

The Frontier and Afghanistan

The Loom of the Bear that had been growing more oppressive since Napoleon and the Tsar Alexander had first planned their joint partition of Asia and India, had greatly increased in the thirty years that followed the Mutiny. It compelled the British to go to Kabul once again to stabilize the Afghan kingdom, and it produced the serious war-scared mobilization that followed the incident between Russians and Afghans at Panideh in 1885. It compelled the Indian and Imperial Governments to undertake a serious strategical study of the North-west Frontier under modern conditions, and confirmed them in the resolution to control the trade routes and approaches between Afghanistan and incidentally Central Asia and India, a control long demanded by traders. It also induced them to make a large fortified camp and position on the uplands of Baluchistan in a climate in which British Indian troops could fight at all times of the year, and it eventually entailed far greater expenditure on frontier roads and railways. It still further emphasized the need for only Indian soldiers of the most reliable races being enlisted in the army, in fact that the Indian tax-payer should have the best result possible for his money.

This meant a prolonged and continued elimination of the softer races of the southern and eastern provinces.

The Long Wars of the 'Nineties

The decision to get a belated control of all the great trade routes that led to India, in the country admittedly within our sphere, could but lead to trouble. With it very properly, went the policy of closing the passes from the Pamirs that were being used by filibustering or exploring parties of Cossacks, and of preventing the Amir of Kabul from over-running small states between Chitral and India or Chitral and Gilgit, which owned the suzerainty of Kashmir. These policies involved the Indian Government in a series of frontier expeditions into the Black Mountain, into the Kurram and Samana, in the Hunza campaign, in the Mahsud-Waziri expedition and the like. The preservation of law and order, and the protection of caravans that were formerly liable to raid and blackmail, exasperated most of the tribes, and when in 1897 the success of Turk over Greek had been magnified and blazoned by the mullahs, and the drum ecclesiastic had rolled and boomed along the frontier hills, that finished it! A great uprising along several hundreds of miles of frontier took place which kept some 70,000 troops busy for eight or nine months of '97–98, and produced many scenes of hard fighting, in which, however, gallantry and devotion were more marked on the part of the troops than of the tribesmen. The attack, however, of the Yusufzai tribes on the British garrison and relieving columns on the Malakand and in Swat in the summer of '97 was characterized by a reckless valour on the part of the swordsmen the *shahids* or 'witnesses' to the faith, that evoked the admiration of those who beat them back with volley, and lance and bayonet. The most remarkable acts of reckless self-sacrifice were those that occurred when the clansmen tried to storm the small British garrison of Chakdara in the Swat Valley and nearly succeeded in doing so. But their valour was largely due to the belief in their mullah's assurances that 'they were immune, that no bullet of the unbeliever could touch those who believed, and when they saw men fall by their side it could only be, because he was a doubter! So with the loud cries in Arabic, *God is Great! Glory for all and Heaven for those who bleed!* the mad 'witnesses' hurled themselves against the loopholed, sandbagged walls and withered beneath the steady Martini volleys from the staunch Punjabi troops inside, in efforts that just were not successful.

There was another astounding attack of courageous fanatics on the frontier in 1888, a story which itself had origin in specially weird and romantic facts. Long before the British came to the frontier, one of the Pindari leaders driven from Central India succeeded in establishing himself in the Frontier hills overlooking the Indus, at a place known as Sitana, and there collecting to himself a group of fierce Moslem fanatics from India, men who would be a thorn in the side of any Government. Bitter was their feud with

An Afridi

An Old Mahsud Waziri

A Shinwari Khassadar

Martial Races on the North-West Frontier

the Sikhs when the latter held the Peshawur valley, bitter were their struggles with the British when opportunities offered. Wahabi fanatics who had made Patna too warm for them, slipped away to join this nest. After the Mutiny, Moslem irreconcilables and wolfs'-heads took refuge among them. In 1863 they had joined the tribes of Yusufzai in their great rising, and indeed it was partly to exterminate the venomous nest that the British had crossed the border that year at all.

In 1888 on the hither side of the Indus, certain Pathan tribes who in comparatively recent years have colonised the Black Mountain or *Kala Taka* in Hazara, and who had constantly been in trouble through raiding into British territory, were again 'for it'. It pleased the 'Hindustani Fanatics' as the nest at Sitana was called, to cross the Indus and assist the men of the Black Mountain. This assistance took the form of a fierce attack of swordsmen on a column consisting of the 18th Royal Irish and the 29th Punjabis. The bulk of the attack fell on the 18th who, steady as a rock, stood up in line to the rush which had come out of a hidden ravine. It was as with the Dervishes at Omdurman, the rush of the fierce, grim, fanatical faces with skull cap on top, and long blades in the hands. But discipline was too much for wild hate even when calling on Allah! and it saved a world of trouble.

The fanatics to the number of several hundred were annihilated, and nothing could have been more fortunate for the peace of the border. "*Yah Allah! Yah Allah!*" yelled the skull caps, *rub-a-dub, rub-a-dub* on the tribal drum, *rip-p-p, rip-p-p*, from the 18th, and "God Bless ould Ireland" when it was over. The Wahabis lay blowing froth bubbles from lungs that were perforated, hacking fiercely at any one who would tend them. The end of such can only be the bayonet, but pity may go out for human folks so possessed. It is the strange power that Islam works over untutored minds, the minds that have the ignorance and impertinence to call Christian folk '*Kafirs*'.

The Wahabi spirit, which is ultra austere and orthodox flourishes, as we have seen during the last few years, as fiercely in the potholes of Southern Arabia as ever it did, and by its fierce iconoclast enthusiasms is always a danger to a go-easy world. This fanatical settlement across the frontier which almost exterminated itself on the bayonets of the Royal Irish in 1888, is always being recruited from the bitter souls that the more introspective form of Islam throws up. The super-simple life with day-long contemplation of the Almighty is their creed and intolerance their practice—cleft of lip and knit of brow is the Wahabi fanatic and the infidel and the luxury lover are his abhorrence. Lyall, as usual, sums up to the life the type which we can admire, despite the application of Shakespeare's saying that 'stone dead hath no fellow'. The earnest Wahabi addresses his fellow Moslems:

> "Your brains are dull with eating and
> your hearts are choked with lust
> And your seat is loose in saddle, and your
> scimitars are rust.
>
> . . . . .
>
> When ye shun the Hindu festivals, the
> tinkling of the bell
> The dancing, the idolatries, the harlotry
> of hell,
> When ye kneel to God in penitence and
> cringe no more to men
> Ye shall smite the stiff-necked infidel
> and rule, but not till then.
>
> . . . . .
>
> So ye are stirred by my words, ye pardon
> my scorn and upraiding?

Eagerly circle me round and ask will I
  lead an attack?
Nay! though your spirits be willing, your
  flesh is but weak for crusading,
When I face Englishmen's cannon I want
  better hearts at my back."

It is the old spirit of the frontier mullah, and it did not die in '88 or in '97, and it is at times quite impossible to cope with save by magazine fire.

It was through these long wars of fanaticism which accompanied the attempt to civilize the trade routes, that the need for only the best of the races in the ranks was apparent. More and more were Europeans necessary to lead, and more and more must the lesser breeds be eliminated.

The Army of Lord Kitchener

By the beginning of the twentieth century two new epochs of war had taken place, the Boer War with its insistent example of the power of the modern rifle, and the Russo-Japanese War with the fierce carnage of Port Arthur. Many were the lessons deduced therefrom, both true and false. Further as regards India, the Russian railways were more and more setting at naught the miles and the steppes of Central Asia.

The Indian Army needed bringing up-to-date in equipments, organization, in training and in self-production and Lord Kitchener was sent East for that purpose in 1902. It is not necessary for the purpose of this book to enumerate his measures. They were measures vitiated to some extent by the fact that no General Staff had yet been formed and no principles of war or of war organization specifically adopted as a starting point, and we are here concerned with the steps taken to re-group the races and make full use of all the new study of the various races and their martial capacities. The Indian Army itself clung often rather pitifully to the old and loyal but no longer truly martial classes of the South and West. Tradition, however, had to be thrown aside. Lord Kitchener with no inside prejudices was the man to do the work. Thus there commenced a careful elimination and re-grouping and a study of all untouched material from the North and East, and from this was the Indian Army of the World War born, with the cream of the selected martial races, with Rajputs of the Sun and Moon—whether in their ancient faith or embraced in that of Islam—Tartar and Afghan, Mahratta and Mongolian, choice young men and goodly like Saul of Tarsus, to be described in their several occasions hereafter.

The Army of the World War

As Lord Kitchener left it, so flocked the Indian Army to Flanders, to Sinai, to the Tigris and wherever His Majesty called and British officers would lead them. The experience and the expansion that followed gave still further knowledge of the few that could and would fight and the many that could not, and while the sour Brahmins in Bengal bit their thumbs and intrigued with Turk and Kaiser and Bolshevik, the masses of the humbler folk who had never shouldered a pike flocked to labour in the great cause . . . for great it was however much we deplore it. Under Lord Kitchener, for his Lordship but provided the cover and the occasion, there were scores of young soldiers with a remarkable and sympathetic knowledge of the people, who were only too eager to be allowed to make the best of such an army. Before the World War the severest foe that the Indian soldier was expected to face was the Russian 'the grey-coat guard' on the Oxus, yet the Indian army, thus re-organized and grouped, was unexpectedly flung into the most desperate fighting in Europe, under the worst climatic conditions—Sikhs, Gurkhas, Pathans, Punjabi, Moslems, Mahrattas, Jats, Garhwalis . . . the cream of India. The strain was indeed more than they should have fairly been asked to face, yet face it they did, always with devotion, often with success, and when they were moved to a terrain and climate more suited to their natures, their services were brilliant.

The Army Indianization Problem before the World War

In the last chapter of this book the problem of what is called 'Indianization' will be dealt with in its modern aspect, but the state of the question prior to modern conditions needs some mention here. The term 'Indianization', so far as the Army is concerned, refers to that of giving higher command to Indians, and enabling them to share the positions of the higher ranks hitherto held by British officers. In the early days of the East India Company, Indian leaders were placed in high positions, especially in the 'irregular' service, attaining high positions and even commanding units. But when the foe to be met changed from the purely Eastern type of soldiery to the large armies of the Mahratta and Sikh states, trained by French and other officers, many from the old Royalist régime, the military needs of the times changed. The down-country troops could not face their enemies without plenty of European leading, and the regular troops, in accordance with the military needs and ideas of the day, became more and more highly drilled. Only in the irregulars was there any scope for Indians, and as military art advanced, the men of heart and thew had not the brains and education to train and command. During the suppression of the Indian Mutiny in which the new Punjab troops were raised on 'irregular' lines, and the Punjab Irregular force from the Frontier sent most of its units down to the seat of trouble, there were few British officers, and the old hidalgos of the Sikh armies and their sons rendered brilliant service. The new army which took the place of the old pattern that had mutinied, was also to have few British officers and was to develop the responsibility of the Indians.

The suppression of the Indian Mutiny and the hunting down of the rebels that remained after a great army from England had dealt with the main rebel forces in Oudh, was a business for which the Indian officer of irregular corps was well suited. But armies were again becoming more modern and scientific, and the enemies now to be faced not the foes of internal India. The stern sacrifice of British officers necessary to stem the tribal attacks on the frontier campaign of 1863, showed that British leading was the principal factor against a determined foe. As the old Sikh had said, it was the '*Chota Sahib*'[1] who did the trick. The Afghan War of 1878–80, as already mentioned, showed the same even more clearly. And when the Russian menace became really serious and the problem of military education became acute, there seemed no way other than to further increase the British officers with units. The question of direct commissions of a general status equivalent to that of a British officer seemed ruled out of court by the defective

[1] Page 215 footnote.

power of assimilating education, evinced by the martial classes. The clever young men of the universities were quite unfitted for military work even if they had desired it, hearts were not in the right place. As an Irish Commander-in-Chief, Sir O'Moore Creagh, once remarked when talking of military learning "Ye can tache a poodle tricks, but ye can't tache him to draa a badger". And this is the commanding sentiment when the selection of military material is concerned.

There seemed no need to spend considerable sums in endeavouring to bring on the superior officer class when there was no immediate demand for such and all argument pointed the other way, while many of the older British officers were painfully conscious of the miserable weeds of clerkly sons who their magnificent old 'Bayley Guard' sirdars, (*v.* p. 342) brought to see them. The men who had 'been to the Bayley Guard', the great suppression campaign against the rebels of '57, magnificent specimens of militant and feudal humanity, in their desire to see their sons prosperous had designed them for civil life, and the process was apparently turning the sons of men into the children of mice. No, the staunch old Indian yeoman who came into the Indian commissioned ranks via the rank and file, or the young Indian land owner of lesser class, made the Indian officer as we know him. They were and are men who have lived and died in the most charming camaraderie with their British officers, the latter very jealous on their behalf of prestige and prospects, and they were all that the times needed. The complications which still endure of the racial and religious difficulties, the inherent tendency to intrigue that lies in the Indian nature, two points which as we now know, bid far to wreck the 'Reforms', all added to the difficulty of any change, even if the need for it were admitted. Again there was no character-building machine of schools and scholarship, nor was there as yet anything in the way of schools corresponding to those in which our fighting leaders are brought up.

Then at the back of all development, was the terrible bend sinister of the Mutiny and the accompanying rebellions, not rebellions made as a sign of disease but a senseless rebellion due almost to chance, accompanied by such astounding atrocities as made the people of the day determined that another occasion should not arise.

That, in brief, is the story of the position of Indians as higher soldiers when the War began. Some half-hearted measure of change had been made at the time of the King's Coronation visit when unattached commissions were given to Indian gentlemen, in the 'Indian Land Forces' but it led nowhere and did not give any opportunity of testing the problems in the supreme trial of The World War.

The Soldiers of the Indian States

Very little reference has yet been made to the armies of the Indian states, since they were hammered in the earlier days in the struggle of the re-welding of India. We have seen the armies of Sindia, of Holkar, of the Khalsa smashed in the old wars, and where annexation has followed victory we have seen them welded into the British service. But in those states which after defeat, or without even seeking it, have entered into treaties and abided by them, their armies remained and still remain. The reasons which made them necessary however have passed away, save the essential eastern duty of ceremonial, but a new one has arisen, that of bearing their share in the defence of India.

Early in the 'nineties a step was taken to organize a portion of the state armies for 'Imperial Service' and in almost every war in which India has been concerned the state forces have taken some part. Now all state troops are so organized and the name Imperial Service no longer designates a portion only. In the organizing of an Imperial Army with the troops of a dominionized India behind it, the Simon Commission clearly saw the share that such troops might take hereafter.

So far as the races in the State forces go, they are but those found in the rest of India. One modern condition has the Government of India wisely insisted on, that with certain specified exceptions, the troops of a state shall consist of the martial races who are subjects of that state. The practice of seeking for grenadiers and such like elsewhere is prohibited. If a state, as is sometimes the case, has no subjects from whom soldiers can be made, the ruler is encouraged to produce some of the non-combatant administrative units such as transport corps.

The armies of the states have traditions behind them sometimes as stirring and romantic as have corps of the Indian Army.

CHAPTER XIII

THE MARTIAL CLASSES IN THE NORTH TO-DAY

A SUMMARY OF THE RACES—THE TRIBES ON THE FRONTIER—THE PATHANS WHO SERVE THE CROWN—THE PUNJABI MUHAMMADAN—JAMMU AND KASHMIR—THE DOGRA—THE SIKHS OF TO-DAY—THE WOMEN OF THE NORTH—THE SIKH REGIMENTS—THE TRAGEDY OF SARAGARHI—THE WOMEN OF THE PUNJAB—THE WATER BAILIFF'S WIFE.

A SUMMARY OF THE RACES

WITH the detailed history that has now been given of all the races that can be called martial, we can perhaps visualise them as they stand to-day, and realise too how profoundly different is the basis of enlistment in the Army in India from that to which we of modern times have been accustomed in Great Britain. From among the people described, the races that retain their martial proclivities and ways of enterprise and courage are briefly as follows:

From the Frontier.

Pathans of many clans (both from the cis-and trans-frontier hills) (Moslems).

Baluchis and Brahuis (Moslems).

From the Punjab.

Sikhs (principally of the Jăt race).

Hindus (a few Jăts and Brahmins).

Dogras, chiefly Hindu and mainly Rajput (from the hills between the Punjab plains and the Himalaya massif, of the Pir Panjal Range).

Moslems of many tribes (principally of Rajput origin).

From Delhi and Hindustan.

Garhwalis (Hindus from the hills between the United Province and the Himalaya).

Kumaonis (Hindus from the hills between the United Province and the Himalaya).

Jāts, Gujars, Ahirs (Hindu).

Rajputs (Hindu for the most part).

Brahmins (cultivators).

Moslems (descendants of Turk and Afghan settlers and converted Rajputs).

From Rajputana and Central India.

Rajputs (Hindu).

Jāts (Hindu).

Mers (Hindu and Moslem).

Kaimkanis (Moslem Rajputs).

From Western India.

Mahrattas (Hindu).

Moslems who are chiefly descendants of Afghan, Pathan, Turk and Arab.

From Southern India.

Indian Christians Pariahs and other depressed classes	Chiefly for special technical corps.

Tamils (cultivators).

Moslems descendants of foreigners as in Western India (a very few).

Of the foregoing, it is to be observed that the men of the Punjab, furnish a very large proportion of the men of stamina and daring . . . men who in civil life are by no means law abiding . . . who come to the Army. To these must be added the Pathans from both within and without the administrative border, and those races of Baluchistan who soldier or who are war-like. They furnish the bulk of the Army between them. And because it is so, Sir John Simon's Commission pointed out that without the disciplinary and psychological control of British officers and without that confidence-giving body of good-humoured, highly disciplined British bayonets, the races of the north would over-run India as they had so often done before. We will now try and look at them to-day in the flesh after a brief survey of the groupings.

The Tribes on the Frontier

The Frontier tribes resolve themselves into certain convenient geographical groups for the purpose of classification, and we must realise that the North-West Frontier runs for close on 1,100 miles.

The divisions are those of the people about

(1) The routes from Kabul.
(2) The routes from Ghuzni.
(3) The routes from Kandahar.

To these may be added two more viz.,

(4) The tribes north of the Khaiber.
(5) The tribes who live within the Administrative Border.

Those of the last category who live within the Border divide into three main groups, viz., The Yusafzais, the

'Sons of Joseph,' who inhabit the plains and foot hills of Peshawur, and the Swat valley and are of many clans, the Khattaks to the south of them, and on both sides of the river, and the tribes cis-Indus in Hazara.

The principal tribes about the routes to Kabul, by Khaiber and by Kurram, are the Afridi, the Orakzai, the Bangash, the Mullagori, the Zaimukt, the Chamkani, and then at the head of the Kurram the Shiah tribe of the Turis who are possibly of Turk or Tartar origin.

Those about the Ghuzni routes, viz., those that come from Ghuzni either via the Tochi or Gomal River valleys, are chiefly Waziris and are in two great divisions, the Mahsuds and the Darwesh Khel.

The routes from Kandahar come through what we now call British Baluchistan. The tribes therein are largely Pathan, some of actual Afghan origin, viz., Kakars, Duranis, Sheranis, Khetrans, etc., but south and east again are Baluch, a people of entirely different and probably Arab origin, and also consisting of many clans, and south of them again some Brahuis intermingle, whose language is akin to the Dravidian of the south, and who are a most interesting survival.

The Pathans Who Serve the Crown

The Pathan varies in disposition and in military value considerably, and his behaviour in his own hills may be very different from that which he displays when serving. But though each tribe and clan has different ways there are certain general characteristics common to them all, and first let us give their good qualities. These wild highlanders as a rule, appeal immensely to most British officers though not to all. They are sporting, high-spirited, adventurous, and jaunty with a jauntiness supremely different from the comparatively unassuming bearing of even the hardiest Indian proper.

Among the many clans some have a far greater reputation than others. For instance, it is not every tribe that has the desire to come to close quarters. The powerful and important group of the Afridi tribes were thought very small beer in the days when sword met sword or clanged on the locking ring of the bayonet. When the fire-arm became a long range arm of precision the Afridi became a first class marksman and took tea at comfortable ranges, with all and sundry.

Tall good looking when young, well-knit, agile, Kipling's line on the young chief portrays the young Pathan well.

> " He trod the ling like a buck in spring,
> and stood like a lance at rest."

The Mahsud Waziris and Yusafzai, on the contrary, stood high among their neighbours for fearless swordsmanship, who would do something better than 'shout hullaloo in the rear', or 'shoot at the strong and slash at the weak' and so forth, up and down the border.

But to live and work among a Pathan regiment at manœuvres or on the border patrol, is an education of itself, a brothership with the most active, strenuous men you could imagine. And since he who drives fat oxen must himself be fat, so the British officer who can control, lead and inspire the trans-border men, must be something more than a man among men. When I see them ending their lives on a Devon golf course with an old brown pipe, and know what they have been and done in their prime, I am astonished. It is like the picture of Landseer's with the lamb resting alongside the dismounted cannon, 'think what

PATHANS OF A FRONTIER CORPS

ADAM KHEL AFRIDI — SAGRI KHATTAK

[Face page 240

he's seen, think where he's been', and the old sea-captain strikes the same note in one's imagination.

Untutored, and at home on their hillside, it is a wild life the clansmen lead, now carrying out a blood feud that has been in progress for generations, 'an eye for an eye and a tooth for a tooth', now sitting all day perhaps, in the fortified, loopholed, solid-butted tower of their homestead, because a neighbour has drawn a bead on you . . . fed and watered by your women-kind, only venturing out at night . . . or else doing the same by someone else. Many a man on leave from the quiet orderly life of a British cantonment must needs enter his home stealthily by night, lest retribution overtake him for the crime of his father. Once the author, during the great campaign of 1897–8 in the Afridi and Orakzai Tirah, spoke on top of the Sampagha pass, with a pensioned Afridi *subahdar*, a retired Indian officer, living on his own homestead. The tribesmen were then wondering if the British would actually take hold of the country and administer it.

"*Sahib*," said my friend, "Does the *Sirkar*, 'The British Government', realise the *takleef*, 'the trouble', the years of guerrilla struggling and unrest, that must follow before the country settles down? I doubt it. But . . . when once it is over" . . . and here he burst into sheer Hibernian, "I can appreciate the heaven it would be to be able to go to sleep one night, and to wake up in the morning without finding one's throat cut!"

Pathans have a passion for arms, and are ready learners on the rifle range. Unfortunately what they learn, in the case of trans-border men, comes back to roost when they are the enemy on the hillside. There is more than one good story of the ex-sepoy signalling back instructions in the most approved style as to how to correct the artillery ranging against him. In the great frontier risings of 1897 and after the Afridi revolt when the British were dictating terms in the Afridi centre, the *jirgas*, the tribal councils who were discussing submission and punishments, were largely composed of ex-soldiers wearing their British war-medals with pride and zest, and no doubt that twinkle of humour which is the Pathan saving grace. As smart as paint in shorts and well pressed jacket, with arms and accoutrements well polished, the alert young rifleman is a very different thing from the 'catch 'em alive oh' searching for *pediculus vestimenti* on his native heath. All over the world the modern Pathan roams and the stokeholds of ocean steamers are one of his popular habitats. In fact, there is no subject on which the modern tribesman has not plenty of enlightenment. The lads who come to enlist often brought by a relative are, if free of pock-marks, very good to look on, often of almost Greek profile, with the down of an incipient whisker on an olive and rose-coloured face, and a love-lock down the cheek, for all the world like a lass of Paris. A Jowakı Afridi is very like the British Yeoman of Signals lent to Admiral Guepratte for the attack on the Dardanelles—a huge moustache and close trimmed beard with rubicund cheeks.

Hospitality is a virtue that is rigorously and whole-heartedly practised, though it does not mean that the guest may not be shot and robbed once he is clear of your definite territory in which hospitality must be rendered.

Before the World War, many of the Punjab regiments enlisted Pathans to a varying extent, sometimes a whole company sometimes even more, sometimes all from one clan such as Khattak or Afridi; others have them by platoons.

Their language of the border is Păshtu or Păkhtu, according as it is the hard and soft variety, spoken in the south about Quetta, and the north about Peshawur, and is a derivative from the Zend the early form of Persian which is akin to the Sanskrit, but it has like most other language incorporated many alien words to meet the need of the generation. It is a musical language and in its literary form is as the Persian phrase has it *bisyar shirin* 'very sweet to the ear'. We are not concerned with it here however, except so far as the come and go of life is concerned. Greetings and salutations are of the overflowing kind, and you yourself or a Pathan meeting another will be received as follows and it is the rule to go through with the series.

The usual salute will commence with,

"*Staramashe!*" "Don't be tired!" and then whether friends be embracing you breast to breast and knee to knee, or whether you meet in more distant fashion, there come in rapid succession the volley of a kindly routine, after "*Kwah mashe*". "Done be down on your luck".

"*Jor-ye?*" "Are you well?"

"*Khajorye?*" "Are you sure you are well?" a sort of "My, that's fine!"

"*Khushal-ye?*" "Are you happy?"

"*Takra-ye?*" "Are you strong?"

"*Taza-ye?*" "Are you cheerful?"

"*Kor Khair dai?*" "Are your family well?"

"*Zaman di jor di?*" "Are your sons well?"

While this boisterous storm greets you, you may be able to interpose "*Ho! Jor-yum!*" or "*Ho! Kushal-yum!*" "Yes, I am well" or "I am happy."

There are other greetings. "*Har kala rasha,*" "Come at all times," the acme of hospitality, "*Loe shah,*" "be great," and so forth, all worthy of highland hearts, but blurred by the scenes of treachery and bloodshed, that so often mar the life across the border. Here is a yarn that my gunner orderly used to tell me with gusto, and he was a Ranizai from Swat, across the British border. His village was separated by a small stream, often dry, from another with which they were at feud, and once when an urchin, he and a dozen others caught a similar lad from the offending village who had strayed across the stream after perhaps a straying goat, but possibly to thieve one of theirs. Without more ado they stretched his little weazand and slit it with a pocket knife, for the Glory of God and his Prophet. *Toba* ! but there you have the trans-border, where there is no authority save tribal custom and the council of elders, and a code that is known as the *Pakhtan wali*.

Within the border all is usually quiet and the King's peace over all. Otherwise the villages are the same, and the loopholed towers often in repair for fear of raiders, but nevertheless, it is reasonably safe and you may watch the great Bactrian camels come down from Ghuzni with the Ghilzai traders, migrating perhaps for the winter to lock up their arms in a frontier police post, and babble instead of *Habeas corpus*. And the families come too, atop the camels, 'knees up Mrs. Brown!' and the sonsy girls making roguey eyes when the *malik* isn't looking, and the asafoetida smells in the bundles and the Persian pussycats spit on the balls. That is the frontier as the Frontier Force and the Mountain Artillery know it year in year out, and the wind comes off the snows and the foot hills show blue in the *brouillard*. The levy-man jogs jauntily by, conscious to-day that with his coat turned outside-in he is an irregular trooper of King George, but that with it turned inside-out, why he is, as Charles Kingsley would have said, just as good a raider as those he is out to stop, nay better. Indeed there are two fat-tailed sheep in that homestead by the *qabristan* 'the burial place', that he intends to have for himself, even if he swears that it was Chikai's men from Tor-garh or whatever other tarry-tiddle the frontier officer may be pleased to swallow or wink at.

Then you will see the hard-featured frontier women, who seem not to have romance, so concerned are they perhaps in fetching water a-donkey-back from far a-field that joy does not seem to enter into their lives. But that can hardly be true, for your young soldier must be some satisfaction to some of those olive-cheeked, pig-tailed lasses who are just growing up and can yet defy the sharp lines that frontier sun and winter wind will make in any woman's face.

But alas, on the frontier, men often think of other things than women, and practices which in the West are the last signs of degeneration and worthlessness are in the East often the trait of the most daring outlaw and wolf's head, for East is East. Alas, too, this state of affairs, the common shame of even the great nobles of Kabul, is also too prevalent even in our bonnie Punjab, and jealousy on this count is one of the causes of unaccountable murders. Again *Toba! Toba!* Shame! Shame!

The Pathan soldier however, though a handy light-infantry man, for light-infantry individual work on the hill side is naturally his *forte*, did not come into great repute in the World War, while some of the other Indian races did. He deserted, especially the trans-frontier man, far too freely, the Afridi more than any other, both in France and in Mesopotamia.[1] Therefore was the Army angered against him, and his enlistment for a while was rigorously curtailed

[1] It may be said on their behalf that neither constitutional faithlessness nor 'cold feet' was the main cause. The inter-tribal balance of power was an important factor. If a company of Malik Din Afridis were wiped out, and the Kukis and Khambars did not suffer equally, the Malik Din could neither hold their grazing grounds, nor maintain their water rights.

and only now is being sparely considered and to a smaller degree re-opened to him. This is a very serious matter in certain of the frontier tracts. In the Afridi Tirah for instance, not only is the number of pensioners dying out, and therefore the country side growing poorer and less in touch with the British Government, but the young men are out of a job. So the good Beelzebub is able to fill his special role and mischief along the border line augments considerably.

THE PUNJABI MUHAMMADAN

Let us now turn from the jaunty inconsistency of the border to the districts of the Punjab in which we find the Punjabi Muhammadan, the 'P.M.' of Army diction. We shall find him on the hither side of the Indus, on the plains, and in the raw red but fascinating hills known as the Salt Range between the Indus and the Jhelum, hard working yeomanry and peasantry, at their fields from early morn till dewy eve, generally clad in a coarse cotton straight smock, slightly coloured with the blue-bag, white pyjamas, and a smallish puggaree—tall, broad-shouldered, often like royal Solomon a choice young man and a goodly, with a clean, high-grade profile and a rather heavy jowl, especially the Awan. The men of the Salt Range, often spoken of as 'Salt-rangers', are ideal soldiers, the better to-do going to the cavalry, but often to be found in the mountain artillery and the infantry, and in many ways forming the back-bone and the back-ground of the modern army.

Not far on the hither side of the Indus will be the Awans, a non-Rajput folk, who claim Arab origin, cultivators to a man, who live in villages, squat mud villages with golden corn-cobs drying on the flat roofs, because no man would be safe in a homestead. They are not too far from the sphere of action of trans-frontier raiders who can easily cross the border, rob, and rob thoroughly, and laying up in broken hills, get away the next night. There are plenty of ways of crossing the Indus, and the country lying about the strategic railway, which runs down the hither bank of the Indus, traverses a country so broken that only a Gustav Doré could do justice to it. It is truly a 'devil' country. Therefore it is that here and all along the uplands of the Punjab Plain, villagers do not live in homesteads, and often have to walk miles to their holding. Despite the *Pax Britannica* and the able police, the whole country side has such a penchant for robbery under arms, yclept dacoity, that homesteading is unpopular.

In the Salt Range and on all the plains between Indus and Jhelum, as well as on the left bank of the latter, the land is covered with the sturdy Moslem folks of the converted Rajput clans, Bhatti, Janjua, Tiwana, and a dozen, more, among them too are some genuine Mogul settlements. Genuine, means distinct from those of the depressed classes who accepting the relief of Islam, have assumed a worldly claim to position as great as that which their new religious position has conferred on them, and often call themselves by the old dread name.

Where the River Jhelum comes down from Kashmir to the sea there in the lesser hills are also Moslem clans, some owning the jurisdiction of the little Hindu Rajput state of Poonch, and some of the Maharajah of Jammu and Kashmir, the very people recently concerned in riots and disturbances against their Hindu Rajput chief. In this connection it is well to consider how the high mountain-locked Kashmir comes into the story, with its modern complication of 'Mr. A's' European amours.

Jammu and Kashmir

We need not go further than Mogul days, in the history of Kashmir, the home of early learning and Sanskrit derivations. Converted by early Moslem rulers, all the inhabitants save the Brahmin clans have been Moslems for many centuries, hardy, muscular, powerful, enduring and yet pusillanimous beyond belief. Conquered by the Moguls who turned its glades and river banks into a paradise with the dreams of gardens, waterfalls, rills and trickles which still remain to enchant us, Kashmir fell to Nadir Shah and eventually to the Durani Empire. It was not till 1820 that Runjhit Singh of Lahore drove out the Afghan Governor and made it a Sikh province. The few Afghan settlers remained there as in the Punjab, Sikh subjects, and furnish occasionally some soldier to the Jammu as well as the Imperial forces, but the soft ease of Kashmir does not harden them.

The fortified city of Jammu, the home of the small Rajput state, and of the three Jammu brothers had, as already described, much to say in the last days of Sikh rule. Gulab Singh the eldest and head of the state who had reduced his Rajput neighbours to feudatories, had as related a powerful army on the Western model nominally in the Sikh service. When he held his troops aloof from the unrevoked invasion of British India, Great Britain rewarded him as part of a very definite policy. That policy aimed at leaving a reconstructed Punjab, but with some drag on it, by detaching the hill Rajputs and Kashmir therefrom. The Sikh Durbar could not pay its war indemnity after the First Sikh War, and Gulab Singh was prepared to do so on terms! His terms suited the British plans, and he was duly made Maharajah of Jammu and Kashmir, though there was no sort of connection between the two principalities save contiguity. A great-grandson of wicked astute rulersome old Gulab Singh of Jammu is the Maharajah Sir Hari Singh of Kashmir, who has lately been reaping the reward of his predecessor's too rigid treatment of the Muhammadan half of his kingdom. The state of Jammu is the home of some of the best Rajput clans, of the *Dugar Des*, the 'Land of the Two Lakes,' Siransir and Manesar, far up in the frontiers of China and Thibet.

In the hills between Jammu and Rajaori and the plains, the Hindu and Moslem tribes are considerably mingled, have the same tribal names and actually count kin, especially in such a group as the Chibs, and in fact racially the whole of these Hindus from the hills belong to the same racial stock as the rest of the Punjab that is not Jăt.

In the old feudal palace of Jammu the ancient whiskered clansmen wear a sword in a velvet scabbard stuck in their waistband, elephants weave in the corner of the palace-yard till wanted, and running footmen with muskets carried in red baize bags stand by, to attend on majesty. Dressed in black sheepskin caps, a few Afghan mercenaries still serve the Maharajah, some his own Kashmiri Afghans, some from his Khagan border, some from Afghanistan itself. Such is the mountain State of Jammu in which blend Muhammadan and Hindu Rajput of the Punjab.

The Dogra

Let us now move a little inland, from the plains and the Moslem foot hills of the *Dugar Des*, and see the Hindu Rajput, the Rajput who has escaped the pressure of the

Moslem invasions—perhaps too missed the call of that simple austerity—and remained in the ancient faith as part of the Brahmin blending. Let us see them step out from the fortified hill capital of Jammu, that city of bastions and white spires and temple gongs and bells, or from the great fortress city of Akhnoor on the River of China, and come down to serve His Majesty or His Highness the Maharajah. Or move a little farther south to the Dogra hills that are within British India, those Rajput countries about Kangra, or see those tall grenadier-like Rajputs who live in the plains, yet in spirit and race are the same as the Dogras.

All comers from the interior valleys are good looking, the better bred the better looking, and the higher in the hills the shorter and sturdier the figure, riflemen and light infantrymen rather than grenadiers. The Mians and Katoch are highest of the Rajputs, blue-blooded and often enough as penniless as the laird of Cockpen, who make the most delightful of faithful and enthusiastic soldiery. The highest in caste will be received and saluted by others with the salutations *Jai Deo*, 'hail deity,' or 'hail great spirit.'

Those who serve with them, the British officers of the Dogra Regiments and the Dogra companies and squadrons of ordinary Punjabi Regiments, have the feeling that they are with men whose doings and feelings are always moved by a code of honour, not always the same as theirs, but one demanding a certain class of action demeanour and integrity, which will not fail.

The Dogra villages, built as a rule of mud and stone nestle against the low hills, but homesteads can exist in safety and by no means all live in villages. The mud houses of the Punjab are much the same, but in the hills even more than in the plains are they the drying and stacking ground of produce, the golden corn-cobs, the bundles of dried maize stalks for the winter forage, with amaranth and 'love-lies-bleeding' in the yards so that a view of the terrace houses and fields from the hill top above is a charming sight. The Mian Dogra is too blue in blood to touch the plough handle; to do so would mean falling to the grade of *Manhas*. His tenants do the work while he stands by as does the Katoch in Kangra, and both are poorer therefor.

THE MODERN SIKH

The term Sikh is a name to conjure with in the minds of the ordinary British citizen. It brings memories of many wars in which the Sikh soldier has covered himself with glory, and the public picture, rightly enough, a tall, often hook-nosed and heavily bearded man. The British memory will be right. The Sikh soldier is nearly always tall and often of aquiline appearance. From this grouping of peoples in a religion that is gradually making its votaries a separate race although but three million all told, are drawn several wholly Sikh regiments and hosts of Sikh squadrons and companies in what are known as class-company regiments, i.e. those whose companies are composed of differing peoples.

The great mass of the Sikh people are as has been explained the cultivating Jăt race of the more easterly Punjab, with them are the lesser cultivators market gardeners, such as *Sainis* and *Kumbohs* whose origin it is not necessary to seek. Then come the trading caravan folk known as the *Labanas*, and a certain number of the trading and clerical class of Sikh known as *Khatri* who claim to be of Kshattriya origin, and who from their education and ability, have often made good officers, and who are invaluable in the quartermastering ranks of regimental life. They possess the physical courage which is unusual in their class, and are a very valuable military as well as citizen stratum.[1]

But it is from the Jăt, the great muscular, hardworking, rather stupid yeoman farmer, the man who is 'born with a plough in his hands' and whose only toy of his childhood is a model plough, that the Sikh grenadier comes, the man to whom perhaps alone in India can the words of Napier be applied in battle, as fighting with 'the majesty with which the British soldier fights'.

By reason of the rules of the brotherhood no hair is cut and no beard is shaved. The Sikh's hair is wisped up and confined with a comb like a woman's, and his beard in its civilian state is long and flowing, and with the old men truly patriarchical. The beard that is wound round a piece of string, and is curled and rolled inwards as known to those who see the Sikh soldier in life and in picture, but follows the Rajput habit, born of the need for preserving clothes and especially government uniforms clean. The Sikhs picked up the trick from the Hindustani soldiery after the annexation of the Punjab. The Sikh army when the British met it, had long flowing beards. Such being a nuisance in private life the military habit has more or less spread to private life.

The three districts from which the bulk of the Sikh soldiery come, and where most of the Sikhs reside, are known as the Manjha the country in the Bari Doab, secondly the Doaba, that is to say the country between the Beas and the Sutlej, and thirdly the Malwa the country east of the Sutlej.

While there is little if anything, to choose between the

[1] Some are even settled as traders in the trans-frontier lands, and as 'Afridi' Sikhs are sometimes enlisted for their valuable local knowledge.

men of these three districts they do to some extent, possess special characteristics. It is from the Malwa that come the great grenadiers of the original Sikh regiments, and the men of the Manjha, who are shorter and perhaps more active, find the best men in the old rifle regiments of the Frontier Force. The Jăt is a better foot-soldier than he is trooper, though there are plenty of good soldiers and fair riders in the cavalry ranks.

It is interesting here to turn aside for a minute and look at the peculiar geographical terms. *Do-ab* means two streams as *Panj-ab* or *Punj-* means five, and while this term is most used for the great Doab between the Ganges and the Jumna, the various *doabs* of the Punjab rivers are known by names made up of the initial letters of the name of each river. Thus the *Bari Doab* is the district between the Beas and the Ravi, the *Rech Doab* of the land between the Ravi and the Chenab, while *Jach* or *Chaj* is that between Chinab and Jhelum. The Chenab or better Chinab is the 'River of China' where it rises, and down the confluences of the Indus and the five rivers we have the *Triniab* or combined 'Three-waters' and the *Panjnad* or great stem of 'Five-Rivers' aforesaid where the five as one join the Indus.

The Jăt Sikhs are composed of many *gots* and clans, of whom several while living within the general Jăt banner claim Rajput descent from Rajput clans who have in later history returned to the Punjab from Rajputana. The names of the *gots* are too numerous to mention, some furnishing more, some less soldiers, but the largest ones enlist freely, *gots* such as the *Sindus* sending a great many soldiers to the army the police, and to the Straits Settlements. The Sikh goes where the pay is highest, and many make for the Far East where police, night-watchmen and the like are well paid. *Gils* and *Dillons* are also numerous but the *gots* are widely split and some of almost every one will be found in each of the districts and also in the cis-Sutlej states.

The Sikh Regiments

The Sikh Regiments are many, but there is a curious muddle in nomenclature allowed to creep in whether through ignorance or to placate Frontier Force opinions, during the re-organization of Lord Kitchener's time. It has been the time-honoured custom of the British to raise corps from a people they have defeated, often from the actual prisoners of war. The first four Gurkha regiments were thus raised. After the first Sikh War in 1845–6 two local Sikh regiments were raised, the Regiments of Ferozepore and of Loodianah, names that they bear to this day. They have always been 'class' regiments that is to say, all Sikh, and almost entirely Jăt. Some nine years later a Sikh Military Police Battalion was raised for service in the Sonthal country on the lower Ganges, after the Sonthal rebellion. This Corps known as 'Rattray's Sikhs' with the Ferozepore and Loodianah Regiments were taken into the Bengal Line after the Mutiny, as the 14th, 15th, and 45th Bengal Native Infantry, and were known as the 14th Sikhs, etc. The Ferozepore and Rattray's Corps did well in the Mutiny though the Loodianah regiment in garrison at Benares mutinied, possibly through mishandling at the somewhat badly managed disarming of the Benares garrison, at which difficult feat Colonel Neil was trying a 'prentice hand.

The principle of enlisting your conquered people was followed still further in 1846, by raising a Punjab Irregular Force to occupy and police the newly annexed *Doaba*, (i.e. between Beas and Ravi), and face the turbulent Rajput tribes of the hills. The Infantry of this Force was known as the 1st, 2nd, 3rd, and 4th Sikh Infantry, the 2nd having the incorrect secondary cognomen of 'Hill' Sikhs, in other words the Rajputs of the Dogra hills, who predominated in the ranks. After the Second Sikh War this force was incorporated with a larger one, the new Punjab Irregular Force, which was to garrison and police the Afghan and tribal border. The term Sikh Infantry meant troops raised from the old Sikh Army of Rajputs, Sikhs and Muhammadans. They were colloquially known as 1st Sikhs, etc. and those who care for such things will also remember how the Infantry for the Irregular Force later named the 'Frontier' Force, had the 1st to the 4th Sikh Infantry, and the 1st to the 6th Punjab Infantry, a truly illogical numbering. But the first four were practically at the outset regiments of the Khalsa Army taken into the British Service, while the latter six were raised in the Punjab largely from old Sikh service soldiers, but from debris and not by corps. In Lord Kitchener's time these battalions, which never had more than one or two companies of Sikhs, were misnamed the 51st, 52nd, 53rd, and 54th 'Sikhs' as if they had been like the 14th, 15th and others, entirely made up of Sikhs. It is a small but very interesting point.

Another interesting point is that after the Annexation of the Punjab every Bengal Infantry Regiment was ordered to recruit at least a hundred Sikhs. The normal commanding officer of the period had no use for the hairy uncouth-looking scoundrels as they appeared to him, compared with his neatly dressed, shako-topped Hindustanis. By 1857 however most corps had some, and even when these were more or less swept away in mutiny, they soon broke back to the British side. Wise Sir Henry Lawrence separated them from the Hindustanis when unrest first showed at Lucknow, and they formed a valuable addition to the defenders of the Residency. In the Punjab his brother also withdrew them to form new corps when the Bengal Regiments were disarmed.

After the post-Mutiny reconstruction, when all corps above 18, and a few below, were constituted from the Punjabi races, Sikhs furnished companies in these 'class company' corps.

After the Second Afghan War and later more Sikh regiments were formed, notably the 35th and 36th, and the 47th, all from the same classes. During the siege of Delhi the experiment was made of enlisting those Sikhs of the sweeper class who had been given, as already described, the title of *Mazbhi* or faithful who have now become a class and almost a caste by themselves. They did so well that eventually three regular battalions of Pioneer Infantry were raised from them, numbered the 23rd, 32nd, and 34th Bengal Pioneers. As the years rolled on and the old Madras regiments were growing unfit, more and more of them were converted to Punjabi regiments and this meant more and more demand for Sikhs so that as already referred to, the net of recruitment was widened, and Sikh classes never before tried were now enlisted. They have been successful as soldiers, and prove once more the uplift in heart and character that Sikhism has brought to those classes that have embraced it. So stimulating are its tenets and practices that it is not to be wondered that the British officers have insisted on its maintenance among their recruits. The result has been referred to, and is gratefully acknowledged by the Sikhs themselves, that at a time thirty or forty years ago when a great decadence was falling on this faith of Guru Govindh, the officers rescued it from slipping away to a very degenerated Hinduism and held it till the Khalsa started their own renaissance.

With the re-grouping after the World-War, the five Sikh regiments other than Pioneer were formed as battalions of the 11th Sikh Regiment, a necessary but tragic reform, in that the numbers that had become more than ever famous in the World-War, have been lost to general recognition.

The Tragedy of Saragarhi

There are many gallant deeds that the Sikhs have done, both in our time and in the old time before, and in this World War, in France, in Palestine, in Mesopotamia, but there is no single incident that remains more vivid in men's minds than the Tragedy of Saragarhi. It is often lauded for the astounding bravery and devotion that it portrays; but that is really a clap-trap note. The party of Sikhs involved, nineteen rifles with two non-combatant cooks, were the most pitiful rats in a trap as the story will show, for whom a surrender meant a cruel death in cold blood. A fight to a finish on the contrary meant going to their God in state with the blood boiling, and many of their enemy to 'open them heaven's gate' in the old Norse style. No, the story really rests on the tragedy and pity of their position, the impossibility of helping them and the majesty with which they, the rats in a trap, fought, not for the glory of the White Queen, who still reigned over us, not for the fame of their regiment, nor for the pride of the Khalsa, but because there was no way of saving their lives from a cruel pitiless foe.

This is the story for those who do not know it, and it shows how the Crown in defending the realms under its authority must now and again call for terrible sacrifices.

In 1897, the great Samana knife-edge on the North-West Frontier, some 6,000 feet above the salt sea, had been occupied by the British Government for five years as the only way of protecting the long corridor of cultivated plains, and the crowded trade route of the caravans to Kabul by the Kurram valley, and the Pass of the Camel's Neck. Northward it faces the great snow massif of the Safed Koh or 'White Mountain' that separates that part of the frontier hills from Afghanistan proper. Between the Samana and the Safed Koh lie the tumbled series of successive ranges and high uplands which form the Afridi and Orakzai Tirah. As an ordinary act of modern sovereignty the occupation of the Samana was a humane and necessary act. But it incensed the raiding tribes and its lofty position overlooks their haunts . . . lifted the '*purdah*' or veil, in their picturesque phraseology.

The normal garrison consisted of one Indian battalion distributed at two stations, Fort Lockhart and Fort Cavignari or Gulistan, and supporting a number of small forts held by tribal military police. In the summer of 1897, the battalion was the 36th Sikhs, a magnificent corps of Jât Sikhs, raised after the Russian war scare of 1885, by Major Cooke and Captain Holmes. The latter went among the villagers offering to wrestle with all and sundry, only stipulating that the competitor should enlist. Since 'All in' wrestling is *par excellence* a Sikh sport, he filled his regiment twice over, and commanded it by his fierce prestige. It was now ten years old but had yet to fight its maiden fight.

But this summer of 1897 the growing distaste for the British policy of protecting trade routes through the border from raiders and blackmail, had bred a fiery dislike for the 'Sirkar'. Highland caterans hate restraining, added to which Moslem Turkey, the Caliph of *Rum*, the *Amir Ul Mominin*, the 'leader of the faithful', had beaten Christian Greece before all worlds. The drum ecclesiastic began to roll on the frontier, *Rub-a-dub*, *Rub-a-dub*, '*Glory for all and heaven for those who bleed*', the fierce mullahs raised the green standards, the *shahids*, the witnesses for the faith, waved their swords, and *jihad* or holy war was proclaimed from the minars and shrines on the mountain side. From pothold and valley forge, from terraced hillside and fortified homestead, the tribes poured forth. Now in Waziristan, now north of Peshawur, now in the Khaiber and down again on the Samana the Fiery Crescent spread. All along the border men flung themselves against the posts and garrisons that stood for law and order, for mercy and good will.

The two military posts on the Samana were over four miles apart, the nearest reinforcement was the frontier brigade of all arms at Kohat forty miles away. Gulistan however, was out of sight of Fort Lockhart, by reason of the rocky bluff of Saragarhi, which blocked the view. Since communication is essential, and wireless was not known, a small fortified post consisting of walled enclosure and loopholed tower at one corner was built of masonry. From the tower, visual signalling could be carried out, in fact Saragarhi was visible from both forts. On the 27th of August the Orakzai lashkars, some 6,000 strong, overflowed into the valley, attacked many military police posts on the ridge and in the plains, and invested Gulistan. By now reinforcements were arriving from India despite the intense heat below. Gulistan was being fiercely attacked, but by September 10th it was relieved and the Orakzais were driven back into the Khanki valley; the relievers however, had to withdraw below for water. By now the Afridi lashkars baffled by the concentration in the Khaiber had flowed over to the south, 10,000 strong. This brought back a combined Orakzai and Afridi force and once more were the Samana posts attacked. Gulistan, commanded by Major DesVoeux, with his wife expecting her confinement and nurse and children with her, had 130 rifles inside. They too fought as rats in a trap, and with astounding energy was the defence made good. Saragarhi, the signal post, was surrounded by yelling, tomtom-beating hordes. A dozen expert riflemen commanded every loophole. The small garrison of Lockhart endeavoured a rescue, but this vain attempt which could only have meant disaster, was recalled, and both posts though invisible to each other could watch with anger and despair the breakers roll round the small garrison, from which the spitting of the defender's fire grew pitifully less.

While the men at the loopholes did their best . . . and the Beau Geste films give an almost life-like reproduction of the scene . . . a party of Afridis under a native bed covered with matting and earth like the 'tortoise' of mediaeval days, were picking a breach in an unflanked corner of the wall. They broke through . . . and all was over . . . how, the watchers could but imagine. A few hours later the relievers' column from below, who had been fiercely assailed during their former withdrawal climbed up again. It was a pitiful sight that met them. Every stone of the post had been cast down, and among them lay the dastardly mutilated bodies of the defenders, stripped and unrecognisable. Later some of the assailants told how they died. How one by one the men at the loopholes were shot, how when the break through came and survivors who could move fought on, a wounded Sikh on a bed in the guard room shot four of the assailants, and how, worst of all, two non-combatant prisoners (cooks), were roasted alive . . . a story which sent the Army boiling with fury for many days. It was all the old pent-up hatred of Sikh and Pathan let loose again, and sent our own non-combatant followers to set light to any Pathan wounded they could find, especially if they could make his cartridge pouch explode on him.

That, ladies and gentlemen, is the pitiful story of gallant rats in a trap, that is so famous in legend. The story of the second and even fiercer defence of Gulistan runs *pari passu*, and the supreme conduct of this 36th Regiment of Sikhs in the rest of that campaign is to be told elsewhere. One poignant remembrance is with those who know. Had the engineers who fortified the Samana thought a little harder, they would have found that a very little dynamiting and shaving off of the Saragarhi hump would have given the necessary intervision and obviated the need for its existence of the Saragarhi Post.

The Women of the Punjab

In all this talk of the Punjab and its manly, martial races, little, if anything, has yet been said of the women, and yet after what Sunjota said close on a thousand years ago,[1] it is neither right nor duly courteous so to disregard them. Let us then turn awhile to the strapping lasses of the Punjab, be they Sikh, or Moslem, or Dogra, or any other kind of yeoman peasant. Except for the really high caste Hindu woman, all women are much more the same in the Punjab than all men. As part of the religious make-up of Islam a Mussalmani will not differ so much from a Sikh or Hindu. 'Judy O'Grady and the Colonel's lady are like enough under the skin'.

They are bonny, sonsy, hardworking women, these mothers and wives of men. Married early so far as ceremony goes the consummation does not take place too soon, either for man or woman, and the erotic early married student is

[1] See page 95.

not to be found in the villages and *jhoks*.[1] Free of limb, straight of figure, strapping and comely, stand these brown daughters of Eve, good wives to good husbands, but not by any manner of means to wear the willow if neglected. I doubt if there are handsomer, comelier women to be seen the world over, where good looks and health are more to be prized than finer beauty, than there are in the land of the Five Rivers. Whether they be clad in the striped gay skirts of Sikh or Moslem, or in the red or white pyjamas that all affect on occasion, but more characteristically those of Islam, the breasts in a *brassière*, the head covered or not by the loosened *sari*, the nose and ears handsomely ringed, anklets and bangles of the family savings, they may be seen at all times about their business in the village. They will be plastering the floor for cleanliness, saying the necessary prayers to the family shrine, pounding rice and grounding the wheat-meal that builds the bone and sinew, which the millet cannot give, milking the cows and goats, winnowing the threshed grain that the bullocks have trodden on the threshing floor, and generally being pretty fair mistresses of their own fate and their men folk; such are the women of the Punjab. Sadly and hardly the war hit them. Tens of thousands of their men folk went away never to come back. Deprived of the husband that means so much to open-air hearty folk, their war story has been one of resignation and actual enthusiasm, and yet somewhat helpless beneath the roguery and chicanery of relative and village officials. So much was this so that the Government of India appointed an English lady,[2] the widow of a colonel of a Punjab regiment, dead in the war, whose knowledge of the women folk was remarkable and unusual, to visit them and report if separation

[1] *jhok*=homestead.
[2] Mrs. G. H. Bell.

allowances and widow pensions were being duly paid and not sticking to the rapacious hands of post office and village underlings, that curse of India which Liberal thoughts and constitution planners affect to disregard . . . the land of tyranny, oppression and petty robbery par excellence for those who are helpless! Much were the visits of this English lady appreciated, and great was the courtesy and kindness extended to her, and deep did she find the loyalty and devotion to the Crown in these simple, anxious souls. And tragedy of tragedies were the grown-up girls whose marriages had not been completed, with the shame that such brings to Indian minds, and whose men folk were away for years and for ever. Sad the world round was the lot of the world's maids in this matter, saddest of all perhaps in the Punjab that trusted but hardly understood. Marriage in India is the most essential matter in a girl's life, for her place in Heaven is determined thereby.

The Story of the Water-Bailiff's Wife

Here by way of lighter vein is an experience of the writer's when commanding a battery, that has its humorous side, but shows both the independence and perhaps the femininity of the lasses of the Punjab. One day outside my bungalow when I returned from the lines, was an old Muhammadan of the Punjab, obviously a yeoman farmer. Under another tree were a young man and a woman. And I asked the old man what his business might be. "*Sahib*," said he after a low obeisance, "I am in great trouble and shame. My son is a driver in your battery. We are Awans from the Salt Range. He is not married but has picked up some worthless woman who is living with him in your married quarters, and passing as his wife. I pray thee compel him to send her away. That is the young man over there."

From the other tree now advanced a lad whom I had often noticed for his good seat on a horse and his smart appointments. He was in white cotton clothes, the white that is tinged with the blue bag, and a regimental puggarree. The skirt also followed in his wake, and a skirt and a half I found her, tall and graceful and sonsy, as I saw a little later. The lad, a good-looking young Awan with almost Grecian features and a well set-up figure, saluted.

"Well," I said, "what is the story and what have you done that your father should have to come to me?" The woman drew her *sari* closer over her face.

"*Sahib*, when I last went home on my way back in the train I met this woman at Lala Musa, and I got into conversation with her. She told me that her husband, who is a water-bailiff beyond Shapur, beat her and that she could stand it no longer. She was on her way to Lahore to try her luck in the *chakla*, the light o' loves quarter, as the more bearable life. I said to her, 'That seems a pity, what's wrong with coming with me? You shall have a quarter in my commanding officer's lines. I will pay the sergeant and say that you are my new wife.' She said, 'I don't mind if I do.' Now I am very fond of her, and she cooks well too. I cannot give her up, and if that water-bailiff man will divorce her I will marry her." The old man wrung his hands. "*Sahib*, this is a great *sharm*, a great disgrace."

So I thought a while and the woman drew near and touched my feet and her *sari* fell from her head. I saw that she was a very proper woman. Tall and bonnie and hearty and modest-looking too withal. She wore heavy bangles on her ankles. "Are these your husband's?" I said, a serious matter. The lad broke in.

"*Sahib*, I have given them to her. I had saved my pay."

The woman gave me a beseeching look, a very haunting look from very attractive eyes.

"If you take her away I shall die," said the young man. It was ever thus. Then I saw the Indian sergeant was waiting too, and I called him.

"You know this woman?"

"She is the young man's wife I believe. She is very well behaved and quiet and keeps herself to herself."

I turned to the father.

"It does not seem that I can do much. You know what young men are. You had better arrange a divorce if you can. She seems of your own class."

The woman had now touched the feet of the old man.

"I never saw her before, *Sahib*. She seems right. I will take this matter further if you say so."

And they left and the young man's dog went with them as the Book of Tobit has it. It was reported to me however that the father had acquiesced in the situation. But that is not the end of the story. A month or two later, I found a party outside my orderly room. There was a constable with a warrant and a terrible looking individual, pock-marked, with a scrubby close-clipped grey beard, dyed red, a regular ogre. In the offing was my friend the young Awan and the lady, who now came up the verandah step. Here she complicated the situation by throwing her arms round my ankles. Happily the sergeant-major here intervened, for a lady embracing your ankles and looking up at you pleadingly is an embarrassment to a workaday soldier.

The heavens had in fact fallen on the idyll. The pock-marked gentleman was the water-bailiff husband, and the constable had a warrant for the summons of the young man and order for his arrest on a charge of abduction, which the constable said would be abandoned if the lady would return to her husband.

The young soldier declared that he could not part with her; that he had spent much money on her, and that she was his all-in-all. Sympathy seemed to run with him, my captain even suggested that it was infernal impertinence the policeman coming into our lines with a warrant, and suggested I should kick him out. The appearance of the water-bailiff, the ogre owner and the beauty were too great a contrast. So I said, "What does the woman want. This choice young man or her red bearded husband?"

Then she drew herself up. What had happened I know not. Had there been jars? I could not tell.

"Do you think" she said sweetly, "that I will stay with *that* creature," and she pointed to the soldier, "when my own good kind husband has come all this way to fetch me?" and she stepped across to his side. Who was I to interfere between man and wife? Whether the lady had seen the game was up and was surrendering handsomely I know not. It was a very crumpled young soldier that left my presence as the lass, the delightful good-looking lass, that was meant to be the mother of generations of good soldiers went off on her rightful arm, the constable and the warrant following. Perhaps Mulvaney would have said "I learnt about women from 'er." But anyway I had seen a typical Punjabi woman of the soldier class at close quarters and I liked the look of her.

That was the end of it so far as I ever heard, but I took the lad away shooting with me to give him something else to think about.

AN AWAN (ONE OF THE PUNJABI MUSSALMAN TRIBES) OF A PUNJAB REGIMENT.

CHAPTER XIV

THE MARTIAL RACES OF THE EAST AND WEST TO-DAY

THE REST OF INDIA—THE ANGLO-INDIAN—THE BRAHMIN AS A SOLDIER—THE HINDUSTANI MOSLEM—THE JĀT—THE MEN OF RAJPUTANA—THE RAJPUTANA MOSLEM AND ABORIGINALS—GUJARS AND AHIRS—GARHWALIS AND KUMAONIS—THE MAHRATTA OF TO-DAY—THE MEN OF THE OLD COAST ARMY—MOPLAHS AND COORGS.

THE REST OF INDIA

So much for the fashionable Punjab whose fighting men furnish the greater part of the Army, fashionable because of their flocking to suppress the Mutiny and the rebellion that accompanied it, fashionable because they gave the British so tough a job in the Sikh Wars, fashionable because they poured forth so many hundred thousand enthusiastic self-sacrificing soldiers in the World War, and because their ways are the ways of men, and for numerous cognate reasons.

But there are other parts of the Indian sea where the fishing is good though not so prolific, where the young men have always served, and whence also many flocked in the World War, and if they could not fight at any rate came to labour. But nevertheless, the rest of India has nothing like the same *percentage* of men that are men as the Punjab, while as for the intelligentsia, it may be said that eighty per cent of those screaming for *Swaraj* did not only not move a finger to serve in the war time, but many were actively concerned with hindering it. Had there not been a Labour Government in power when such questions would have been invidious, it would have been no bad jest to have summarized and made public the war services of those who came to the Round Table.

The races that are not of the Punjab and which serve India and the Crown with credit, must now be enumerated, and it will be seen that some of them have a special romance of their own, often deeply connected with some of the more glorious of both British and Indian traditions.

The Anglo–Indian

Anglo-Indian is the name now applied officially to people in India born of British and Indian parents, or the descendants of such. It has taken the place of the term Eurasian, an obviously unsuitable one, which may equally apply to Franco-Chinese or any other combination. Speaking generally it applies to those of the first generation whose fathers are British and whose mothers are Indian and their descendants, but as there is a growing number of unions between Eastern men and Western women the term may in time be widened. We have yet to discover how the latter are to be brought up. The Anglo-Indian at present is almost invariably brought up as a Westerner. This community is just as much an Indian one as were the earlier progeny of Aryan and Dravidian, or of Turk and Indian, and so far as they have martial proclivities they are entitled to a place in this chapter, and I have placed them between the Northerners and the others.

There have been in the last 150 years many famous soldiers

and frontiersmen of mixed parentage. The famous Colonel Skinner will be described in this chapter under the story of the Hindustani Moslems, and he is one of the most distinguished in history, and in his generation have been also Robert Skinner his brother, Hyder Hearsey and many others, while a generation or so later there were several who came to fame, and among them no less a person than Sir Richard Warburton of the Khaiber. Many generations of Hearseys served the Crown. Sir John Hearsey, the famous cavalry soldier, had no Indian blood, but his cousin Hyder had, and also had married Zenat-ul-Nissa, one of the Begums of Cambay, wards of the Moguls, Sir John marrying Hyder's daughter Harriet. There were several of her sons in the Army. Hyder himself when sixteen years of age had a cadetship in the French trained forces of M. Perron in the service of Sindia, and only joined the British service after Lord Lake's victories. Then he served the state in many campaigns and in many capacities, and was a great character well known in his day. Among the many stories that used to be current was that he had a *Pachesi* board tattooed on his abdomen and that his wives played *Pachesi* (Homeward Bound) thereon while he slept!

This half-bred race is a peculiar one, handicapped in many ways, and having varied origin. Some of the women married were of the highest families, others of the humblest. Some of the mixed race were the children of officers, others the miscellaneous progeny of the rank and file. The women in the south were probably Dravidian, in the centre Aryan and in the north often of Tartar blood. But the well-to-do of the mixed race have of modern years retired to England and failed to be a support to those left in India. It has been said that this community 'leaks at both ends', the upper end to England and the lower to the native

Christians in the bazaars who wear European clothes, but whose European names have often been taken from the tombstones in the British burial ground. In no other race do those who come to success tend to disappear from among their community.

In many periods of Indian history the young men of mixed blood have rallied to the service. There have been many in the ranks of the Company's Europeans, and during the Mutiny many served in the Volunteer cavalry, notably the Lahore Horse, and took a part in the Defence of Lucknow and Cawnpore. Since the Mutiny their services have been made little military use of save in the subordinate medical services, and indeed some want of sympathy and imagination towards a community that is of Britain's own making must be laid at the door of the authorities. The Volunteer force of India, however, has seen them by the thousand, and in the World War they flocked to serve, both in such corps as the Madras Artillery (who shared in the Defence of Kut), and in every sort of technical service. The community have a grievance that a battalion has not been raised from them for the permanent army. That is not based on sound reasoning, for the life of the normal rank and file does not offer a career. They would not have been the better for such an opening, nor do they turn out sufficient men of physique to form a battalion, the better grown members looking for some higher role in life than that of the rank and file, which is but a preliminary to unskilled work in civil life. A battery of coast and inland artillery should certainly have been raised for them, and the Signal Service is one that should have been opened to them in earlier days.

Unfortunately, white people still have the instinct, even when repressed, to look down on the offspring of miscegenation, and those who condemn the Aryan contempt for the depressed classes, the descendants of miscegenation, are not themselves free from an exactly similar complex. This mixed race which gets so complicated as the generations roll on, is a serious problem, for the name Anglo-Indian covers so many varying elements and stages, but its military record is by no means negligible, and the memorials for the World War in the schools of India, mostly in the hills to which such boys go, contain just as sad, and in proportion, just as numerous tablets to young lives lost as do the schools in Merry England. Its fostering and its care, especially under changing Indian conditions, are a peculiar duty for Britain, and it is satisfactory to know that after some delay Christian boys of mixed descent are declared as eligible as any other Indian-born lad for the position of 'Brindian' —the slang phrase for an Indian-born lad who is to have a British officer's status in the army.

Let us hope in justice to the memory of James Skinner, Hyder Hearsey and Richard Warburton of the Artillery, that such boys may come to great fame.

The Brahmin as a Soldier

Those who are not well acquainted with the story of the Indian races will be surprised to know that the Brahmin has for many generations been renowned as a soldier. The ranks of the Bengal Army were largely recruited from the agricultural Brahmins of Oudh. The sepoy ranks that helped carry the Union Jack to China, to Egypt and to the Hindu Kush contained many men of the priestly race, stalwart young yeoman peasants from the farms on the plain of Hindustan proper. Their defects as soldiers were largely their ceremonial and other inhibitions regarding food. The obligation to strip to feed made the Afghan winter a sad trial, while the question of water and sick attendants was most complicated. After the mutiny of the Bengal Army their numbers were greatly reduced, but in almost every war the Brahmin soldiers of His Majesty have gained some special distinction. The intense veneration however that they demand and receive has always made their position in a disciplined army anomalous, while the overpowering penchant for intrigue has always made them a troublesome asset in their grouping. Before the World War they had all been concentrated in two battalions entirely Brahmin in the hope that their pride of race might be enhanced and that they might well exhaust their power of intrigue on themselves. As two fine corps they went to the War, but they unexpectedly refused to abrogate their feeding and cooking peculiarities as they had promised in the face of the enemy, were starved in consequence and lost any reputation they had acquired. Now except a clan known as the Gaur Proper, whose habits are simpler, there are very few to be found in the Army.

As members of the Indian race their future must depend on the line which they are to take. Hindu reformers of non-Brahmin castes have always held their pretensions in enmity. The Westernization of many ideas may alter their outlook, but a race and a pretension which survived a thousand years of Buddhism, and eight hundred years of Islam, is not likely to give up lightly the position in the minds of men that is theirs by three thousand years of custom. What is likely to do them more harm than anything else is a display of such hostility against British dominion and leadership as will exasperate the British spirit against them. For a race of such intellect a joint alliance alone can promise well for the fate of India and themselves in the next few generations. Beyond that the human vision cannot look, but can however draw deductions from the centuries that fall away behind it.

The Hindustani Moslem

The term Hindustani Moslem is an inclusive one and comprises all those who profess the Moslem faith in the United Provinces, which include Rohilkand and the Delhi districts. They include the converts the Sheiks, the descendants of settlers of all kinds, Afghan, Pathan and Turk, and the people of traditional Arab descent, the Sayads. But round Lucknow are descendants of many and varied breeds of foreigners, Turks and Persians, so that the Moslems who live in 'Hindustan', the name by which the country of the earlier Gangetic settlement is known to the Eastern world, are of many origins.

Many as they are, it cannot be said that all are of any martial strain or proclivities, and it is not till we get nearer to Delhi that we begin to touch the real soldier strain.

In the districts round about that ancient capital are a large number of land-owning and cultivating smallholders, yeoman peasantry and the smaller lairds, all of whom at one time or another have received land from the kings and emperors of Delhi. Ethnologically they may be Turk, Afghan, Persian or Pathan. They call themselves by the term Turk, or rather 'Toork' for the tongue dwells on the 'u', and in the sense that Toork has come to have, already referred to, of 'professional hereditary soldier'. They all have tied tenants under them to whom they still refer as their 'slave'. Other of the hereditary professional soldiers are the Rohillas, the descendants of the Afghan and Pathan settler of Rohilkand, of whose history so much has already been said. It is from these men that the old Irregular or *Silladar* Cavalry drew their best men before the Mutiny. It was such men as these who in Afghanistan would fight single combats with Afghan horsemen, and it is they who when they mutinied were so often killed in single combat by the young British leaders of the retributary horse—and at times killed them. But it is also the fact that many of them, especially the 'Toorks', remained staunch.

It was from this class that 'Old Sekunder'[1] Colonel James Skinner, raised his men whom he brought to Lord Lake's service from that of the broken army of Sindiah. Two regiments of Skinner's Horse served the Company and the Crown from the beginning of the nineteenth century to the end of the World War when they were amalgamated in one only as 'Skinner's Horse'. The 1st was the original corps of old James', the 'Yellow boys' in the canary-coloured *kurta* that they wear to this day, and the 3rd Skinner's Horse was a corps raised by his nephew. Old James himself was the son of an officer in the Company's service and a *Rajputni* and entered the cadet service of De Boigne under Sindiah. The stories of him are legion. He wore a British dragoon helmet and a yellow light dragoon jacket trimmed with silver braid. The church he built at Delhi is well known but not perhaps the mosque and the Hindu temple, all erected says the story, because of a vow that he made when once abandoned wounded on the field of battle to make the many mansions that might appease—and who shall say that he was wrong?

The Skinner family still abide on the Skinner estates near Delhi, and little old ladies in beaded capes and black

[1] Sekunder—fortunate—the name for Alexander of Macedon.

crêpe bonnets still sit in the Skinner pew, while the head of the family still holds an honorary if undistinguished commission in the ancestral corps.

There is an old Irish saying 'the tribe of Flynns know their own whiskey skins', and Skinner knew his Moslem men. He enlisted only the Toork from Delhi as his *silladars*[1] with a few of their slaves as *bhargirs*, and he left it in his will that never should the Rohilla be allowed to dim its ranks as he considered them always untrustworthy and full of *fisad*, i.e. treachery and intrigue. To him as to all others Indian born the old tag held good "*Afghan! Afghan! Be iman! be iman!*" which may be interpreted "*Fie! Fie! Faithless Afghan!*" This is a reflection which the friends of the Afghans would fain explain away and which the Afghans would like to live down. They do not find it easy, and old James' will came straight off the ice!

Now Skinner's Horse under Crauford Chamberlain was staunch as a bell during the Mutiny and practically held the frontier city of Multan, disarming the Poorbiah sepoys, connected with which is the terrible shooting at Gurgaon of the ressaldar-major of the regiment on leave from Multan during the Mutiny by Hodson, the one act that no-one has ever been able to explain or exonerate. Another famous corps, the two regiments of Sind horse, afterwards the Sind Horse and Jacob's Horse, swore by them as the finest soldiers in India, and they kept the whole of that fierce Baluch border quiet and put the 'Fear of God' into the Baluchis for all time. The cavalry regiments of the Frontier Force also enlisted them. But the upset of the Mutiny, the prevailing passion for Punjabis, and no doubt the dying of

[1] *Silladars*, men who bring their own horse and arms and are paid accordingly. *Bhargirs*, men who are brought by a superior who provides the needful for them.

the martial instinct among some, has brought about a fewer number in the ranks than formerly. There are magnificent young men among them, and certainly the present older generation still speak with awe and veneration of *Lik Sahib*, Lord Lake, the general who drove the Mahrattas from Moslem Delhi.

There are still choice young horsemen too among the Rohillas, but the record of Rohilkand in '57 has taken a lot of living down, and it is not from that province of ill-omened name that many come who serve the Crown.

The Jāt

We have seen the great Jāt or Jăt race of history contend and mix in earlier times with those who had obtained their footing in the great fraternity of Rajputs, and how they had for reasons not explicable remained outside. We have also seen how a portion adopted Sikhism to found the solid basis of the men of the religion that is becoming a race, and we have also seen how some have turned to Islam and have noticed the warning that 'Jăt' in the Punjab is almost synonymous with cultivator, and cannot be taken entirely as denoting race.

Among the Hindu Jāts of Rajputana and the territories round Delhi to-day it is very different. Here you find the Jāts as they were when they came into the hierarchy of Brahminism, probably at the reconstruction. You have the peasantry, the yeoman and the small landowner, the lads that flock to the army, also choice young men and goodly, with all the good traits of Hinduism of repute and status and few of the bad ones.

The Jāt with a long ā is exclusively Hindu, and in British

India is found in all the districts in the vicinity of Delhi, as well as Rajputana and in portions of the United Provinces. They are grouped into two fairly distinct sections known as *Hele* and *Dhe*, but in Rajputana the *Hele* are also called *Deswali* and the *Dhe Pachade*; the *Hele* and *Deswali* have a higher social status than the others, which may date back far into history, the *Dhe* being said to be much later arrivals in the country, and also to be perhaps the ancient *Dahe* who were spread from the Caspian to the Persian gulf.

The Jāts were a very definite power in the days of the Mogul waning, and the defiance of the British by the state of Bhurtpur, then in alliance with Holkar, resulted in the only setback that Lord Lake met with, having four times been repulsed with heavy loss from its high mud walls, despite the greatest gallantry of British and Sepoy stormers, in which the famous 76th Foot was specially pre-eminent. It was not till 1826 that fresh arrogance on the part of a usurping potentate resulted in the final capture by Lord Combermere. The defence was then equally stout, but the British brought more heavy guns and worked under better conditions. The Jāts then had entertained a large contingent of mercenary Pathans who suffered severely.

The Jāts in Rajputana are for military purposes divided into Western and Eastern, the former from the bulk of the larger Rajputana states, and the latter from Bhurtpur, Dholpur, and the district of Karauli. The largest number of Jāts are found in Jaipur, Jodhpur, Bikanir and Bhurtpur. The modern Jāt like the Jăt Sikh is stolid and unimaginative, but never forgets what he has once learnt. He is sturdy and independent in character and does not subscribe to those Hindu customs which have been the ruin of so many of its votaries. Marriage is usually at adult age, and the young men, like those of the peasantry in the Punjab, are not victims to the early eroticism which so injures the classes of the intelligentsia. Widow marriage is practised, and the Jāt in fact stands at the top of the classes who permit it, caring naught for ordinary Hindu opinion. The opinions of experienced officers and the experience of the World War have placed them among the best of the Indian martial classes. Indeed one of the Jāt battalions like the Mahratta and the Garhwali has the high distinction of the title of 'Royal.' The women of the Jāt classes, and indeed of all Rajputana, are sturdy, jolly wenches. They dress in a flowered corset, laced at the back, which acts as a brassiére, wear a picturesquely bright skirt of coarse dyed cotton, and a bright head scarf.

The number of *gots*[1] or clans among the Jāts is legion, the larger clans noticeable in the Punjab not existing, and for this reason a man's *got* is not so important in his estimation as among other classes.

The regiments that wholly enlisted Jāts under the class system existing before the World War were the 6th and the 10th Jāts now battalions of the 9th Jāt Regiment, the 6th having earned the title 'Royal.' There are also Jāt squadrons in some of the cavalry corps as well as Jāt companies in other Infantry regiments.

The Men of Rajputana

There are, as has been explained, but two centres where the genuine unadulterated clan-bound Hindu Rajput is to be found, the arid hills and valleys of Rajasthan, to which the Rajputs of the Gangetic plain betook themselves before the hosts of Islam, and the Dogra Hills. The men of the former both Rajput and other races of martial proclivities inhabiting

[1] *Got* has a different significance here from what it has with Rajputs who use it of marriage groups, rather than clan.

Rajasthan enlist into the Rajputana Rifle Regiments, the 7th Rajput Regiment and some of the companies of the former Hyderabad Regiments. More could be obtained if needed, but as in Jammu and Kashmir, the state armies themselves have first claim on their own men. There are eleven true Rajput clans still recognized in Rajputana or Rajasthan, and they are the names famous in the Rajput annals that have already been briefly described. Among the more notable are Rathor, Kachwaha, Chauhan and Jadu.

The Rathores always have pride of place and by predilection are cavalry men only. The only Victoria Cross gained by a Rajput in the World War was won by a Rathore, Jemadar Govind Singh, 28th Light Cavalry. Their martial spirit in modern times has largely been sustained and stimulated by that Paladin among modern Indian heroes, the Maharajah Sir Pertab Singh of Jodhpur, the first gentleman, it is not too much to say, in the Empire.

The Kachwaha are another very numerous tribe with many sub-clans, divided into three main groups of which the Shekhawat find more soldiers than any other, and from them the Shekhawati regiment of the Bengal Line was recruited, now the 10th Battalion of the Rajput Regiment. The Jadus, the Rajputs of the Moon, have often been mentioned. The Bhattis who are found all over the north, Hindu and Moslem, are a branch of the Jadus, and in the Punjab gave their name to the city of Bhatinda. The Bhattis have long been laughed at as simple coves. One of their chiefs of Jaisulmer is said to have ordered the jackals in his forests to be clothed because some one had said that their howling at night was due to their feeling the cold.

Every tribe is the centre of many legends of origins and prowess, and the sagas of chivalry and derring-do are the constant subject of popular song and recital. If you march and camp with Rajputs you may sit late into every night by the camp fires listening to all that is to be told, each yarn more stirring, more romantic and more imaginative than its predecessor! The people of this countryside far removed from many of the so-called ways of progress that are to be met with at any rate in the great cities of India, are much as India has been through the ages. Elephants weave at the Palace gates and hoot at the Chief's silver motor car, gaily caparisoned horses and camels are ridden through the great city gates and archways into the crowded, picturesque bazaars. Retainers carrying often enough the arms and even the mail of the middle ages throng the palaces, and a paternal feudalism is everywhere in evidence, though that does not mean that modern ways are necessarily absent from the framework of the administration.

The Rajput chief however is still the father of his state, his clan, and his people, and the descriptions that Lyall wrote hold good in this the twentieth century, save that the widows will not burn unless surreptitiously. It is he who makes the old dying hidalgo mourn for the ways of war that are gone:

> Eight months my grandsire held the keep
>   Against the fierce Mahratta hordes
> It would not stand three winter suns
>   Before the shattering English guns.

and the fierce uncompromising spirit that still remains when the old man tells of his unwilling penance for the death of a Brahmin:

> But I must offer gifts and pray
> The Brahmins stain be washed away.
> Saint and poisoner, fed with bribes
> Deep-versed in every traitorous plan.
> I told them only to kill the scribes
> But my Afghans hated the holy man.

The end of such needs Kipling's gift to see him go on his funeral pyre, when his prowess and his titles are chanted in sonorous Persian *Dost-i-Inglishia*, *Bahadur-i-Bahaduran*:

> Friend of the English, Free from Fear,
> King of the desert of Jeysulmere
> Lord of the jungles. Go!

And the young men leave the simple old paternal lands, and follow the Union Jack round the world, deriving pleasure and profit thereby, and so the world rolls on.

The Muhammadan and Aboriginal Peoples in Rajputana

There are in Rajputana many Moslem peoples of distinct military value more exploited in the days now past of the local corps than in the Army of the Line, but still happily not entirely overlooked and to be found in the ranks of what is now the 6th Rajputana Rifles, and the 7th Rajput Regiment. The Rajputana Rifles has for its components the regiments known before the recent regrouping as the 104th, 120th, 122nd, 123rd and 125th Regiments, three of them being the famous Bombay Rifle Corps.

The races are not sufficiently prominent to merit a long description. Perhaps the most important are the Minas, regarded as some of the aboriginal inhabitants who live in the long mountain range known as the Kalikho Hills, which run from Ajmere to the Jumna. Many of the clans, however, claim and undoubtedly have, some Rajput admixture. There are six main divisions and countless clans, and as many stories accounting for the origin of each. Some of those who claim Rajput admixture are admittedly of high status, and from some of them, such as the Ujlash, Rajputs will take food and drink. They make useful soldiers.

The Mers come from Merwara, which state at one time had quartered in it the local Merwara battalion, afterwards numbered in Lord Kitchener's day as the 44th. They are it is said but the highlanders of Rajputana and of aboriginal origin. Mers are both Hindu and Moslem, the latter being usually called Merats, yet to make the problem simpler there are also Hindu Merats to be found. Military service is extremely popular with Mers who flocked to the new corps during the War. It is because they have never been known outside the local corps that they have not been made more use of. Mers and Merats have been known to eat together in spite of the latter being Moslem, but on the other hand many of them are anxious to be recognized as having Rajput status.

Kaimkhanis are Rajput Moslems said to be descended from Chouhan stock converted in the fourteenth century when Feroz Tulaq was Emperor at Delhi. They are not very numerous but living in Rajputana have retained many Rajput habits and make fine horse as well as foot soldiers. Meos are the inhabitants of Mewat, the term for the hill country in the states of Alwar, Bhurtpur and the Delhi district, and are probably folk of pre-Aryan origin. They are all Moslems in name and are cheery, sturdy soldiers, of whom perhaps more might be made. A small high grade Moslem people are known as the Khanzadas from whom soldiers are taken.

It is to be understood that the number of battalions required from the races of Rajputana is small and that the contingent from these races is as nothing compared with the enlistment in the Punjab. Nor is it probable that they are, taken all round, up to the Punjab standard of physique and general suitability.

TYPES FROM RAJPUTANA. (PRE-WAR CORPS AND DRESS). MER, MINA AND KAIMKHANI

[Face page 282

GUJARS AND AHIRS

Reference has been made in Chapter III to a people of obscure origin widespread in northern India, viz., the Gujars, many of whom are Moslem and who are largely graziers. They live in considerable numbers in Rajputana and round Delhi, where they have always had a reputation for turbulence. A few of them are taken into the Army among the Rajputana classes, and in the Punjab as Punjabi Muhammadans and are a class from whom, if need be, a larger number of soldiers might be drawn. Rather independent, and agricultural or rather pastoral, they have many of the characteristics of the Jāts but live in a lower social plane in the eyes of Hindudom generally. Gujars are to be found all over the Delhi districts, the Doab and in Rajputana as well as the Punjab. Gujars were and probably are the acknowledged experts and addicts in cattle thieving, and whenever law and order is at all below par, the addiction will break out, for at all times as on the Highland border your neighbour's cattle are fair game.

Among the Jāt and Gujar races and the Eastern Rajputs will be found another useful people, the Ahirs, not taken very largely as fighting soldiers save as drivers in the Artillery, and recently even as gunners. The Ahir group known as Jadubans, however, have always been taken in the corps that were in the Hyderabad contingent. They are chiefly lesser cultivators and dairymen to whom the producing of milk for the ghee market is an important industry. Ahirs are perhaps a respectable Hindu class rather than a race, but keep themselves to themselves, and are one of the most reputable classes in their districts in a minor way. Their usefulness in their special line is considerable, and though in the past they have no doubt shouldered a pike in the military rag tag and bobtail of Eastern armies, they cannot well be described as one of the martial races of renown, yet their reputation is growing.

The Eastern Rajput is the modern recruiting name for the class that formed the mass of the Bengal Army, the Rajputs of Oudh and Behar, and what are now known as the United Provinces. Fine athletic young men under modern conditions, a certain number are taken in the 7th Rajput Regiment and a few in other corps. They, as has been explained, did furnish the bulk of the old professional soldiers of northern India, faithful like the cat to the house rather than to the master, and in days gone by have marched to the Hindu Kush and beyond with the Mogul armies as well as under the Union Jack, and it was they who sang the old patient chant of the foot-soldier:

Khăbhi Sukh aur Khŭbhi Dŭkk
Angrez ka naukar

which may be interpreted

"Sometimes pleasure, sometimes pain
The soldier of the English."

Garhwalis and Kumaonis

The Gurkha both past and present has been dealt with in a separate chapter, by reason of his commanding place among the martial races. Allusion has been made in that chapter and elsewhere to the Aryanization, the penetration by the old white colonists into the lower valleys and hills of outer Himalaya, and how there were evolved races which in the reconstruction were accorded Rajput status. This was especially the case in the hill tracts north-west of Nepal known as Kumaon and Garhwal, from which, as already related, the ruthless invading Gurkhas were driven by the British in the war of 1814–16. Kumaon is now a British district of which Garhwal is a part, the northern half of the latter, however, being the state of Tehri-Garhwal. The Garhwali Rajput has come to great fame and status in the Indian Army, but especially so in the World War, when not one but all regular battalions were among the very few to earn the distinction of the title 'Royal', a distinction shared with one Gurkha, one Jāt, one Măzbhi Sikh corps, and the Deccan Horse. The Kumaoni, a little hillman who of late years has not been very favoured, supplied battalions during the War and one of them has been retained since.

The history of the Garhwal hills has been little written of, and such as it is but records the constant wars between chief and clan and baron, and the attempts of the Moguls to bring the country into their system.

We know and the people know that the twelve years of Gurkha dominion were exceedingly bitter. All old families were destroyed, all persons of rank and importance were banished or murdered, villages were burnt and many of the people sold as slaves. The British rule which succeeded was unalloyed bliss by contrast.

Nine-tenths of the people of Garhwal belong to the mysterious Khas race, of which Garhwal is now the true *Khas desh*, or Khas country, a race mysterious because we find geographical traces of them in many a place-name, Kashgarhas, Kashmir and the like, and because no one can quite locate them in the Aryan cosmos. Were they a separate and advance wave of Aryan, or were they earlier folk, whiter than Dravidian, who mingled with Aryans? No man knoweth. We see the same folk also in Nepal, and along the

Himalayan foothills towards Assam as Khasas, amid the Khasya Hills. However that may be the *Khas* have now Rajput Aryan status sufficient for the purposes of modern Hinduism. The remaining tenth of the people of Garhwal are the Tibetan Bhotyas, the Nagas, also the remnant of some lost race, and certain immigrants as well as the universal black servitors of India, the *Doms*.

For modern grouping the terms Upper and Lower Garhwal are used, the people of Upper Garhwal being by physique and by character, the better soldier. The broad divisions are Brahmin, Rajput and Dom. The Rajput includes both Khasas and the Rajput immigrants of later coming. The various groups and clans in the first two categories are innumerable, some being better for military purposes than others. A few Brahmins are enlisted, but the major portion of soldiers comes from the Rajput class. The Garhwali is slighter and lighter than the thickset Tibetan and Tartar folk, and unless there has been some Dom admixture they are fair of countenance. The wilder and less sophisticated man is the better soldier, the man who only wears blankets; he who wears cotton is always less desirable. The dark man of Dom colour is also to be avoided. In former years many Garhwalis were enlisted in Gurkha or other corps, and their good qualities were not so supremely developed till they were grouped in all-Garhwali corps. They have been clothed by the British in rifle green, and dressed like the Gurkhas in Kilmarnock cap. There is a faint trace of the Tartar often in their faces, as if some miscegenation had been admitted in the past, and in appearance they resemble faintly the Gurkha, especially the *Khas* Gurkha, though taller and slighter. To the Garhwali however the Gurkha is anathema, and they would indignantly disclaim any resemblance. A good many of them were serving in the Gurkha Army under

Gurkha officers in 1914–16 which accounts for their being found in days gone by in the ranks of our own Gurkha corps. It was a sad jar to their pride that, when a company or platoon gave trouble in 1930 in Peshawar and the whole corps was disarmed, they should have been sent to the custody of the Gurkha brigade at Abbottabad.

The disaffection was happily only in a small portion of the corps, which was shortly after re-armed. The evidence of the British officer who commanded the errant company at the military court was significant because it so exactly tallies with the tragic behaviour of hitherto loyal corps in 1857. "I did not know the men, they were transformed from the men I knew." It was the same in '57, a really loyal corps, clamouring one night to be led against mutineers, would have turned sour in the night like milk in thunder. A virus cherished by some evil cell would have spread from some slight indisposition. For some years the military authorities had been dinning into the hypnotized ears of the Civil Administration that congress seditionists were very active in peaceful happy Garhwal, and could bode no good. It does not pay in the East to disregard the omens.

The great record of the Garhwalis as loyal soldiers, however, can carry off this strange if ominous incident. They went to the World War as the 1st and 2nd battalion of the 39th Garhwal Rifles, and eventually expanded to four battalions. After the War in the re-grouping they remained as the 18th Royal Garhwal Rifles, the title 'Royal' being conferred on the *whole corps*, but because the Army is human and suspicious of favourites it was not unamused at the Peshawar incident.

It was in France that the regiment earned such undying fame as almost to be classed as 'storm troops'. So far as it is an accurate gauge, the list of honours is significant:

Out of 5 Victoria Crosses won in France by Indians 2 went to the 2 battalions of Garhwalis.
Out of 10 Military Crosses 4 do. do. do. do.
Out of 68 Indian Orders of Merit 7 do. do. do. do.

grants far above the proportion likely to accrue to them. Losses were peculiarly heavy and amounted to 60 per cent, 15 per cent being killed.

The State of Tehri Garhwal maintained a Company of Sappers for the Imperial Service, which also went to the War, and was not undistinguished, and of course furnished many recruits. That in brief is the story of martial Garhwal.

The Kumaonis, who inhabit the district south of and adjoining Garhwal, are very similar in type, but in appearance show rather more of the leavening Tartar blood. Were India at all short of soldiers, several more corps could be raised from this Hindu race.

The Mahrattas To-day

The Mahrattas of to-day, or of any period, are born and bred among very different scenes from the men of the frontier and the sun-swept Punjab. Theirs is neither the heat that rattles mens' skulls and brains, nor the fierce cold that makes men among men. Not the wholemeal of the '*atta*', the coarse-grown wheat goes to their composition, nor the grapes and apples of the northern fruits. They live a life and eat a diet that produces the wiry mountain rats of the Shivaji legend. We must try to visualize the great jungle-clad wall of the Western Ghats that catches the clouds of the south-west monsoon, and all the year round is green and even luscious. Nevertheless the terrain is hard, and only fit for the agile little men who live among the scarred ravines and terraced fields which spread down to the Konkan, the lower lands below the Ghats. Their slightness is not the squat diminutive pug-dog build of the Gurkhas and Kumaoni, but the active litheness of the wildcat. All along the Ghats where trade routes pass through, as related in the earlier chapters, the old fortresses frown down atop the openings, and the stone horses of Siva stand in line at the village entrance. The Mahratta is like all the Indian soldiers, a cultivating peasant, or the land-owning yeoman who works his lands with the help of Kolis and other humbler folk. He is the child of the soil and talks the local prakrit that we know as Mahratti.

He is intensely sensitive of the story of Shivaji, and is, as already outlined as national in a local sense as the Sikh in the north and with a truer reason.

On the upland atop the Ghats live a burlier type of the race known as the 'Dekhani' Mahratta, the inhabitant of the plains of the Dekhan. Those are the great plains that stretch inland from the mountain wall, where people tell you that the hoofs of the horses of the *Panchhazari*, the Five-thousand Corps of Baji Rao the last of the Peshwas, are heard o' nights beating their way out before Sindia and the British.

The men still affect the little cap rather than the puggaree, and such folk as the police, the night watchmen and the *peon* or footman, the pawn of the chess-board, still wear with satisfaction the little Kilmarnock cap that the Crimean Army wore, and which the Indian Army at one time adopted.

It was the Mahratta soldier that played so stout a part in the suppression of the Indian Mutiny in Central India, a service which made the Bombay Army grow slack with a pride and self-righteousness that was to be its undoing in the Afghan War of 1878-80, all the more because by that time a cult of grenadierdom had eliminated most of the mountain rats, the *Untoo Goorgas* of Lord Lake's day. In the revival and the systematic study of race and caste, that in its intensity dates from Lord Kitchener's day, the cult of the Mahratta, especially the Konkani Mahratta revived. Several class corps came into being composed very largely of Konkanis, and went to the World War as the 103rd, 105th, 110th, 114th, 116th and 117th Mahratta Light Infantry, six battalions in all, and in the post war re-grouping became the 5th Mahratta Regiment, consisting of six battalions. It has been explained that no Indian corps had ever been given the supreme and envied title 'Royal' till after the World War. The 117th Mahrattas now carry this blazon of pride.

The Men of the Old Coast Army

One of the sorrowful things that the years have brought forth, the years of the Pax Britannica that have prevailed for over a century in Southern India, is the elimination of the men of the Madras Presidency from the fighting forces of the Crown. So much has this been the case that there now remain but the 1st Madras Pioneers, and the Queen's Own Corps of Sappers and Miners. That is to say the corps primarily concerned with fighting have gone, and those remain whose primary duty is construction, a duty which may bring many dangers in its train, but secondary to their main purpose. Before dwelling on the races that join these technical Corps, a glance at the story of this Army in continuation of the historical account already given, will be of interest. The so called Brahminization of the Army has been referred to which a century ago meant the enlistment of the agricultural classes rather than the outcasts and the children of the foreign soldiers of fortune. The faithful attitude of the Madras Army during the disturbances following the Mutiny of the Bengal Army left that army like that of the Bombay Presidency with considerable prestige. Its caste constitution was largely Hindu, viz. Tamil and Telegu cultivators, with some companies of the hardy outcaste Pariahs and Christians, and with a certain number of Moslems largely the descendents of Turk and Afghan settlers, notably in the cavalry.

Now there has never been any question but what the Madrassi soldier has been most efficient under arms, and capable of a very high degree of training. Smart, well drilled, alert, obedient, apt to handle arms, and good shots, they have many of the qualifications that make good soldiers. German officers from their point of view have more than once said that only in the south of India had they seen 'regular soldiers' on parade.

But at the bottom of it all a stout heart comes first, and the rest of the Army in modern years have asserted that the Madras soldier failed in stout-heartedness. Years of the Pax Britannica had removed the familiarity with danger which is a small portion of the requirements. Another and very important factor was the fact that the best officers wanted to be near the frontier, and that the garrisons of Madras were too far off for their Madras Corps to be brought up into the field for anything save a very large war. Every regiment must in the course of human nature carry two or three officers who are less good by nature than the others. The spirit of the regiment carries them along. But there was a tendency for more than a normal share of the lesser characters to gravitate to the comparative ease of a 'down country life'. The result of this must have effect on the men. The annexation of Burma brought an unexpected call in 1885 to the Madras Army, and it did not fulfil expectations. Shortly after, a number of its units were reconstituted with up-country men, and ever since this process has continued.

There have always been some shining lights in the Madras units, men who would carry any race over the top, and under their stimulus certain corps maintained a high reputation. Enthusiasts themselves they endeavoured to bring everyone to belief in the superiority of the Madrassi soldier. During the war however, the call for men and more men, extended to Madras and the older military castes who had mourned both for financial reasons and for those of tradition, their lessening opportunities, sent forth their youth once again. The writer well remembers in 1920 inspecting a large depôt for Madras units in the field, and watching recruits at physical training. The adjutant who showed him round was bubbling with enthusiasm, and implored him to use his influence that such material should not be lost. Eager, willing, muscular boys thronged round, ideal soldiers to look at and in every way promising. But there is many a promising lad who does not realize that he is deficient in animal courage till the hour of trial comes. Military public opinion held that it was not right to spend the Indian tax-payers' money on one article when a better article for the purpose could be had elsewhere, and this sternly utilitarian view prevailed.

But older men with wider knowledge have always put forward two arguments in favour of the Madras soldier. First is the utter want of sympathy with feelings that may sway the north, and secondly that for this reason loyal second-class troops may often be better for the British purpose than first-class troops who may be disgruntled. A subsidiary argument was the great stimulus that military service has always brought to the character-building of the countryside, and the great loyalty to the Crown that the presence of retired Indian officers and N.C.O.'s in the districts produced.

Nevertheless the modern point of view has prevailed, all those choice young men are about their business and the Army of the Carnatic with all its accumulated story of glory is no more, save what the Sappers and Pioneers perpetuate, while some of the new Punjabi battalions carry on their colours, the old Coast honours.

The races of Madras consist chiefly of those classed under the main name of Dravidian, a people from the north who entered India at some remote period, subduing aboriginal tribes of negroid and perhaps Turanian origin. How or when they became to some extent Hinduized, or when the Brahmins came to settle among them, is but very dimly known, but that there were large and powerful kingdoms ruled by non-Aryan rulers is well known, and has already been referred to. Of the two great divisions Telegu and Tamil, the latter only have been taken of late years for the Army.

Among each division are certain of the depressed classes, like the Pariahs or Parayans, and these with the native Christians, also as a rule converted from the depressed classes, form the bulk of the men in the Sappers and Miners and the Pioneer corps.

The inherent Indian tendency for new castes to arise and for some form of social uplift to occur, is amusingly illustrated by the fact that outcaste races who serve in the Queen's Own Sappers and Miners form in civil life a new and inclusive caste known as *Quinsap*, holding their heads distinctly higher than the remainder of their own people, and confining their marriages to the daughters of those who have served. Long after the British Army is forgotten, the caste *Quinsap* will remain, and even puzzle ethnologists.

The Christians are largely drawn from the outcaste tribes and of late years the call has reached vast numbers, and total several millions. The old form of Christianity which is spoken of incorrectly as Syrian has flourished men say since the legendary visit of St. Thomas. This Church has broken into several by an attempt to gain touch with, and enjoy the support of the various Christian Churches of the Middle East, and for that reason some may be Syrians, others Nestorian, Chaldeans or Jacobites, though originally belonging to one Church. One or two lads of good family among the Syrian Christians have received the King's Commission (as distinct from the Viceroy's Commission given to ordinary Indian officers) and have therefore joined the class already referred to as Brindian.

One of the most gallant soldiers the writer has ever known was an ordinary Indian Christian, of the 23rd Wallajabad Light Infantry, one Naik Anthony, who was mortally wounded in a sortie from the beleagured post of Sadon on the Chinese frontier of Upper Burma. It has always been a matter of regret that he was too late to read the funeral service over him which he found being done by a Christian jemadar of the Queen's Sappers and Miners.

Moplahs and Coorgs

An interesting story is the attempt of the 'nineties of the last century following on their experience of Burma to find more martial classes within the Madras Presidency. A battalion of Coorgs from the highlands abutting on Mysore, the 73rd, and two rifle battalions of Moplahs were raised (77th and 78th) with that pomp which is permitted in our Army to rifle-dom.

The Coorgs, whose chiefs and retainers had more than

once assisted British arms in times gone by, could not furnish enough men to make the experiment a success. The Moplahs or Mapillahs are a race of Dravidians from the Malabar coast with some touch of Arab ancestry, who have become extremely fanatical Moslems. From time to time agrarian distress, possibly the oppression of landlords, added to the roll of the drum ecclesiastic, has brought them out in fierce opposition to the local police and stern and unyielding resistance under arms to detachments of European troops.

It was thought that such material might have some military value, and two battalions were raised. After some years, the more advanced of the two was sent to the Frontier at the most favourable time of the year, especially well clothed and equipped for the winter that would come. The battalion, however, was a failure, and though it contained two or three hundred lads who might with infinite care make in time soldiers, it was realised that there was not enough of them to maintain one, let alone, two battalions. Moreover there seemed to be no social class from which Indian officers could be drawn. Their own language was hard to learn and had no military vocabulary, and altogether it was not considered worth while 'going through so much to achieve so little'.

Those who were on the Frontier when they arrived wearing their tarbush, a dress hitherto unknown to the Army, but eminently a martial one, and saw them drag their weary limbs after a fifteen mile march, past such corps as the 20th Punjabis and Coke's Rifles to the frontier tune of *Zakhmi Dil*, their regimental quickstep, will sympathise with their officers and agree that they were wisely disbanded. Very small races are not fit material on which to base a battalion.

So ended the attempts to find more warlike material within the confines of Madras.

Chapter XV

IQD-I-GUL

THE CHAPLET OF ROSES—THE KING'S PAWNS—THE WHITE LIE—THE SUBAHDAR'S TITA BHAI.

The Chaplet of Roses

THOSE who have read any Persian will know their *Iqd-i-gul*, their Bunch or Chaplet of Roses, the collection of stories which begin "*Badshah-i-ra-shanidam*" . . . "Once I heard of a king", though what he heard of that king was not always quite presentable. The same name has been given to these few stories which show something of the personality of the Indian soldier in its most lovable side. The story of the King's Pawns has been told before, told, too, to His Majesty, as it was told the author up the Nile by Mr. James Breasted, of the University of Philadelphia, historian, and Mr. Oscar Straus, formerly United States Minister at Constantinople as told them by an officer of the Turkish General Staff who was present.

I have told the story at length and used the title of *The King's Pawns* in a book of short stories about the World War,[1] but cannot resist giving a brief outline of it here for the sheer beauty that it contains. Considerable efforts were made to trace the men, lost on the desert of Sinai, to whose glory the story might remain for ever, but there were several small parties lost, some perhaps deserters for

[1] *The Kings' Pawns.* (Sheldon Press).

whom the appeal of *Jihad* had been too much, and identification has not been possible. Like the Unknown Soldier they must remain as one of those to whom I always apply that beautiful text from Malachi, "for they shall be mine," said the Lord of Hosts, "in that day when I make up my jewels."

The story of the *White Lie* comes from my personal experience in Mesopotamia, and that of the *Subahdar's Tita Bhai*, from the life of a brother officer and a mountain battery with which I am 'well acquaint'. The first two happen to be stories of the same class, the Moslem of the Punjab who constitute the backbone of an ordinary Punjabi regiment.

The King's Pawns

For many months of the World War, before the growing might of Britain made the invasion of Judæa a military possibility, the British Army, largely its Indian components kept watch and ward on the Spine of the Empire, otherwise the Suez Canal. German and Turk desired to seize it, to prevent that astounding carriage of men and munitions that the East and the Pacific were sending to the struggle in the West. To break this spinal cord, to overrun Egypt and dominate the Red Sea was the object of the Central Powers. Early in '15 they made the first attempt and failed, but after the evacuation of Gallipoli they essayed it in strength, actually driving a railway line from Beersheba across the Desert of Sinai.

So come hot season come cold, the Indian troops, horse and foot and camel corps, held the line of the Canal, and sent their patrols out into the desert peering across the wind-swept sand dunes, watching the lizards and the mere-cats scuttle amid the tussocks and the camel-thorn, and the dust devils pirouette aimlessly in the track of the setting sun.

Bleak and barren are the desert and the Canal zone as even the first class passengers on the great liners know. You know it better still if you have patrolled Sinai in summer and seen as did the Children of Israel, the miraged cities and lakes, the wonders in the Land of Ham and the Field of Zoan.

A patrol finds its route by compass, and comes back by the great searchlights of the Canal, but in summer months when the dust devils dance and the dust storm blows and the scene is blotted, our compasses will not work nor do arc lights show. So it happened one day that a patrol setting forth from an out-post hard by El Qantara, the bridge where the ancient Pelusiac channel of the Nile now long dry, was crossed by the great trade route of the world, the Way of the Philistines, found itself trudging over the dunes in a dust storm. Fiercer and fiercer blew the dust, till it frizzled and sparkled over all their accoutrements, and on and on the party trudged, eyes and ears full of dust, their puggarees tied close over their brows and noses, till all sense of direction was gone and only a numb sense of duty remained. At last these Mussalmans of the Punjab, men of those Rajput Moslem clans already described, for such they were, lay down utterly lost and weary, with their heads buried against a thorn bush, in the hope of mercy. And thus they dosed till the late afternoon when the sun was falling and the wind had dropped and the fiery desert was assuming its innocent, peaceful evening aspect as if even butter would not melt in the rose and petal-grey light.

They were rudely awakened by the lance point of a Turkish cavalryman while a patrol with an officer of the German General Staff attached stood round. Dazed they got up and shook themselves free of the sand. Secured by a head rope each man to a Turkish horse-soldier, they were hustled parched and hungry into Beersheba. After a drink had been flung at them they were pushed into the presence of a Prussian officer, shaved and bullet-headed, with some trace of Tartar cheek bones, an unpleasant type. Interrogations were thrown at them through an interpreter which they answered none too truthfully for their own *Sahib* had warned them to lie heartily if caught and questioned.

Then the Prussian snapped this at them:

"You have heard that the Caliph, the Sultan of Rum, the head of your faith has proclaimed a Holy War, a *Jihad*, against the infidel, and has summoned all good Moslems to fight on his side. How is it that you are still fighting for the British—you who say you are orthodox Moslems?"

The *havildar*, or sergeant of the party, who was acting as spokesman, said:

"We have heard about the War of Religion, *Sahib*, but we don't accept it; we know that this is a political and not a religious war and so we serve the British King."

"I don't care a rap about that. Here are five Turkish uniforms. I will give you five minutes to put them on and join the army of the Caliph or you will be shot, so!"

The *havildar* said, "May I speak to my comrades and see what they say?"

"March them out," snapped the Prussian.

In five minutes the five British Indian soldiers were marched in again before the *General-stabber.*

"Well," he growled.

The *havildar* saluted, held up his hand, and with one accord the party shouted:

"Three cheers for King George!"

That was the end of it, and the officer gave the sign. A few minutes later a volley rang out.

That is the story of five simple Indian peasant soldiers of the Punjab, and how they were *Nimak hallal*, 'true to the salt that they eat'. The story is one of which it may well be said that it "fills strong men's hearts with glory till they weep."

THE WHITE LIE

Some reference has been made to the implacable hatred that flourished between Hindu and Moslem, and of the fierce periods of mutual destruction which characterised the rise of the Sikhs and their share in the fall of the Mogul power. The recrudescence of this bitterness, the horrors of the Cawnpore massacres of 1930, and the trouble over the relationship between the creeds of Islam and Hinduism that lays at the door of Mr. Montague, are to-day a matter of commonplace knowledge. So long as the British governed with impartiality and held the scales the hatred lay dormant. The heat of politics has revived the ancient enmities never very far from the surface. In His Majesty's Indian Army, however, the enmity has always been frowned down, and Moslem and Hindu and Sikh have been very good comrades, especially in those thrice famous corps of the Punjab Irregular and later Frontier Force corps in which the companies comprised men of differing faiths and races.

The following story which happened in the author's command in Mesopotamia in 1920 during operations in Kurdistan is a stirring proof thereof.

One of his columns had been in a mess up. Undue confidence that sometimes seizes the best of troops had resulted in the head of a small force in the Kurdish mountains being badly and quite needlessly ambushed by a Kurdish Agha. This is the scene that followed as the survivors who had been captured were brought before the victor.

The Leader of the Kurds stood on a ledge, a high felt Noah's-ark cap on his head and a bright silk scarf round the cap. Two rifles, four bandoliers and knives innumerable completed his armament. Before him were ranged the captives, a few Muhammadans, the remainder black-bearded Sikhs. A surviving N.C.O., a smart young Muhammadan *naik*, was addressed by a Kurd who had been an interpreter apparently with our own troops.

"What is your name?"

"Murad Ali Khan Ghakkar."[1]

"Shiah or Sunni?"

"Sunni."

"The Agha knows that these men on the right are Moslems, but who are those? They look like some uncouth Hindki unbelievers."

And the *naik* looked at the Sikhs and remembered that Sikh or Moslem was of no matter in the Frontier Force. To belong to the regiment was to be one of a brotherhood. And he swallowed a mighty swallow, for there was a fingering of knife-edges around him.

"They are as good Moslems as I am," quoth he, "I will swear it on *El Qoran*. They are, it is true, uncouth, they come from a savage part of my country. But they are Moslems true."

The Agha had a worked leather haversack over his shoulder, and from it he drew a Qoran, bound in painted papier-maché covers . . . an illuminated Qoran.

"Will you swear it?" quoth he. "For I misdoubt their looks."

"I will swear," re-iterated stoutly Murad Ali Ghakkar, "If you don't believe me, strip them, and you will see that they are as good Moslems as I."

"Nay, let him swear," quoth again the Agha, failing to call the bluff, and bluff it was with a vengeance as those who

[1] *i.e.* Punjabi of the tribe of Ghakkar.

know the Semitic rite which Moslems undergo, will recognize.

And then and there with uplifted hand that steadfast *naik*, to whom the faith of his regiment came first, swore that the black-bearded sons of Hind were true and honest Moslems of the Sunni or órthodox variety. Then the knives went back into their sheaths, and the prisoners were led away and fed.

It was a lie of the whitest, one of those good white lies that no recording angel dare enter, but to the Moslem's heart it should have spelt damnation, save for an agricultural conscience that a frontier regiment had improved on.[1]

That night the prisoners slept in a cave and the eyes of the Sikhs followed their sponsor as those of a disciple follows his *yogi*.

The Subahdar's Tita Bhai

There are many things that the British officer does for his Indian soldiers, or, for the matter of that, that Britain does for India which are not as it were in the contract. The following tale is told here, because it is so typical of the inner relationship between British and Indians and this simple village story is one of those lesser, unrecorded but long remembered benefactions which help to form that happy liaison and *camaraderie* between the British officers of the Indian army and their men. It is also a story of one of those remarkable little coteries of blood brothers which men call an Indian Mountain Battery. There are now nine-

[1] I am happy to record that I was able to use the authority then vested in Commanders-in-Chief to give an immediate reward of a decoration for valour to the *naik* who had so taken his own life in his hand for his comrades, and who with the other prisoners was rescued next night by a surprise counter-raid of some reinforcing troops.

DOGRA RAJPUTS (HINDU) OFFICERS

MAHOMMEDAN RAJPUT GUNNERS OF THE PUNJAB PLAINS

THE MARTIAL CLASSES OF THE PUNJAB (I)

teen such, but there were originally only six; four of the Punjab Frontier Force, and two of the Jacobabad frontier found by the Bombay Army. Late in the 'eighties of last century two more were added and now inherit the ancient prestige. For many years these batteries were commanded by captains of the Royal Artillery, and were undoubtedly the finest captains' command in the world. The job bred the men, and it would be hard to find officers more enterprising and efficient, if at times somewhat masterful, than these captains of artillery in permanent high command. They were characters and personages, commanding units of fame and reliability, and some were great characters, who lived entirely for their batteries, their men, and their old brown mules, and had little other interest in life than that of their command.

Of this type was James Osborn, captain of Royal Artillery and commandant of what we will camouflage under the name of the Paniala Mountain Battery P.F.F. The latter letters mean that it was part of the Punjab Frontier Force of pious memory, the renowned Punjab *Hatha* in which every Sikh and Punjabi Moslem, worthy of the name, desired to serve. Now Osborn was the son of the distinguished officer who had raised and commanded for fifteen years, from captain to lieut.-colonel, the well-known corps Osborn's Rifles, one of those loyal corps that marched from the Frontier to Delhi when the Bengal Line blew up. From Delhi it had '*Bayley Guard gya!* which being interpreted means had gone to the Bayley Guard, in which the Lucknow garrison and their charges were besieged. The men who have '*Bayley Guard gya*' have now almost all piled their arms, at the order of Death to the old musketeer "Pile your arms! Pile your arms! Pile your arms!" Yet now and again if you go to the fighting villages in the Punjab, there will still be some old tyke who will be helped out, to salaam to you, and put his hand in your hands, helped out by a grandson in the same corps, while the pensioned son looks on.

The Paniala Mountain Battery held its head very high, and still bought its own mules, by favour of the Remount Department who would not wrestle a fall with Osborn, and magnificently muled it was; bays and browns with a grey for the pioneer, not a light grey for tribesmen to shoot at, but a douce grey with the blessed donkey mark in deep black, for mules take after their mothers. Every mule was every man's friend, and would lie down in the lines while you sat on their bellies and smoked a cigarette, which is only done in the best batteries. If Osborn was not in the mule lines watching the mules clipped till their silk undercoats showed, he would be in the gun park with the gunners or cheering the wrestlers in the sand pit, or watching the tug-of-war team, all the while sucking a pipe which bubbled and squeaked in a minor key.

Then one day it happened that he had come out of the orderly room after seeing the Sikh recruits sworn in over the seven-pounder, firing a blank round as they swore, and was going across between the maneges when he heard a rattle and the sound of hoofs against a mud wall, and a small scurrying figure ran into him screaming. Round the manege lane came two of the remount mules just arrived, terrified by the new sights and not yet initiated into the holy calm that should reign in a battery mule lines. They had broken loose from the paddock and had not yet learnt to make for the forage barn, and were raising Cain. The little figure that ran into him had five plaited pigtails flying out behind, and her little gold embroidered cap was in the leading remount's teeth. She was dressed in little red pyjamas and a little muslin shirt and was sobbing with fright.

Osborn, uncle Osborn of the Paniala Battery was equal

to the situation. He waved his whanghai cane at the runaways who turned back in the lane to find a driver havildar with two nosebags close behind. Then he knelt on one knee and drew the child to him.

"There, my lass. *Daro mat, badmash chalagya.* Don't be afraid, the rogues have gone, see".

And Tita Bhai looked up.

"Who are you, *piari?*"

"I am Tita Bhai".

"Without doubt! But whose Tita Bhai".

"I am the subahdar's Tita Bhai".

Ah! That was it, she was Subahdar Jowand Singh's daughter.

"But a subahdar's daughter should not mind run-away mules."

"*Dar gya* Sahib, *Bahui dargya.* I was very much frightened," whimpered the little maid.

"There, there, *piari, kuchch dar nahin,* there is now no fear. See rather this," and Osborn struck a light with a patent pocket lighter.

"Ooh-ee. Do it again *Sahib!* Do it again!" Sunshine had returned at the *Sahib's* wonderful *hikmat,*[1] and Tita Bhai was all smiles.

"Come along, *piari,* and we will seek thy house. See the wicked mules have been caught by the havildarji". "Wicked mules," piped Tita Bhai, as hand in hand with the *Captan Sahib* she danced across the parade ground, and there, already half-way across, putting a crooked puggaree straight was stout old Jowand Singh hurrying towards them.

"Oh! shameless one, where have you been? Thy mother will surely whip thee."

And Tita Bhai clutched her protector's hand more closely

[1] Trick.

and whispered "Tell him, *Sahib*, I don't want mother's slipper". And the *Captan Sahib* explained very gracefully and cleverly and all was peace.

And thus it came about that the little maid of the five plaited tails, became a fast and inseparable friend of the commanding officer and established herself as deep in his heart as he in hers. Did Osborn sit watching the hockey or football, Tita Bhai sat between his knees. Did he judge the wrestling, Tita Bhai would judge it too, telling Osborn by a pat on his leg which champion had her favour, and when the sections played inter-section hockey Tita Bhai would say by the pat which side she wished to win. If Osborn was inspecting the forage or seeing the *ghee* board sample the *ghee* Tita Bhai must take part and dig her little finger into the tempting butter-tin, as the grown men did, sucking the finger appreciatively like her betters. Around, the great seedpods of the acacia trees would clatter in the wind, the click clack which made the Punjabis call the trees *chǎjna*, the 'clatter of women's tongues!' and the grey squirrels would scamper up the mulberry trees hard by, and men would say that Tita Bhai was worth placating, and giving lollypops to. And then perhaps the gun of high twelve would go, and bedlam would break out in the mule lines, like hell let loose, at the sound which meant the midday feed was due.

Sometimes she would trot behind Osborn and the Havildar-major when they went to look at the guard, where the six pug dogs of war stood in line and a big Sikh in very loose artillery knicker breeches with a very large crimson puggaree on top, and a very curly sword in his hand stood sentry. The guard would turn out with curly swords drawing them with a flash that made Tita Bhai clap her hands and rattle her bangles, more bangles, folk said, than she should have, but then her father spoilt her.

Sometimes they would watch the mules in the paddock and see them squabble to graze near the ponies, for mules are faithful to the memory of their mothers, and it is very swagger to crop your grass alongside a pony. If you are a mare mule and can graze by a foal, and nozzle and pet it, then your poor frustrated mother instinct is soothed, for mules are sterile, save the famous mule of Tirah which is a mystery, with a Merkoman pony thrown in. Hashi the red roan gun mule in No. 6 gun, could kick so hard that she generally was cock of the grazing paddock, and grazed by the pony she liked best and none to say her nay, save a piebald pioneer mule that had been bought as a brown and was dyed with permanganate when you went to war. Tita Bhai specially loved the piebald, who was known as Mr. Binks or Binks *Sahib* by the men, no-one knew why. Tita Bhai would beg a little gour from the Baniah and keep it in the pocket of her muslin waistcoat, till it was all pocket-jammy, and take it to Mr. Binks if she knew the line sentry. But the line sentries knew she was a favourite and privileged after the immoral instincts of the East, where the highly connected can do no wrong. There was a squat little pot of a Labana Sikh driver-naik, who was her slave and when he was about they would do what they liked and even set Osborn's terrier to hunt for rats in the gram-orderly's shed. Once the orderly subaltern had come round to find half the grain sacks over-turned for Tita Bhai's amusement, and had received a very smart salute from a very hot driver naik. Seeing that he was not in disgrace, Bhola Singh became confidential and explained that small girls with pig-tails were '*Bahuti piari chiz*' 'very dear things'—and how his own had died of malaria last rains.

And since Tita Bhai was at times all woman, and all men fish to her net, why she in the shelter of her privileged position had taken the Moslem camp by storm, and made old Nizamud-din, who really hated all Sikh and other *musheriks* or idolators, bring her farings every time he went to Rawal Pindi Bazaar.

It was three years more before the two-handed step to Osborn came, the promotion which meant that he must leave the battery in which he had served so many years. Burma Manipur, Waziristan and Tirah, good marching, hard fighting, a wonderful vista, with the smell of the mule and the camel, of the heaped tobacco in the bazaars, and the wood smoke in the lines for a memory. For fifteen years and more had he 'climbed in his old brown gaiters, along of his old brown mule'.

Tita Bhai was growing with the years and would soon go back to her village and be betrothed, and Osborn was due to be promoted. And the news came at a final rehearsal of a tug of war, and Tita Bhai had just patted her hopes as to the victory on Osborn's right or left leg as the case might be when the telegram came that announced promotion and a posting to Europe.

The whole battery was aghast, and the day of departure was a sad one. All the battery had come to the tonga station and had brought half the mules, and many *sahibs* of regiments came too. Tita Bhai had wept for days, and had scorned the suggestion—that she must be a grown-up girl and soon be married. Never, she said, could she be married unless he was there to see to it, as she and the subahdar said a last farewell to the *Captan Sahib* who now felt he was an old major.

II

Osborn went home to serve in that important part of the Royal Artillery then known as the 'Gambadiers'. A Gambadier is a gentleman who wears the article of dress known as a 'gambadoe' which is said to be but the Spanish name for a gaiter. As the Garrison Artillery alone in that branch of the Service wore it, it delighted the more lively young gentlemen to know that portion of the Artillery by that name, a name of humorous affection. But ere two years were out it pleased the authorities to decree that henceforward the commandants of Indian Mountain Batteries should be of the rank of Major, the same as the British batteries. Before long it happened that Osborn was offered the command once again of the Paniala Mountain Battery, which he with joy beyond compare accepted, and you could not see his heels for the dust in his haste to rejoin. He had not taken unto himself a wife, though the famous captain commandants in days gone by, did not of necessity disdain such aids to efficiency. They usually married douce philosophical ladies to whom mules and camels and frontier stations were not anathema, and who perfectly well grasped their place *vis-á-vis* the other and senior mistresses of their masters' affections.

To Osborn however it had been 'he travels the fastest who travels alone'. He returned to the Paniala Battery with no rival interests, and great was the scene at the re-union. The Battery had changed its station, but all the old friends were there to help carry his kit, and half a dozen of his favourite mules were brought down too, and the battery tonga with the best of them was waiting to spirit him up the road to the cantonments a dozen miles or so away. Second editions are never quite the same as the first, and three years makes a difference. The old subahdar had gone to 'pension' and of course there was no Tita Bhai. Tita Bhai was at home and probably married, for she was growing fast when he had left. A dozen or so of the old gunners were gone including the old specimen who had been extended, and extended, because he had been with Bobs to Kandahar, and that was about all.

He asked for news of the old subahdar, but no one had been to his village lately, and no one knew if Tita Bhai was married. A week or so later, however, a man rejoined from furlough from the village who said there was the devil to pay. Tita Bhai had refused absolutely to marry. Instead of being smacked and married without more ado, her father had listened to her. There were two candidates, said Indra Singh the informant. The son of the headman, a very prosperous young fellow was one. The other was a havildar, a young havildar in the 19th Sikhs, not such a swell as the headman's son, but still an important personality in the village, which was taking sides over the matter, the military families, of which there were several, favouring the havildar.

Ah well, that was interesting, and the talk of the Punjab village was all good and natural and like old times when he had shot and fished among them.

And the affairs of the battery engrossed him till one day just before Christmas came a letter from the subahdar, thrice rejoiced at his return to the East and especially to the old battery, and then followed the gist of the matter.

"There is much trouble in this village, and I know Indra Singh has told you of it. Tita Bhai should have been married long ago, but, *Sahib*, I have spoilt her and let her do as she likes, and now she says she won't marry anyone unless you tell her to. The Lambadar is making an enmity with me over the matter, and the havildar's family are making botheration and all the village is quarrelling. That headman saying it is my fault, and that I should compel my daughter to marry one or the other, he does not care which, he does not want my daughter, but his son does. My petition is that you come soon, *Sahib*, and settle the matter. The village will make a Durbar for you. I also thinking that my master will shoot the black partridge. Your devoted Subahdar," and to the screed of the writer the old man had put his signature in Gurmuki.

Osborn considered the matter. He might very well settle the matter for them, for no doubt the woman's wits of Tita Bhai would tell him in some fashion what she wanted. The battery was in excellent order, and there was no reason why he should not have a few days Xmas leave. Black partridge there were he knew in the *beyla* near Jhok Sayanwallah, and of all the good birds to shoot let alone eat, the black partridge was hard to beat. "Write oh Munshi-ji and say that I will be there by the mail train at Pindar Khan station the day after the Big Day (Christmas Day), and that if I come his daughter must do as I tell her."

With alacrity his old orderly and bearer got out his shooting kit. He would stay at the dak bungalow near by and would not want tents, and Boxing Day found a contented and amused officer undertaking the dusty journey in the train across the Thal, to Pindar Khan. His journey was uneventful, save that in changing trains at Shahpur, and getting into a second-class carriage he found a scene of distress. Two subalterns had flung their kit in, where an educated gentleman of the clerkly class was already sitting, had tied their dogs to the legs of the seat and had gone off to get a cup of tea. The dogs had started fighting, and the clerkly gentleman was evidently disturbed. He was hanging out of the window calling "Oh Station-master! Oh Master of the station! Come quickly. Come quickly mashterjee! Fighting dargs are here."

Osborn came to the rescue, pacified the terriers, and reassured the intelligent one. "Cheer up, Babuji, that is all right. Keep quiet you devils."

And then in discussion with the babu, he found that he too knew Jhok Sayanwallah, and knew of the trouble. "This is mischievous case, Sar, and that woman must be she-devil. Those men taking sides and fighting soon, and perhaps beating that subahdar. These women are beelzebub, Sar."

On arrival at Sayanwallah, Osborn whose fame had gone before him was met by a crowd. All the old soldiers in the district were there, horse, foot and artillery. The village headman had been in a cavalry regiment too, and it was not a question of the civil versus the military element. Each side had soldier supporters and it was a wonder that the peace had not been broken. In fact the village constable, who was on the platform too, as much as said so, and had already made a report on the matter. A pony was waiting for the *sahib* and a two-wheeled tuntum for his servants and luggage, with a pony fresh plumed and tasselled in the shafts, and it was a regular procession that escorted him to the bungalow. After some chat he was asked if six o'clock that night when all were home from work would do. Osborn agreed that he should not speak to Tita Bhai who was half locked up in her father's house.

Many were the visitors to the bungalow that evening. The headman himself came and presented after ancient Mogul customs his nuzzar of two gold coins, which were nothing less than Russian ten-rouble pieces, to be touched and remitted. It was a great honour he said that his village should be visited, and more especially that the *Sahib* should have come to settle so momentous a matter. Women, as no-one knew better than he, were the devil, and that the Sahib should of his own kindness put his head into any sort of mesh where they were concerned, was amazing. But such were the English, in the call of friendship. He himself had no great wish for this marriage, but his son . . . ah well, the *Sahib* knew what young men are. 'Give her to me to-day or I die' . . . and his son was so upset . . . and such like and so forth. Came also the old Sikh *Grunthi* from a neighbouring temple, who had met him before, with an offering of the Sikh communion dough, and a dozen old soldiers, Mehtab Singh who had '*Bayley Guard gya*' among them. Very old and stiff but still erect was Mehtab Singh, great uncle of the subahdar, wearing not only a Mutiny medal but one for China, bringing his sword in his hand, that Osborn might touch the hilt after the courtly custom of fealty. Among them too was an old Moslem sirdar, a man of the Guides, also with the Mutiny medal, bent but still hawk-eyed on a grandson's arm. He had come to make *salaam* as in duty bound and as was his social right. He was not going to be out of anything of interest, and besides the *Sahib* among these Sikhs might want some outside support. Ho! he'd like to see any daughter of his having airs and graces and bringing a *Commanding Sahib* all this way to settle her affairs. Then he fell a-chuckling, and was fain to tell a Rabelaisian story of the return of the Guides from the taking of Delhi in '57, that fabled event of which men still speak in the up-country villages, to every man a veiled cart and inmate, and more to the sirdars, with many other valuables besides. One forgets but the village does not. The story did not lose by Akram Khan's telling, and then came the subahdar when the press had gone. He would not speak of Tita Bhai save that she was well and said the *Sahib* would deal fairly by her. But his chief remarks were to his sense of gratitude for the supreme honour that the *Sahib* had done him, and how his izzat was exalted for ever, which could easily be imagined in a country where honour and consideration are so prized.

Ten minutes before six an escort of two stalwart young soldiers came to bring the major to the eventful durbar. The space in front of the subahdar's house in the middle of the village had been cleared and a fire burned in the centre, of a ring round which were sitting the notables of the village. There was a semi-circle of chairs for half a dozen, the rest were squatting, and in the centre was a low armchair for the *Sahib*. By the side was a table arranged with lemonade bottles and tea cups, and a lad was blowing hard on a samovar. As Osborn approached every one rose, and the headman conducted him to his chair within the circle. It was dark and in the distance he could see spectators and even women who would draw in as they sat down. Osborn took his seat, and to his surprise the village schoolmaster, known as *mashterjee*, read an address of welcome, full of allusion to the brilliant sun and British friendship and kindness and then a reference to "grave matrimonial squabble now disturbing our beloved village contrary to propriety and custom."

Osborn had been considering procedure in so delicate a matter, and decided to call on the headman to address him and the durbar. This that notable did but briefly and said that it would be well that the son should state his case, but before doing so he dwelt on the advantages to any girl who should marry his son. and alluded to the strangeness of the times that a girl should not abide by what her betters had decided. Here Osborn interrupted. "Had her betters, had the betters of the two young people come to any decision?" This, as a matter of fact, was an important point and was of the nature of a bombshell. The headman was fain to admit, that for some strange and unfair reason the father would not give orders and have them obeyed.

Then suddenly there arose an altercation, a sound of protests from the outer darkness, in the direction of the subahdar's house and outer court. There was a shuffle and a rush and a figure heavily shawled sprung high over the fire, and scuttled to where the major was sitting. Squatting on the ground it nestled between his knees and he felt the confiding pat on his knees that he recognised of old. The disturber of village life, the prize herself had come into court. One or two had risen.

Osborn called on all to remain seated.

"It is mete and right that the girl should be here. Let her hear through her veil what people think of her conduct," and everyone said "Wah. Wah! Let her hear."

So Tita Bhai remained, and Osborn knew that he would have guidance as to which of the two she herself favoured. He said "I presume *Subahdarji* that neither you nor your daughter object to both suitors, you are agreeable that she should marry one or the other."

Here the subahdar rose and said "Without doubt."

"And will your daughter marry whichever of them I say?"

Here there was a pat on his knee. "Without doubt, *Sahib*." Then the counsel addressed the parties.

"Do I understand, oh *Lambadarji!* oh *Subahdar Sahib!* that you and your son and your daughter will abide by my decision, do I understand that also from you two young men who want the girl, you Havildar Ganesha Singh of the 19th Sikhs, and you Bikram Singh son of the Lambadar of Jhok Sayanwallah, will abide by it too, and that there shall be no enmity between you, and that there shall be no enmity between the Lambadar and the Subahdar, and between Ganesha Singh's friends and the Lambadar or the Subahdar? Because unless that is said here before all the village I will not put my hand into the matter at all."

And here the crowd said Wah! Wah! and the women in the shadow who had drawn near put their palms to their mouths and made a sound of approbation.

Then up stood the two parents and an uncle of Ganesha Singh and made declaration, and then the two young men. "Let Bikram Singh, the Lambadar's son speak first, what are your claims on Tita Bhai."

"*Sahib*," said the young man, who now rose in his place and the firelight played on his six foot figure, verily a choice young man and a goodly. "My father has half the land in this *charak*, I have only one brother, my mother will gladly receive Tita Bhai, but she shall have a house of her own and a girl to grind the wheat. She will go to town in an ekka, and manage all my affairs. My sheep and goats are my own, and men say I shall be lambadar after my father. Tita Bhai is the light of my eyes. The *Sahib* is a *jangi nafar*, a man of arms, and his sympathy may be with the *havildarji*. But *Sahib*, we too are *jangi nafar*. My father was Lance Duffedar in the Sam Brown Rissalah, and went to Kabul with Roberts *Sahib*, he did not make a jemadari, as he was to be lambadar. We are *jangi nafar*." And here the court said Wah! Wah! But Tita Bhai gave no sign.

"Now Ganesha Singh," said Osborn, "spout up."

Up jumped the other young man as well favoured as the first, with the aquiline features that showed less of some ill blood than the first suitor. The nostrils were finer and better set on the face, the which is a better sign of breeding all the world over than anything else.

"*Sahib!* That we too are *jangi nafar* need not be demonstrated. My father was an artillery officer in the Kohat Battery, so what more suitable than that I marry an artillery subahdar's daughter? I have no mother and my house will be my own, but my wife shall come for a while with me to the lines, and where the regiment is there shall she be. I hold my father's land, but my great-uncle looks after it for me, till I am quit of soldiering. When she wants to, my wife shall live in my house. I have not all the money that the Lambadar's son will have, but I have enough, and

A JĀT SIKH OFFICER

A DOGRA OFFICER

THE MARTIAL CLASSES OF THE PUNJAB (II)

[Face page 316

Sahib I have *izzat* (prestige), I have the *Arder of Merat* (the Order of Merit) that I won in Chitral, and ere long I shall be jamadar."

There was not much more to it, and Osborn was puzzled for Tita Bhai gave no sign. No doubt she was enjoying the holding of men in the balance.

"Both young men have spoken well, and both are desirable husbands for any Sikh lass. Ganesha Singh is truly a soldier. There he stands before you on the right, he will go far in the services of the Sirkar and will be some day '*captan*'. There on the left we have this fine young Lambadar, he will be headman, and can keep a wife even better than Ganesha Singh, parents might well favour him. So equal and desirable are the two, that perhaps it would be well if I cast lots." Here at last came a sign. He paused. But . . . and he thought some time "Tita Bhai is born of the barracks and though Bikram Singh is of a family that does *jangi naukri* (military service) he will remain 'civil'. He will wax rich and fat I make no doubt. The subahdar has been all his life a soldier, it is right that his daughter shall marry a soldier. This is my decision, Tita Bhai will marry Ganesha Singh as soon as the priest can find the propitious date. I have spoken. . . ."

But as a matter of fact when he spoke of spinning a coin Tita Bhai had patted his right calf very distinctly and again and again, as in the old hockey days.

But all the while the refrain of the Punjab lyric remained in his mind.

"Oh Wars should be made by men without wives
Bangles ring softly and sadly."

And that is the story of the subahdar's Tita Bhai.

CHAPTER XVI

THE INDIAN RACES AND THE WORLD WAR

THE ARMY OF 1914—FRANCE—THE PROBLEM OF THE MAINTENANCE OF CADRES—MESOPOTAMIA—PALESTINE—THE LESSER THEATRES OF WAR.

THE INDIAN ARMY IN 1914

THE Indian Army in 1914, so far as the personnel of its units went, was quite the finest that India had ever seen, largely due, as has been explained, to the principles on which the martial races were enlisted and grouped therein, and the enthusiasm of the British officers. The war organization, however, was by no means complete for Sir Douglas Haig's solemn memorandum on the subject, written when he was Chief of the General Staff in India, was deliberately burked as a result of the pernicious appointment of a committee under Lord Nicholson to examine Lord Kitchener's work. The Indian Army has always failed in its war organization largely because it was tainted by the memories and practice of the old Mogul system of '*debrouillez-vous*', to use the slang expression from the France of 1914. Nothing was ready for severe war, and all systems of maintenance were inadequate and amateur. As it had been in 1878, and 1897, so in many ways was it in 1914. The Indian military authorities and the Indian Government were eager enough to assist, but their whole outlook was inadequate. Nevertheless the Commander-in-Chief in India Sir Beauchamp Duff, who had not long succeeded to the command, a man of great vision, realized all that India could do in this crisis of the Empire. First and foremost, Egypt and the Canal could be held and British garrisons in Egypt released. The oil supply in Mesopotamia could be guarded and the German possessions in East Africa attacked. The idea of sending Indian soldiers to take part in a war on the Continent had often been considered by the General Staff as a subject of study and mental gymnastics, but had never seriously entered into the head of statesmen. It was, except in the terrible circumstances which fell on the world, an impossible thought to ask these simple Indian peasantry to undergo so terrible a trial.

Sir Beauchamp Duff was prepared, so far as his advice to Government and his own responsibility for the defence of India went, to go to the furthest length in the Empire's cause, and accordingly with astounding promptitude on the part of embarkation marine and naval authorities, five different expeditions sailed out of the ports of India in the autumn of 1914. Those for Mesopotamia, Aden, Egypt, and East Africa went with the consciousness that they were going on a duty well within the competence of the Indian soldiery, but with the Army Corps that went to France there may well have been grave misgivings in the minds of the more sober. The Indian soldier, sacrificing, gallant, staunch, as he was, had never been trained to the thought of heavy casualties, and it was well known that his fighting strength was comparatively feeble without the unlimited initiative and fearless and abnormally prominent leadership of his British officers. While the younger minds only dwelt enthusiastically on joining in the great struggle in Europe, the older heads knew that a terrible trial was before the soldier and his leader. History will probably say that only the direst need justified bringing the Indian soldier of the Crown to the assistance of the Crown. Had the whole of Indian opinion been in sympathy there would be no guerdon too heavy to give to a people who have so generously shouldered the burden of Empire. Unhappily certain classes, especially among the intelligentsia, worked desperately to produce anarchy and revolution in India. Indeed it would be more interesting to ascertain how many of those who are at present taking so active a part in the more questionable portion of the Indian political movement, did anything whatever in the World War to earn the gratitude of the British Commonwealth or of civilization. Incidentally it may be mentioned that the Kaiser sent addresses in embroidered leather cases to all the Princes calling on them to rise and join him. How indignantly such overtures were scouted by the six hundred odd ruling chiefs history can proudly state.

The five different great Armadas leaving Bombay and Karachi were a marvellous demonstration of amphibious power and might, but it was the sight of the great forest of smoke-stacks and masts, heading up the Gulf of Lyons and entering Marseilles harbour that brought the climax of glory and drama, and sent the frightened French wild with joy and enthusiasm. The scene has already been alluded to in the opening chapter, as one that should be retained on the Empire's retina. The hosts of Indian soldiers marched through the streets of Marseilles with the population, especially the female portion, hanging on the arms of bewildered Sikhs and Pathans. Struggling with the crowd were to be seen the somewhat grim faces of the British officers now realizing, perhaps, for the first time the great struggle into which they and their men had been thrown. How the latter could be sustained therein was from first to last the anxiety of their officers. After the World War there sat in India an Esher Committee, no one quite knew why, on army matters. Among its members was an old Bengali judge, and what struck him most, he said, in hearing the evidence of many Army officers on pay, promotion, etc., was the fact that it was always the interests and good of the men that seemed to perturb them . . . quite a new aspect to him. And so the Indian Army officers were anxious in their minds, especially at bringing their men into an approaching European winter, and under a heavy artillery fire. To such they were quite unused both in experience and in contemplation, though indeed this must equally have been the state of mind of all those citizens who were already being hauled from their homes to share in the terrible catastrophe that had overtaken the world.

The officers of corps composed of the more famous martial races had fewer fears, or if they had they suppressed them, as to their men's power of resistance, but it was felt that some of the lesser races, despite their discipline and training might not be up to it.

What did eventually come to pass had often been foretold, and it is as well that those who spend their enthusiasms on the idea of an Indianized army should realize it, viz., that the strain fell on the British officers, who while too many for the training and superintendence in peace were too few for the leading in modern war. In the terrible strain put on all the troops that first autumn and spring in France, the British officers of the Indian Army poured out their lives like water. Staunch and magnificent as were the Indian officers, the drive, the *élan* and the initiative had largely to come from the former and the flower of this eclectic army fell. The best of all ranks were lost, but the drain on the British cadre was out of all proportion to its numbers. Small wonder that for many years after the War the gutting of the middles of the regiments was severely felt—the loss of the senior captains and the majors, and also the '*Chota Sahibs*' of whom mention has been made. The latter, however, were not so many as with the old Bengal Army in the Sikh Wars.

The troops, British and Indian, had left India with great enthusiasm, and Indian men of wealth subscribed freely for comforts and hospitals, while the disloyal and Prussian-fed element kept aloof. In the villages whence the soldiery came, enthusiasms were always great, the old soldiers offered service, and reservists flocked to the colours. A few regiments were in the hands of the fierce, bitter seditious elements, derived from the Bhabbar movement, and had to be treated accordingly, but disciplined enthusiasm was the note of all others, enthusiasm for the *Raj*, for all the good that His Majesty stood for in the world they knew of.

One scene of departure always takes my fancy, that of a regiment marching over the Indus to entrain from out a frontier station, the subahdar-major's wife usually strictly *purdah*, in the arms of a British officer's wife—the farewell at the bridge of boats, tears mingling with enthusiasms and the common touch—the various races shouting their war cry '*Wah Sri Khal sa Ji ki jai*' from the Sikhs and so forth. Then a touch of scandalous humour—when there came a hustling bustling *tonga* pushing folk from the path, and in it some ladies of the town, and the house on the wall. They too must say a farewell to some of the '*Chota Sahibs*' of their acquaintance, and in the phraseology of Tobit 'the young men's gardener drove them,' for so is laughter and tears, good and evil mingle, when the drums begin to roll and human nature transcends all barriers.

The doings of the Indian units in the years of war are outside this story, but the great features that stand out among them may perhaps be touched on—those special deeds which now sparkle for ever on the fore-finger of time. Certain of the races now took great pride of place, often those who had attracted no great attention before. The Punjabi Muhammadan gained great opinions for his unvarying steadfastness as also the Moslem of the Dekhan whose antecedents have been referred to. The Dogra covered himself with quite well-bred glory, and the Hindu Jāt came to a fame beyond that expected of him, as did the lithe little mountain rat the Konkani Mahratta aforesaid, so that some brief account of typical doings will not be out of place.

The first Armada of the Indian Army Corps arrived in Marseilles on the 26th of February, 1915, as has been said with such pomp of shipping, such forests of masts and strength of escort, as the world had never before seen. The renowned and sympathetic Sir James Willcocks, from the Northern Army of India was in command. The enthusiasms of the French knew no bounds so that both the British and the French Press spread themselves in hyperbole and inaccuracy. The French even stated that it was the armies of Indian Princes who had come to the world's aid, who were themselves installed in the finest Marseilles hotels, Prince Sykia, Prince Ghorok, and Prince Baluckin, apparently the eponyms of Sikhs, Gurkhas, and Baluchis; but who cared. The Eastern troops of the great Ally had arrived and Phœnician Marseilles disported accordingly in a manner which was at times none too edifying. It has even been surmised that some cheerful and imaginative subaltern had been poking fun at the Press, a favourite habit since the days of 'trying it on Billy Russell' was so popular in '58.

But the Indian Army was to start under many disabilities. It would have been expected that it should concentrate in fine autumn weather, straighten itself out in peace and quiet, and then as a corps, advance into some portion of the battle line in a style to do itself justice with its own leaders and staffs in charge. Unfortunately, it was fated to fare far otherwise and this adventurous force had to face its trials under the least favourable conditions. To begin with the leading division had had, for unavoidable reasons, to leave a brigade in Egypt for a while. Then, as has been mentioned, the Indian Army was singularly ill-equipped for modern war, partly from parsimony, partly from the different nature of the role for which it was maintained, partly because of the terrain in which its premier role was to be set, partly alas, from the supreme ignorance of the administrative staff as to how war should be organized. Still worse was the inefficiency with which some of the mobilization improvisations inseparable from an expansion to a war footing, were given effect to by those responsible, an indelible blot on the military escutcheon of India, not fully atoned for till the War had long progressed.

The Indian Army being prepared for war in mountain countries naturally had not the transport system fit for the West. It left its camels and its masses of pack animals behind, bringing only first line transport and the ever useful mule cart trains. It was to be fitted out with the complete wagon trains and other transport from Great Britain, but the expansion there in progress had outrun provision. The preparations for transport were not ready. The factories had not yet got ahead with the mass production of wagons nor could the Army Service Corps depots improvise at the rate that improvisation was demanded. The first transport therefore, was fairly inefficient. The Indian Corps concentrated forward very properly, but alas, the weather had broken, and it arrived at Orleans to find disorganized transport swimming in a sea of mud, and was thus severely handicapped. The British General Headquarters, only too anxious to give the Indians a fair start, were in the grip of circumstances they could not compel. The move to Flanders was taking place immediately after the Indian Corps arrived, and by the time that corps was assembling in Orleans, the new British line was being thinly held, often by cavalry alone. Into this hell on earth, for hell it truly was, the new comers were precipitated piece-meal, and every single corps was broken up by wings and even companies to patch the bulging cavalry line. To European troops such a treatment would have been trying enough and it may well be conceived what a supreme trial this was to Indians. Staunchly and heartily did they do their best. It was the 21st of October, 1914 that the Lahore Division of the Indian Army moved up into the battle area round Wallon Capel and Lynde, less its brigade still in Egypt. The 57th Rifles of the Frontier Force was detached and broken up among the 4th and 5th Cavalry Brigades, much as sandbags are thrown into a threatened embankment. A little later the rest of the Ferozepore Brigade to which they belonged, shared the same emergent duty, especially the 129th Baluchis and the Connaught Rangers. The British Cavalry Corps of 4,500 sabres was holding an immense length of front, and it was the broken up units from India that helped them to stand the strain. In the years to come, that should be a memory wherever great deeds are held in reverence.

It was the Dogra Company of the 57th that first saw the raw red war of the West, and who drove back a German night attack. In the first few days the Ferozepore Brigade lost heavily, and the 57th and 129th were torn to pieces, their British officers pouring out their blood like water, to save to stimulate, and to lead, their bewildered yet staunch following, thus strangely thrown into the supreme and unexpected trial.

The brave story has been told in full by Colonel Merewether in collaboration with "F.E."[1] who was in Press liaison with the Corps, and also by no less a pen than that of their Commander, Sir James Willcocks, and cannot be long dwelt on here. But it was in these days that Garhwali and Jāt came to take pride of fighting place alongside Sikh and Gurkha as *primus inter pares*, and commenced the trail of glory that gained them the title 'Royal', which will stand for all time among the regiments of the British Line. Some of the bayonet work of the 57th in conjunction with the 5th Dragoon Guards, was of a very fierce and determined nature and fully showed how the famous Indian regiments could square up to trouble. Many Indians, chiefly men of the Punjab and the Frontier, at this juncture gained great personal distinction and reward. The Indian Corps, moreover, in due course attained its desire to fight in its proper formations and in the slang of the Army had its 'belly full' thereof, at the First Battle of Ypres as well as in the later fights of that first eventful year.

An event of romantic importance at this time was the pushing up of the three Indian battalions of the Jullundhur Brigade, the 15th Sikhs, the 34th Pioneers and the 59th Rifles F.F., to the assistance of the French cavalry under General Conneau, who were filling a gap in the British Line. This cavalry had had ten devastating days in the breach and as soon as a lull came, the Indians after first supporting them relieved them so that they could return to their own part of the line.

At Neuve Chapelle the Indians had some desperate street fighting in which they gained well deserved applause but lost heavily. During the winter two remarkable occasions behind the line took place, viz., the visit of His Majesty, and that of Lord Roberts. In the first case the supreme

[1] Lord Birkenhead.

affection and enthusiasm for the Crown were evinced in a remarkable manner, as they had been as a mass movement among the country folk at Delhi, two short years before. The coming of Lord Roberts in the bitter winter weather which caused his immediate death, was equally dramatic if different in tone. For years, since in fact the Afghan War of 1878–80, Fred Roberts had been the name which had stirred the Indian soldiery from North to South. Leadership and *camaraderie* were concentrated in his name. His coming after he had left India for many years and had become to the younger generation a myth—a resounding myth of which their fathers ever talked—was an occasion beyond belief. Of great age in their eyes but full of activity and life and kindly enquiry, with a gift for stirring men's blood and hearts, the visit was an uplift and a pouring forth, a feudal scene amid a feudal people. Extremes of Indian military story and legend were meeting. The officer of the old East India Company, the Field Marshal who never retires, the new age and the old, were to meet on this astounding occasion of India in Europe which had not happened since the days of Darius the Persian.

The swift death that followed the Field Marshal's effort was a tragedy, that all realized, as Kipling wrote:

> " He had touched their sword hilts and greeted each,
> With the old sure word of praise."

and again

> " Three hundred miles of cannon spoke
> when the master-gunner[1] died."

That tragedy to the Indian mind only paled before the even greater one of their other renowned Chief falling to a German deep sea mine.

[1] Lord Roberts held the post in the Household, of the " Master Gunner of St. James".

The Problem of Maintenance of Cadres

It is easy to realize that the British officers of an Indian Corps are a highly specialized product. The losses that swept their ranks were made up with difficulty, partly by transfer from India already squeezed dry, with a frontier still to defend, partly by the rejoining of any younger men from Britain who had retired but were fit, and who eagerly stepped into the vacancies. Another source was the selected portion of the Indian Army Reserve of Officers, men of knowledge and sympathy, with the usual training as reserve officers or in the Indian Volunteer force. The Indian Corps, however, was soon to fall into some disrepute at General Headquarters, whose watchword had to be efficiency, by reason of the sad state of the effectives. Battalions of but 200 rifles filled the great front in a forward line. The Indian regimental officer was now to reap the result of his own want of vision. An Army Reserve had long existed, but it had never caught the imagination of the regimental officer whose eye only looked to intense efficiency on the Indian frontier. Instead of encouraging good young soldiers, whose holdings often called them back to their villages, to go to the Reserve, they had used it as a dumping ground for any man they wanted to get rid of. Nor were the arrangements of Army Headquarters as to the training and prompt discharge of ineffectives up to date. When the first parties of reservists arrived they were the laughing stock of the depots, feeble old men who were of no use and of whom large numbers were rejected in Marseilles, and who only could have left India by reason of gross neglect of duty on the part of both medical and depot officers. The defence of the Frontier prohibited yet awhile the drafting of many able-bodied serving men from the garrison and the linked battalions. It was some time before the recruits could be enlisted and trained fit to fill the gaps. Sir James Willcocks and his staff were in despair. They felt too, that the severely wounded Indians should not be sent back on recovery, but return to India and let fresh transfers fill their place. But immediate needs were inexorable, the kindly hospitals of England returned them as cannon fodder once again. This was a condition indeed which our British soldiers also had to undergo, however cruel and bitter, but the two cases were not quite on all fours, though as the years rolled on ideas perforce grew harder on this subject.

By the beginning of 1915 in addition to the Indian Army Corps a cavalry corps of two divisions from India was also assembled to reinforce that vast concourse of French and British squadrons with which both Joffre and Haig dreamed of a break-through—a stream of cavalry and horse artillery over-riding and mopping up everything behind the German line. Alas it was never to be, but the Indian Cavalry Corps was a notable addition somewhat handicapped by the fact that Indian horses and Walers are born to move on the top of the land, while the horses of Europe have often to move through it.

It was the writer's privilege to be present at a review of the massed Indian Cavalry Corps, commanded by that famous privateersman General Mike Rimington, drawn up in the snow on the plains of Hazebrouck. There eighteen regiments in line of mass with six batteries of horse artillery were reviewed by Sir John French in January 1915, the bare woods as a background, the snow light on the ground, a Meissonier picture come to life.

As the first twelve months drew on, the Indian Corps brought itself to more glory in the great battles of the period,

Neuve Chapelle, Festubert, second Ypres, Givenchy and the like, and then it was fought to a standstill, the British officers dead, the staunch veteran soldiers killed and broken. Many devices to supplement its deficiences had been adopted, Territorial battalions came into the brigades and shared their troubles. But the Indian Army had already huge responsibilities on its shoulders, in Gallipoli, Egypt, Mesopotamia and many lesser fields. The New Armies of England were now in being, the Territorial forces were at the top of their form, the flood had been stemmed, it was now possible to remove the temporary dams behind which the builders had been working. The Indian Corps was to be withdrawn to refit in Egypt and India, and to start perhaps in new fields that would try it less. As a matter of fact the health of the Indian troops had been a surprise to all. They had stood the damp cold of Flanders marvellously. Not only had great care and attention been given by their medical authorities, but above all things had they re-acted to the European conception of a good ration. Meat every day to a people who have only had it once or twice a week, worked marvels, while ample sugar and tea had warmed their hearts and kept the internal fires burning. Nevertheless to get them to dryer lighter climes was a fate they well deserved and so they were removed, all save the cavalry corps who were to stay on for months awaiting the Armageddon which they were in fact, to achieve elsewhere. Never was the cavalry heart of Lord Haig to see its desire blossom in Europe.

So gradually restored and re-fortified, the Lahore and Meerut Divisions, now to be known as the Third and Seventh Divisions, started eastwards and were rebuilt in Egypt and in India.

A change indeed was coming over the face of the Indian

Army and over the whole style and principle of training the Indian levies. Not only had the drain on the existing corps and their recruiting sources been severe but more was to follow. Mass production and mass production methods were required. The Imperial Government had asked India to raise another quarter million of men. The whole field of possible soldier-bearing strata was explored, races that had never yet cared to present themselves as soldiers were tried. Many of these never took the field. Others did and some of them won a place in Indian martial life that they had never looked to acquire. The training of new soldiers was intensified and greatly improved by the use of British drill sergeants, an entirely new departure. Men intensively trained were found to do well under temporary officers who knew little of them. The discipline and needs of war time had produced a psychological submission to authority and an emulation in danger which had not been looked for. The mass-produced Indian soldier while not in the least resembling the majesty of the old regular sepoy army had very fair military qualities which sufficed. It was only when subjected to the individualist fighting against the Mahsud Waziri that the great gulf between it and the old line was apparent. For mass fighting it was a very creditable imitation. Then in India had also been established two factories for *Chota Sahibs*, boys who were to have commissions in the Indian Army which Sandhurst and Woolwich had no time or space for in the war days. Very creditable cadet colleges they proved, though the World War was over before the cadets could be swept in to the receiver of the cannon machine. They would have been as self-sacrificing as the *Chota Sahibs* quoted who saved the situation in the old Sikh Wars. The story of the mass production is almost forgotten, but it left in the memory of the Adjutant-General's branch at Headquarters data for the enlargement of the recruitment basis which bears good fruit in the Army of to-day.

Mesopotamia

In Mesopotamia, as all the world should know, the Indian troops had a far worse campaign for the first year and a half, than in any other theatre. Not that the casualties were more severe, for the actual fighting was less appalling, but the climate was most trying, and fighting in a Tigris summer defies realization. So long as the force there was a small one, things went along reasonably well in shirt-sleeve fashion. But the Government of India and the Indian Army as then constituted (1916) seemed congenitally unable to realise the implications of a river campaign with no road and rail, or the organization necessary to cope with such, or with heavy casualties and a large ammunition demand. The fatal unbalanced decision to move up the Tigris without any adequate transport facilities, taken bravely enough to help the Allies out of their Gallipoli situation, produced untold misery. As the troops pushed on up stream, every mile made feeding and maintenance generally less possible. In face of this blindness unpardonable, three reinforcing divisions were dragged up the Tigris without any possibility of adequate supply. The big battles for the relief of Kut were undertaken without ammunition, hospitals or hospital transport, the misery of the troops was very great and the humiliations of unnecessary defeat still greater. For a while the stoutest of the Indian troops quailed, deprived already by war casualties of their best officers and best men. Cold feet supervened, religious objections to operations on the holy ground of the Tigris and Euphrates arose. At the commencement of the campaign the Turkish divisions, at this time of inferior troops, were driven out of Basra and up the Tigris and Euphrates, and then the tables were turned. Turkish reinforcements early in 1915 made a determined attempt to drive the British into the sea. Just as Sir John Nixon was taking over the command from General Barret, was fought, chiefly by Brigadiers Delamain and Mellis, what history will pronounce to be one of the most decisive battles, not only of the World War but of all time. A strong force of Turks was endeavouring to drive the British out of Basra. The tribes of Arabistan had been raised against us, the pipe line from the oil wells to Abadan had been cut, and a strong corps with hordes of Hamidieh cavalry was advancing on Shaiba, which is old Busorah of the days of Sinbad the Sailor. Only four brigades of British Indian troops were available to oppose it and were terribly hampered by floods which practically cut the eight miles of dry connection with Basra. All Asia was watching, and had the British been beaten the Gulf tribes would have been up, Afghanistan and the frontier would have joined the *Jihad* already proclaimed by the Caliph, and the age-old sedition in India which has seethed for a thousand years would have broken into rebellion. The roll of the drum ecclesiastic would have upset the usually loyal Moslems of India. In this fight fought on the edge of the arid desert in considerable heat, many corps distinguished themselves.

It was not till General Maude and several new commanders took charge, and above all developed *bandobust* on the line of Communications came into being, that the troops with adequate food and fresh vegetables, with hospitals and ammunition galore, got back on to their perch. Once back nothing could stop them. When Maude at the end of 1916 went forward with a swish, neither could the hospitals retain the sick nor the dockyard the river steamers. '*À Bagdad*' was the cry, and the fighting form of all the classes rose to its best, and stayed at and even beyond the top of their ancient form, till the final victory at Mosul in 1918 assured the Arab world that the Turk should not dominate the ancient land of the Caliphs.

By 1916 India had begun to organize seriously, so far as war material was concerned. The War Office poured out its resources and the Tigris as an organized waterway five-hundred miles in length, with a modern port at Basra, left little to be desired.

The Poona division with which General Townshend advanced to Ctesiphon had fought splendidly against heavy Turkish forces. It included some of the finest of the troops in India, and as all the world also knows, was driven back into Kut, where the unfortunate decision was made to stay. By now the two divisions from France, the war-battered Indian corps of Ypres, of Festubert, and of Givenchy, patched, repaired and refitted arrived in the Tigris. With these, dribbled up bit by bit on the unequipped river, and the troops already in Mesopotamia, General Aylmer attempted to relieve Kut and smash the covering force of Turks. To support the Indian divisions from France the 13th all-British Division from Gallipoli, already broken and twice replenished at Anzac and Helles, was brought up the Tigris. It is but fair to the memory of these three divisions smashed once more on the wheel of heroic but unsuccessful endeavour, and to their commander, to record what should be written in letters of fire wherever staffs are taught, viz., that General Townshend had reported that he could not hold out after the middle of January. Therefore, before artillery ammunition or hospitals had arrived

General Aylmer put his men at the Turks on both sides of the Tigris, only to be beaten back again and again. And General Townshend held out till April! He had not surveyed his supplies and his available substitutes in the Kut bazaars. Had he given a better estimate Aylmer would not have gone off half-cock in the belief of the urgency of the case, but would have waited till all his guns, his ammunition and his hospitals were to hand, and success his to command.

After the fall of Kut all the torrid summer was spent in refitting and preparing. There were to be no mistakes this time. When Maude advanced some of the Indian units distinguished themselves greatly. The storming of the Turkish trenches in the Muhammad Hassan below Kut by the 45th Sikhs, the crossing of the Tigris at the Shamran bend, the latter one of the most remarkable river crossings in the annals of war, are epics in the military records of the races involved.

The remainder of the campaign, now supremely victorious, is well known. After the capture of Bagdad which had considerable effect on the *moral* of the whole world, the Turkish divisions based on Mosul were steadily driven north and destroyed. Before this however, some of the best of the troops were transferred to Palestine.

The resources of the whole East were drawn into this campaign—several thousands of Chinese artificers worked in the works of river and railway—Egyptian labour corps dug out the dockyards—the Indian jails sent their organized convicts who earned both freedom and bonus by good behaviour, while the Clyde sent its shipbuilders to work on this ancient river at the erection of tugs and barges.

Sinai and Palestine

It was Indian troops who held Sinai and the Canal zone for a year and a half, beating off the attempt of Kress Von Kressestein to get into Egypt in February, 1915, and guarding it through the long monotonous days of Gallipoli, when ward without excitement was the order of the day. In the first days of the advance when the war worn troops from the Dardanelles were recouping, and the slow advance to the River of Egypt and Gaza was commencing, there were few Indian troops involved. Indeed in the first two battles of Gaza and Allenby's successful break through into Palestine, India was poorly represented. By the time that the advance into Judea had commenced Indian brigades had joined the force, and troops with frontier experience were extremely useful in piquetting the hills in the valley of Ajalon and the passes leading to Jerusalem. A little later came the India Cavalry divisions so long retained in France for the possible break-through, and now to assist materially in the great cavalry move that destroyed the Turkish Army.

The first guarding of the Spine of the British Empire referred to, saw the 2nd Rajputs, the 62nd Punjabis, with the 2/10th Gurkhas engaged in beating back the daring Turkish attempt on the very banks of the Suez Canal itself. The Bikaneer Camel corps during the long months that followed, made the Sinai Desert its own, but it was not till the autumn of 1917 that the 75th Division constituted from various Indian units with a Territorial battalion in each brigade moved into the active area of the force in Palestine. In January, 1918, arrived those 'battered cowries of many markets', the 3rd and 7th Indian divisions, the Meerut and Lahore Divisions of France, back into the West after their trying but victorious career in Mesopotamia. These divisions took a notable part in Lord Allenby's final campaign, and the 7th finished far up the coast beyond Beirut forming the principal unit whose doings are inscribed on the rocks of the *Nahr mal Kelb*, the Dog-River, below those of Darius the Persian, of Alexander, of the Legions of Napoleon the Great, and of the French in Syria in the 'sixties.

At the end of 1917 the Indian Cavalry, after their long sojourn in France, were also moved to Palestine, and the Yeomanry Division which had sent many of its yeomanry units to France as machine gunners re-appeared as the 4th and 5th Cavalry Divisions, largely composed of Indian Cavalry, under two famous Indian cavalry officers, Generals Barrow and McAndrew. They were then to take a leading part in the famous ride of the cavalry corps round the Turkish flanks over the Musmus pass into Jezreel which destroyed the whole Turkish army, whence they moved to Damascus and Aleppo, an astounding adventure and military operation. In these operations the Indian cavalry as a whole, earned an opportunity of brilliant service which had to their great chagrin been denied them earlier, save in Mesopotamia under the later leading, where notable cavalry occasions had arisen.

The Lesser Theatres of War

In the lesser theatres, at the same time as Indian troops, often those from the Indian States, held the Canal, an Indian expedition went to German East Africa, to meet at first with a severe reverse at Dar-es-Salaam. The whole of South Persia was cleared of bitterly hostile German agents, held, and organized. The Turks, threatening Aden, were kept at bay by an Indian force, and as the war rolled on the

Indian Army went to the Caspian, from Bagdad, while after barring the long Perso-Afghan Frontier against the Pan-Turk plans of Enver Bey, Indian troops actually found themselves in Merv and Trans-Caspia. An Indian brigade and several mountain batteries took part in the Dardanelles in the rugged country behind Suvla Bay, with great distinction and heavy losses, while several Indian formations served in the long and weary campaign that at last cleared the Germans out of East Africa, and last but not least, in the final destruction of the Turkish Army in Palestine.

Far East that famous corps the 36th Sikhs helped to take Tsingtao, the German port in China, while at Singapore the other side of the shield was unexpectedly displayed. An Indian Moslem battalion seduced by German intrigue joined the merchants of the latter nationality in trying to seize the port, and had to be destroyed.

After the war, Indian troops occupied Batoum, and thence went inland into Trans-Caucasia. And all the while that this went on, the Indian Frontier simmered and re-acted to every yarn, although the staunch friendship with the Amir Habib-Ullah Khan prevented the situation from getting unmanageable. Several expeditions to punish raiders were necessary, however, in the long four years of war.

The record is an amazing one, and had the administrative services of the Indian Army been adequate, and the organization of its resources equal to the conceptions of its General Staff, the fame of the Indian Army would have had few dimming happenings.

A word in respect to the Indian Labour Corps which were eventually flung round the world by the tens of thousands before concluding. The countless folk of India who till the soil but have never been equal to handling a pike and shouldering a musket went to the war freely in its later stages as organized labour, in addition to the strange feast of jail birds in Mesopotamia. From the simple hereditary almost slave-cultivators in Hindustan to the wild hillmen of Burma and the Himalaya, the recruitment spread. Their services were invaluable and it is worth trying to imagine what the result has been in their untutored but often astute minds. In many ways this recruitment has produced the effect in Hindustan that the Black Death produced in England. It took the men from the villages in which they lived for hundreds of years and broke the hereditary serfdom of ages. Whatever good such an happening may seem likely to have to the apostles of "divine discontent", it has ruptured an economic system without replacing it by a better. The old relations which alone made life possible in the economic conditions of India were shaken in many districts to a remarkable extent, and this is one of the factors in making India lie unhappily in the post war world.

One special feature should be held in affectionate memory and that is the Indian Mule Corps, pack and draught. On the great *chaussés* in France, the mules leaning intently inwards, the drivers heads and faces wrapped in their puggarrees, plodded steadily day in day out, oblivious of bombs and long range guns. Under constant fire, in Gallipoli pack mules carried on with supreme content on the shell swept beaches of the Peninsula. For those who can see the fun of it it may be mentioned that every muleteer came away wearing three grey-back shirts from the ordnance stores abandoned at the evacuation!

Once the author met a long train of mule-carts in a dust storm marching down through Persia, the drivers' faces as usual, wrapped in their puggarrees and he demanded:

"*Kahan se ate?*" "Whence come you?" and the muffled patient reply came from the leading cart, "*Karspian se ate,*

Mosool ko jate!" "We come from the Caspian and are going to Mosul," just a trek of close on a thousand miles, these simple drivers from a Punjabi village.

That is the end of the war story, which has hardly yet been realized. It begins and ends in glory and in pathos. Glory that the men came so eagerly, pathos that they should have had to die so freely far from home, and that too at first because administration was not equal to endeavour. And at the head of it, first in death and glory, were the colonels and the '*chota sahibs*' who died so freely at their heads and whose sons I hope will remember.

Let us spare a thought however, not for the widows but for the unmarried girls, whose marriages ten times more essential to them than in the West, never took place—who waited far beyond marriageable age to their great disgrace and who had to let the propitious star-blessed dates go by—never in many cases to come again. Those who know the Punjab village will know the super-tragedy of the *jhoks*[1] and their daughters.

[1] *Homesteads.*

Men of 55th Cokes Rifles (Frontier Force) pre-war (1912). Showing admirably Punjab and Frontier Types: Sikh, Pathan, Afridi, Dogra, Muhammadan Rajput. Now 1/13th F.F. Rifles (Cokes). Known as *The Cookies*

[*Face page* 340

Chapter XVII

THE INDIAN ARMY AND MARTIAL RACES IN THE FUTURE

THE FUTURE GENERALLY—THE FUTURE OF THE INDIAN ARMY—AN INDIAN SANDHURST—THE INDIAN ARMY AND THE SIMON REPORT—THE CONCLUSION OF THE WHOLE MATTER.

The Future Generally

It is hardly possible to have said so much about the Indian Army and the martial races, of their past, their valour and their services, their glories and their tragedies, without wishing to peer into the future. It is only as people in a country in which British and Indian are working a condominium that they will interest us hereafter. If India is ever allowed to break from a friendly control, if false sentiment and feeblemindedness are to lead Great Britain to let go her Imperial hold and return to the heptarchy, then India and her races may go to the devil their own way. But on the assumption that the British intend to remain a sovereign and adventurous people, and that India will run in friendly and gently controlled double harness, then the future is of great interest to consider.

The martial races, as has been explained, are without exception, small landowners, yeoman farmers and farming tenants. As such, the passage of one or more lads of each family through the ranks of the Indian Army, has brought discipline, knowledge and progress into the homesteads to which they return. It has also brought wealth and prestige, as is clearly seen by the improvements and signs of prosperity in those villages that harbour and breed the *jungi log*, 'the men of war'.

The ex-soldiers form a very valuable nucleus bringing to a very simple, ill-informed country knowledge of the world, of the British Empire and all that the Crown stands for. They, all without exception cultivators, form the vanguard of those who support and endeavour to understand the many improvements in agriculture, seed, irrigation, and the like which the Government is always endeavouring to introduce.

Very real is their support of Government in times of trouble and rumour. Whenever there are rumours of war the reservists hasten to join, often when there is no intention of calling out the reserves. During the World War the pensioned Indian officers hurried to serve in any capacity and were to be found all over the world like the retired British officers of the Army and Navy, taking any duty that might be required of them. I well remember an old Sikh *subahdar* who had come to Mesopotamia in charge of a labour corps. He had a flowing beard that was pure white, and I said: "How long, old soldier have you been (in the Persian metaphor) eating your pension." He had a very deep voice and he replied, "Ho! Ho! Ho! I've been eleven years eating my *pinsin*, but when the war broke out father said to me and my brothers (also pensioned officers) 'Get out of this and go to the War, I won't have you young fellers loafing about my farm.' Ho! Ho!" And father was what is known in the Northern Army as '*Bayley guard gya*', one of those men from the North as already explained, who had gone with Sir Colin Campbell to the Relief of Lucknow, or its subsequent re-capture, for the Residency at Lucknow was known as the *Bayley Guard*, the garrison which served as escort to Colonel Bayley, a resident in earlier times, and the Indian memory is a long one.

The old pensioned officer in the Punjab, in Mahrattaland, in Madras, wherever it may be, is a tower of strength to the administration. Knowing what he does too, he is one check on the utterly incorrigible propensity of the lesser Indian official to victimize his neighbours or exact illegal gratification. In the good old days of Indian kings some potentate would lose his patience and have such an official crushed by his elephant, or punished by a similar summary method, to the delight of the public. To-day the evil subordinate is rarely treated as he deserves and the retired soldier in many districts acts as a check. He has a method of access to authority which scares the evil doer into moderation.

The more the administration 'Indianizes', the more will this check on roguery be important.

The future of the martial races runs in two directions, one as citizen, as a yeoman and farmer, the other in the role we know him best, that of a soldier. As a farmer, a man of the martial class whether he has passed through the ranks, which can only apply to a small proportion, or whether he remains all his life on the land, provides the stuff from which the only effective supply of ruling personnel can be drawn. The merchant class and townsman who takes to politics by way of the law, and from which class most of our Indian civil servants are drawn shows no great sign of having sufficient 'guts' to be a public servant in responsible positions.

There are, of course, certain brilliant exceptions who could be quoted but *en masse*, the personnel of the railways, of the active professions and of the administration, if it is to be Indian, must come from this class, the martial land-owning or land-cultivating class, who can and will say boh! to a goose and more.

THE FUTURE OF THE INDIAN ARMY

The constitution-makers and those who follow in their wake, have been busy finding and framing arrangements for the Indian Army of the future, but as they all seem to assume that Great Britain is not going to dominate India in the matter of general direction, we need not pay very much attention to them. The real problem is how far the Indianization of the Indian Army can be carried without jeopardizing the British Empire, and without destroying the fighting efficiency of the Indian Army as a fighting machine, bearing in mind that the Indian soldier of to-day is only able to meet his probable opponents if he is at his very best, and if his moral and physical qualities are very fully developed.

Indianization of the Indian Army means the substitution or rather the introduction of Indians into some of the positions held by British officers, and eventually it must also postulate that some of those officers, if fitted, shall be permitted to take higher command alongside and at times over Europeans.

The writer has long been of opinion that we have been slow, lamentably slow, in bringing forward a few military Indian officers into the positions of British officers. He has always held that, as in the civil and medical departments and the other services where partial Indianization has been introduced, it should perforce have been tried in the Army also earlier. He was one of a small clique at Simla who urged this should be done when Government was searching for boons to announce to the Army at the time of His Majesty's visit to India in 1912. Older heads, notably

Lord Roberts, advised against it, with the result that it has been done in response to agitation after the War, and the valuable experience of the World War has been lost. The difficulties were great no doubt, the other services of Government were not a parallel, in that the cheek-by-jowl life of mess and the close daily association that army life means both in peace and war, makes and made then, the proposition a different and a difficult one.

Differences of religion, difference of outlook on life, different standards and ethics all make the close mingling difficult. Especially is this the case in so small a social circle as an Indian unit.

But nevertheless the problem needed facing in some form, and there was this much in favour of its consideration, viz. that the British had infinitely more respect and affection for and more in common with the martial classes than with, to use the Indian idiom, the *clerkly-werkly* classes.

In Chapter XII some outline of the 'Indianization' question in the past has been given and it has been shown how, in the early days of the Indian Army, Indians rose to very high positions and occasionally to the command of irregular corps. It has been explained that it was the need for regular highly trained units, on a western model, to meet the harder, fiercer foe and their troops trained in western methods that saw the elimination of the Indian in higher positions a hundred and fifty years ago. It has also been explained how, after the Mutiny, the 'irregular' system with a few British officers was introduced and how it failed in the first hard fighting on the North-west Frontier. More British officers alone then could combine the knowledge of modern ways with the power to lead.

The Russian War scare increased the need for British leading. Unfortunately the World War gave us little experience of how Indians would re-act in the higher command, . . . and this opportunity has been lost. Happily, however, the experiment has been made since the War, and young Indians at Sandhurst have joined the Army in the place and status of Britons. There has not been a very wide choice as yet for the reasons aforesaid, and in the earlier days the young officers joined units exactly as a young Briton would do.

Later when Lord Rawlinson was Commander-in-Chief, it was decided to Indianize entirely a certain number of corps, that is to say, all junior officers would be Indians so that gradually the units will be filled up from the bottom, and become all Indian as the years roll on. There have been two reasons for this decision: one because in the early years after the War it was thought that the fact that there would be Indians in the ordinary regiments was deterring British officers from coming to the Indian Army. This was not mere dislike of colour. The outlook of peoples with entirely different personal codes of honour, morals and conduct, though not necessarily less worthy, could not, it was felt, be the same, while the close life in a mess, and thus the possible diminution of those amenities which alone make the Indian exile bearable, would suffer very much where the varying Indian races were mingled with the Europeans in such association. The other reason was the difficulty of Indians eventually having command over British officers. The young Indian himself was seriously displeased. His ambition was to live in close association with the European, and felt that the Indianized unit would have a lesser status in the estimation of Indians and the world. The writer believes that an error of judgment taken *on a long view* was made, and that the mixed mess on the whole would have been best for all, but as it seemed that any such step would alienate the better British boys from the Indian Army, the segregation policy appeared unavoidable and was adopted.

In the meantime the Army officers had long realized that the Indian intelligentsia as a rule, save perhaps from the northern Khatri, would never make officers, and that the only real source from which to draw a reliable 'Brindian', the term colloquially applied to the Indian officer with British officer's status, must come from the class that now furnishes the 'Indian officer' and that the sons of the *subahdars* and *ressaldars* would be far more likely material and might have the character necessary, if caught young enough. Therefore, there were started King George's Schools for these very boys, in which an education on British boarding school lines for several years, prior to selection for Sandhurst, could be given. These schools ere long should give good results.

In the desire to meet the demands of the politician the Government of India have announced their intention of Indianizing enough new units to form a complete Indian division. Already there are eight units to which the experiment is being extended, and four or eight more with the technical services is no great addition. The theory is that the sooner the worthiness of Indian officers is put to the test, the better. The trouble is, however, that the test is principally war, assuming that the more difficult peace duties of war training can be successfully performed. The test of war postulates the possibility of failure, and failure in war in a test that is any value is a bitter business. The proposal does indeed contain the idea that Indians can be trained to lead units in serious war, and we have yet to see that they can do so. There is already a hint, made in all good faith and with sorrow and disappointment, by those who are anxious for success, that the delightful young Indian lads who come through Sandhurst, are a little less efficient each year that they are longer away from the college, rather than passing each year from strength to strength. They go down the hill instead of up it. If this be true it is tragedy that has not been unexpected.

There is another anxious point. The age that the Army officer is entering on to great responsibility which calls for character and energy, is about the age at which, probably from the climatic conditions of centuries, the Indian is inclined to evince a desire for ease, that will ruin him as an officer. Those with experience do not believe that the Indianized division will ever be possible, and feel that merely to please political talkers the Government is but sacrificing a slice of an Army they must now do without. Others feel that the proposal is one of despair in that perhaps those who are responsible for it have relinquished all hope of getting truth and hard facts faced by responsible ministers of the Crown, and by Viceroys . . . faced indeed by those who like the juggler are thrice happy if none of the balls fall to the ground during their turn of handling them. It will be for the Indians concerned to show that the croakers are wrong.

The Commander-in-Chief in India is naturally only anxious to give the considered policy of Government the best chance of success possible. If it is left in his hands, it will be properly watched and controlled. If taken from his hands strange events may result.

There is one point that all in authority may be sure of, viz., that if British officers are certain that wisdom and strength and not sheer opportunism are behind Government intention, and that they are not being asked to forge a weapon which is to destroy the British Empire, they will throw themselves heart and soul into the task. They will use their best efforts to make the men of the martial races as fit leaders as they have hitherto been soldiers and any others who so aspire.

It has been announced that it is the Mhow Division which is to be Indianized as a whole. Within that District lie the battlefields of Mehidpore, of Assaye, and Argaum, three battlefields on which it has been necessary for a British force to destroy an Indian Army. It is to be watched that history is not compelled to repeat itself.

A working difficulty is the future of the non-commissioned officers, whose prospects at present lie in the position as Indian officers of the present type and status, and whose education precludes a higher position. In the Indianized regiment, this type of officer disappears, the 'Brindian' alone being in charge.

This diminution of prospects is causing some alarm among those who form the backbone of a corps. Alarm and discontent among a valued indispensable class, is a danger at all times and in the Indian army even more than elsewhere.

An Indian Sandhurst

The all important matter of the final cadet training of the 'Brindian' has been carefully considered. A committee of the intelligentsia went round the Empire examining the systems and some of them learnt a good deal, although it is said the distorted minds of others were more intent on ascertaining how much the dominions hated the mother country than on the business in hand. It has now been decided to start a normal 'Sandhurst' in India, which was really necessary if a large number of cadets is required. At first sight it had seemed also that it was hard to expect parents to send their boys so far from home as England but as a matter of fact, they actually prefer to do so, exactly as they also send their sons in large numbers to British universities and other colleges.

Rightly or wrongly, and the writer ventures to think that the balance of arguments is in favour of it, an Indian 'Sandhurst' there is to be. He hopes that some British cadets joining the Indian Army may even spend their last term there.

If the British dominion is to remain on sound lines the less that 'separation' takes place the better it will be. There are plenty of British officers who will make a great success of this cadet training so far as success be possible, though how far that may be, as in the matter of Indianization at all, is a question that time alone can solve. The training of youth is a British *forte* and there is no doubt that there will be plenty of enthusiasm in the new College. In fact ere long British cadet officers will be declaring that their boys are the finest in the world! All of which brings us back to the same point, viz. that if India will turn its face from the Ghandi madness, and the age-old bitter Brahmin-inspired venom and put a shoulder to the wheel in the way of comradeship, there is nothing that India cannot do, within her 'possibilities' and the 'length of her cable tow'.

The Indian Army and the Simon Report

The Simon Commission went very fully into the major conditions of the military problem and they recorded their opinion that without the British garrison and an army of the northern races, India could not be defended. They also showed a grasp of some of the salient facts about India, by saying that without the discipline and control that only

British officers could exert, the Army of warlike northern races could not be prevented from dominating India and forcing its will thereon, and the same remark undoubtedly applies to the Mahrattas and Gurkhas in the Army. Then the Commission proceeded to infringe British canons of business by making a logical proposal for the future. They went so far as to say that all the British troops and that part of the Indian Army officered by British officers must be an Imperial Army, an Army of the Crown, commanded by a Commander-in-Chief responsible to the Crown through the Governor-General and not responsible to the Government of India. Further, besides that there should be provincial troops available to support local law and order, and welded as would be the forces of the 'Princes' states into one major mobilization scheme for the defence of India on a large scale. In the local troops would be the opportunities for the 'Brindian'. The existing Territorial force, the State troops, and possibly some of the newly Indianized regular regiments might be the first fruits of the policy of local forces behind the Imperial first line.

That is a normal, logical, strategical, conception. There might be plenty of 'Brindians'—this semi-slang word is so useful that it must be retained here—in the Imperial portion of the Army. There are already clever young men among them to whom the Staff College will be a possibility, but at any rate, for many a day the place for the higher employment of such would be in the 'local' forces. In the Simon scheme there is plenty of room for re-adjustment within the general framework, and that is the secret of a good scheme formed on so indeterminate a basis as the British position in India. There must be room to recoil as well as to advance, to retrace steps that are false without a bouleversement. Development and evolution and not revolution is the key note on which alone India can thrive and British rights be maintained.

There is another interesting point that we may well remember. Those who are at all familiar with the story and the system under which the Government of India by the East India Company was conducted, are aware of its many excellences, and of the fact that it squared much more readily with a more logical basis of British dominion than the system which succeeded it. It had many weaknesses, it was also, as is the magnificent Indian structure of to-day, the butt and the cock-shy of every one with bile in his composition or who suffered from an inferiority complex. It came in for an excess of abuse largely unmerited, after the outbreak of the Mutiny of the Bengal Army and there is much to regret in the passing of the form of statesmanship that lay behind its arrangements and the principles which animated both the Court of Directors and the Board of Control. Especially was this so in its military principles, which were better than its military practice. Each local Government produced and maintained its own native army, and its forces were of two kinds, general and local. The local supplemented the police and were for the maintenance of law and order in the wilder parts which still exist. Their place is now taken by the armed police. The European Army consisted of two quite separate forces. There was the Imperial garrison varying with circumstances but paid for by India and there were its own European forces, maintained by and enlisted by the Government of India. The control of the Company's, that is to say its own Europeans by the Government of India, especially a more Indianized Government, would be simpler than when all the Europeans belonged to the Imperial Army. It will be seen that this original arrangement has many of the same germs as the

Simon proposals, more permanent in principle than the arrangements introduced after the Mutiny when the Indian Government's Europeans were abolished as such and amalgamated with the Imperial Army.

The Simon proposals do embody some of the more logical premises which underlay the Company's system, especially in the sense of a Crown Army garrisoning a more or less 'dominionized' India supplemented by the local 'Dominion' troops.

The Conclusion of the Whole Matter

The conclusion of the whole matter may briefly be summarized, and it can only be summarized here by the light of the faith with which this whole book has been written. That tinge and that faith is this. *Firstly*, that Great Britain has just as much right to rule in India as any other of the conquering races that form the martial classes, in view of her conquests, and a thousand times more right in view of the fact that she, and she alone, has spent all her energies in good Government and in the re-constitution of a broken continent. *Secondly*, that all the lives lost and capital lent for India constitute a deep-set right. *Thirdly*, that *pari passu* with the maintenance of those paramount rights and the safeguards which shall ensure them, the advance of India shall continue as a sacred duty, and that the growing sense of responsibility in India shall be fostered to that end.

The races that are likely and fit to take the lead in an awakening India can only be those races which have been described in this book as the folk who have the character and physical characteristics that fit them for the more energetic side of a native life. From them only can the more active national servants be drawn: The curious temperamental feud between them and the effeminate intelligentsia which is as old as India itself, is likely to endure, and as the Simon Commission states without British control can only end in the complete and ruthless domination of the masses by the martials. Given however, sufficient discipline and control from the outside, it may safely be said that the martial classes present the great hope of India in all more virile development.

With this faint attempt to peer into the future, this story of the martial races, which is really the story of India, must come to an end. In every town, in every village in Great Britain, the officer with happy memories, often enough pathetic memories, of his life with some or other of the races just described, 'eats' as the Eastern has it, his pension, and cultivates his memories, memories of men who have followed him, fought and died by his side. In the villages of those Indian districts whence come the combatant races a similar case exists. The old soldiers both commissioned and otherwise cherish their memories, as has been told in the story of the *Subahdar's Tita Bhai*, quarrel with the civil officials, attend their regimental re-unions, flock to meet some *sahib* who is shooting or recruiting in the neighbourhood. At seasons of the year greetings often speed on across the waters to their old leaders, and the leader's son when he joins his father's regiment is eagerly and heartily received.

Les enfants poussent toujours, the races increase and the land gets full. For a couple of generations have the great canals by which British engineers have spread the snows of the Himalaya on the parched Punjab land, catered for the increase by the million. But the new land is nearly finished, and it remains to be seen if the close scrutiny of the just distribution of water can be kept up, without which the land cannot produce its fair crop. It is these hardy races who will keep the new land productive, it is they from whom some at least of the engineers must come and indeed are now coming. Government is the matter of men of character, and character must in the end, be dependent on a modicum of personal courage. It is the descendants of the men who fought Alexander, of the women who took part in the Saccas of Chitoor, and even of those fierce Turks who drove them to it, on whom such future as India may possess must rest, not on the millions of the lesser folk who swarm on the land like myriads of ants. They and their intelligentsia alone, have no promise for India, nor unless the regime is directed by the strong men from the West is there any chance of physical uplift for such. The strong men of the North, as Sir John Simon has pointed out, are more likely to work their own will for evil on the feebler folk of the South.

So that is the pith of it. The virile men must lead, and someone must see that they can lead, and do not set about to misuse or run the land for themselves alone. Guided and controlled, a great feature remains for them. Loosed, we may expect centuries of *Poppa Bhai ki Raj*'.[1]

For years the old cry, when the nominal Raj of the Mogul still remained, ran thus:

Khalk-i-Khuda
Mulk-i-Badshah.
Hukm-i-Sahiban Alishan.

which may be interpreted:

Mankind belongs to God.
The land to the emperor.
But the ordering of things to the mighty English.

[1] See p. 85

How the enfeeblement of a ministration brings *Poppa Bhai ki Raj* already, the following extracts from the Indian papers of the spring of 1932 show, all during the month of April. In Peshawar a Moslem Inspector of Schools is found with his head chopped off, and none to say how or why. At Cawnpore nine villagers are tried for conspiring to break the law by burning the living widow on the funeral pyre of her dead husband Bhure Singh, in the presence of between two and three hundred sympathisers, and resisting the police who tried to save the unfortunate woman.

At Lucknow a party of women-singers finding themselves hoarse offered as a sacrifice a nine-year old girl Musammat Kunia to the Goddess Bhagwani, the Wife of the Great God Siva, as a sure and certain cure, having first hacked her to pieces with a sharp mattock. In the Southern Mahratta country an amiable gentleman, obviously a Mahratta, by name Vithoba Karanjalkar of Pimple, was sentenced for ill-treating and roughly consummating his marriage with a girl of thirteen. He had been married to her several years, but she, according to custom resided with her mother till of marriageable age. He having demanded her and been refused, removed her by force, tied her hands above her head and secured her feet by driving double-pointed plough nails into each foot. The kind Indian judge remarked in sentencing the prisoner that it seemed a pity that among the poorer class husbands still asserted their right in this manner!

. . . . .

Perhaps to set such things right even with the help of the martial races and to lead them to their eventual destiny, the *Hukm-i-Sahiban Alishan* is still necessary. It is one thing for a continent to have thrown up through the ages the martial races that have been described, it is another matter for them unaided to control a country with the proclivities that these cases show. Without the *Hukm-i-Sahiban Alishan* it looks as if the road might still lead to the 'Saccas' of Chitoor, but given this *Hukm* there are plenty of stout willing hearts to develop the land.

A book of sympathy about India can never do better than end with a verse from Sir Alfred Lyall. Thus West —some kindly Lord Irwin—speaks to East,

> " Let the temple moulder in gathering sand,
> Let the stones lie strewn in the cedar grove,
> Ye shall rule like Gods in a glorious land
> Ye shall live by knowledge and peace and love."

But East replies to West somewhat hopelessly viz.,

> " The burden of thought and the travail of care,
> Weigh down the soul in its wandering flight;
> The sun burns ever, the plains lie bare
> It is death brings shade and the dreamless night."

For it is but the spirit of Hindu complacency that is content. . . .

> " With the dirge and the sounds of lamenting
> And the voices of women who weep."

Thus tolled the knell at the Cawnpore Massacre of 1930 —the fierce communal riots in Bombay of 1932—the immediate results of the weakening of the great psychological bonds of authority and peace which India owes primarily to Mr. Montagu's attempts to stir 'pathetic content', and upset the finest Government in the world. For a century and a half has Great Britain rebuilt, fitted together the broken pieces, while amateur modellers are now anxious to apply to an enormous country a system working fairly well in these small scale islands, which have taken a thousand years to create it. By trying to build in the last ten years a system which Britain trained herself for since the Saxons landed, we have built on foundations that have not yet been dug deep enough. We have now to grout our too hasty jerry-building. The educating of the manly and martial classes to control is sadly in defect yet, and the effervescence of education is in less settled minds. How those manly classes have been formed and evolved, how great and how dangerous they can be to themselves and everyone else, and how splendid under control and leading, this short account has endeavoured to show.

The ineffective outlook of the Ghandi mind would but throw the country back, would get rid of the West and its millions of miles of life-giving water, its thousands of miles of rail that prevent famine, and would bring it where it was, like China with her bandits and war-lords.

> "Scored with the brand of the burning heat,
> And the wrath divine and the sins of man
> And the fateful tramp of the conqueror's feet,
> It has suffered all since the world began."

The men of those races whose hands have never kept their heads cannot be expected to do so, nor do they seem to be worthy of the trust that the Crown would otherwise wish to place in their hands. On the other hand the men of the Rajput, Jat and kindred races and groups have it in them in due course to lead and control. And as this book is about soldier classes in a land that soldiers have made and marred, it is perhaps not out of place to quote once more the saying of a wise old Irish Commander-in-Chief in India, who was emphasizing the value of character at an important conference of the military *alumni*. "Ye may tache a poodle tricks but ye can't tache him to draa a badger". Our energies in India have let the education that is so essential pass to the clever un-manly classes, who cannot alone use it effectively. That was not the method of one of England's wisest kings of whom Kipling wrote:—

> " There are four good legs to my father's chair
> Priest and people and Lords and Crown.
> I sit on all of them fair and square
> And that is the reason it don't break down."

THE END

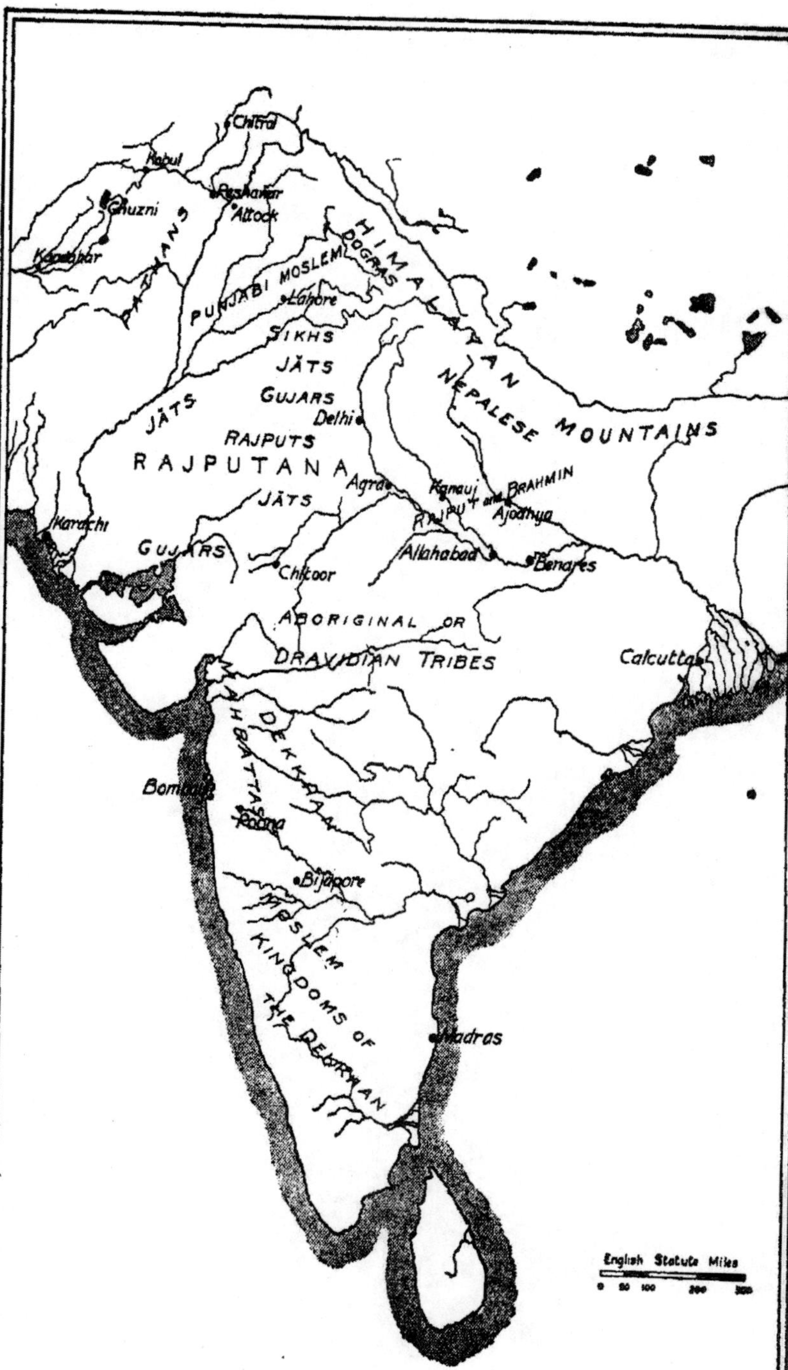
Chitral
Kabul
Peshawar
Attock
Ghuzni
Kandahar
PATHANS
PUNJABI MOSLEMS
DOGRAS
HIMALAYAN MOUNTAINS
Lahore
SIKHS
JÄTS
GUJARS
Delhi
NEPALESE
RAJPUTS
RAJPUTANA
Agra
Kanauj
BRAHMIN
RAJPUT and
Ajodhya
Karachi
GUJARS
Chitoor
Allahabad
Benares
ABORIGINAL OR
DRAVIDIAN TRIBES
Calcutta
MAHRATTAS
DEKKAN
Bombay
Poona
Bijapore
MOSLEM
KINGDOMS OF
THE DEKKAN
Madras
English Statute Miles
0 50 100 200 300

INDEX

F

G

H

I

By the same Author

The ARMIES of INDIA (1912)

(ILLUSTRATED in Colour.) (A. & C. Black), 21/-

PIKE and CARRONADE

(Stories of Wars). (Blackwood & Sons), 7/6.

A FREE LANCE in KASHMIR

(John Murray). (A Romance of the Indian Anarchy), 7/6.

AFGHANISTAN from DARIUS to AMANULLAH

ILLUSTRATED (G. Bell & Sons), 20/- (1930)

Recognised as the Modern Classic.

BEHIND the SCENES in MANY WARS

ILLUSTRATED. (John Murray), 15/- (1930)

"A very entertaining book and a solid body of most valuable experience."
—*Times.*

"The happy record of a man who has been at the centre of the great events of recent history."—*Sphere.*

GUSTAVUS ADOLPHUS. The Northern Hurricane

(Hodder & Stoughton), 18/- (1930)

"A brilliant study of a man who could organise war."

The KING'S PAWNS

(Sheldon Press), 5/- (1930)

(War stories with a difference).

"Fifteen stories interwoven with some delicate romance."

"A born story-teller."—*Week-end Review.*

The INDIAN MUTINY in PERSPECTIVE

ILLUSTRATED. (G. Bell & Sons), 12/6. (1931)

"Written with great sympathy and understanding of the Indian Army."—Sir Frederick Maurice in the *Observer*.

"Admirable and most timely . . . Clear and dispassionate . . . read it carefully."—Sir Walter Lawrence in the *Sunday Times*.

"A wise, broad-minded and impartial survey."—Sir Michael O'Dwyer in the *Morning Post*.

The RELIGIONS and HIDDEN CULTS of INDIA

ILLUSTRATED. (Sampson Low, Marston), 15/- (1931)

"Handled with remarkable skill—Judgment sound—Colouring is brilliant."
—*Times*.

"A floodlight on India . . . This is a remarkable book, and will be widely discussed."—*Evening News*.

"An accurate, vivid and most readable account of its vast subject; it is a book of exactly the kind that ordinary readers require."
—Bishop Whitehead in the *Sunday Times*.

The ROMANCE of the INDIAN FRONTIERS

ILLUSTRATED. (Jonathan Cape), 16/-. (1931)

"A romance of battle, murder and sudden death, irradiated by heroic deeds, eloquent in scholarly setting . . . could not have been in better hands."
—Lord Meston in the *Sunday Times*

THE ARMY—Life and Work Series

(Geoffrey Bles), 3/6. (1930)

"An Army career, its charm and advantage."

VIGNETTES from INDIAN WARS

(Sampson Low, Marston). 12/6. (1932)

The latest of a series of noteworthy books in no way inferior to his well-known works, in human interest and historical value."
—*Illustrated London News*.

"Our thanks are due to the author for so lively and vivid account of episodes deserving long remembrances."—*Times Lit. Supplement*.

Published by

Facsimile Publisher
Ashok Vihar, Delhi-110052 (India)
Website: www.facsimilepublisher.com

Distributed by

Gyan Books Pvt. Ltd.
5, Ansari Road, Daryaganj, New Delhi-110002 (India)
E-mail: books@gyanbooks.com, Website: www.gyanbooks.com

8 888000 388166